Travels of a Country Woman

Travels of a Country Woman

By Lera Knox

Edited by Margaret Knox Morgan
and Carol Knox Ball

Newfound Press
THE UNIVERSITY OF TENNESSEE LIBRARIES, KNOXVILLE

Travels of a Country Woman

For all other uses, contact:

Newfound Press
University of Tennessee Libraries
1015 Volunteer Boulevard
Knoxville, TN 37996-1000
www.newfoundpress.utk.edu

ISBN-13: 978-0-9797292-1-8
ISBN-10: 0-9797292-1-1

Library of Congress Control Number: 2007934867

Knox, Lera, 1896-
Travels of a country woman / by Lera Knox ; edited by Margaret Knox Morgan and Carol Knox Ball.
xiv, 558 p. : ill ; 23 cm.
1.Knox, Lera, 1896-—Travel—Anecdotes. 2. Women journalists—Tennessee, Middle—Travel—Anecdotes. 3. Farmers' spouses—Tennessee, Middle—Travel—Anecdotes. I. Morgan, Margaret Knox. II. Ball, Carol Knox. III. Title.
PN4874 .K624 A25 2007

Book design by Martha Rudolph

Dedicated to the Grandchildren
Carol, Nancy, Susy, John Jr.

Contents

Preface

The former Lera Margaret Ussery, born in post-Victorian Tennessee, began her colorful adventures in 1896. That early portion of her life is described in *Goodness Gracious, Miss Agnes: Patchwork of Country Living*, the first book to be published by the University of Tennessee digital press, the Newfound Press. She described her family background from pioneer days in Middle Tennessee. From her phenomenal memory she recalled the life of a shy, bookish child in a small town, on her grandparents' little farm, through her experiences as a student, then as a teacher. She told of the continuation of her education as she moved from being "a city girl" to being "Mrs. Alex Knox," a farmer's wife and the mother of two.

She described the early years of hers and Alex's life, from the arrival of the newlyweds in the hundred-year-old manor house of a former plantation, to life with their two children, Margaret and Jack. (She said later that was the happiest time of her life when the children were small.)

Little did Lera know at that time that she had many more adventures ahead, many of which she was to describe in newspaper articles in the *Nashville* (TN) *Banner*, the *Columbia* (TN) *Daily Herald*, and the *Maury* (TN) *Democrat*. Described in her own words, the accounts have been collected and put together lovingly here by us, the daughter Margaret, and son Jack's daughter Carol.

Travels of a Country Woman, begins with the family's emergence from the Depression, initially by way of a trip from Columbia, Tennessee, to the Chicago World's Fair in 1933. They traveled by "Elizabeth T," the family Model T Ford and Lera wrote articles about the "Flivver" trip for the *Nashville Banner.*

Those articles marked the beginning of a career as a columnist—a career that she pursued for the rest of her life. She wrote articles about her travels from Hollywood to Copenhagen, from having tea with Eleanor Roosevelt to attending the Coronation of Elizabeth II.

Lera Knox, who had become a farmer's wife in 1918, always maintained that for farmers the Great Depression began, not in 1929, but at the end of World War I. That was particularly true for Middle Tennessee farmers like the Knox family. In the business of breeding, "breaking," and selling mules, they experienced hardship when at the end of the war the bottom fell out of the market for mules.

By the spring of 1933 the family had had about as much Depression as they could take. So when an item appeared in the newspaper that the World's Fair would be held in Chicago that summer the family did not hesitate to say, "Let's go!" The family began putting whatever change we could muster under the living room rug, but by June there was only $3.81. Everybody knew that would not get us very far. Daddy said he had gone to school with Jimmy Stahlman, who was by that time publisher of the *Nashville Banner*. Mother had written for several farm magazines. Daddy asked her if she would consider trying articles for the *Banner*. She did. Her account of how she overcame her doubts follows.

Margaret Knox Morgan, the daughter, and
Carol Knox Ball, Jack's daughter, Editors

A Note from the Newfound Press

Margaret Knox Morgan and Carol Knox Ball collected, organized, and transcribed these newspaper articles by Lera Knox. In doing so, they have preserved detailed and spirited firsthand accounts of travels and special events during the first half of the twentieth century. Through this collection, they make available to readers and scholars a unique and joyful perspective on life during difficult Post Depression years.

To promote ease of reading for this collection of articles, Newfound Press has made minor changes in punctuation, capitalization, and italicization. For instance, the name of the Model T, which sometimes appears in the newspapers as "Elizabeth T." has been standardized to "Elizabeth T" for consistency. The name of the Nashville newspaper, which often appeared as BANNER, becomes *Banner* in this collection. Titles of novels and films that originally appeared in quotation marks have been italicized, as have names of ships. In a few cases, we have corrected misspellings of people's names rather than interrupting the flow of the ideas with notes about spelling.

The content of the articles remains intact. That content belongs completely to the active mind of Lera Knox and to the other writers featured here. The editors have enhanced that content with narration and explanation where appropriate. Newfound Press has adapted the format for present-day readers. We accept responsibility for typographical errors that may have occurred in that process. Please join us for the lively travel accounts of a Columbia, Tennessee, country woman at home and abroad.

Newfound Press thanks the following newspapers for their permission to reprint the columns by Lera Knox.

The Nashville Banner (Nashville, Tennessee)

The Daily Herald (Columbia, Tennessee)

The Dickson Herald (Dickson, Tennessee)

The Abilene Daily Reporter-News (Abilene, Texas)

The San Jose Mercury-Herald (San Jose, California)

The Knoxville News-Sentinel (Knoxville, Tennessee)

Stars and Stripes (Washington, D.C) [*Used with permission from the Stars and Stripes, a DoD publication, © 2006 Stars and Stripes.*]

PART I

The Chicago World's Fair

PART I

The Chicago World's Fair

THE NASHVILLE BANNER,
SUNDAY, JULY 2, 1933

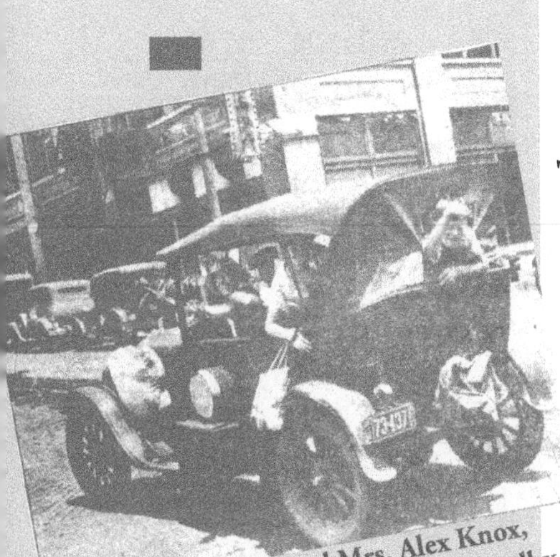

Typical Middle Tennessee Farm Family 'Flivvering' To Chicago's Century of Progress in 'Elizabeth T'

Here are Mr. and Mrs. Alex Knox, Margaret and Jack, waving "goodby, Tennessee," snapped in front of the *Banner* just as they departed for their history-making trip to the Century of Progress Exposition at Chicago. On the right is shown the attractive old home on the Knox seventy-acre farm six miles out from Columbia, where cows, chickens, hogs, cat, dog, and goat have been temporarily "farmed out" until their return.

THE NASHVILLE BANNER,
SUNDAY, JULY 2, 1933

Mrs. Alex Knox to Write Humorous Account of Its Peregrinations

How a typical Middle Tennessee farm family, which for more than a dozen years had been struggling to pay off an inflated farm mortgage with deflated farm prices, went to the Century of Progress Exposition in Chicago in a Model T Ford and what they saw there will be graphically and humorously described for *Banner* readers in a series of articles to be written by Mrs. Alex Knox of Columbia, who with Mr. Knox and their two children, Margaret, 14, and Jack, 12, left their seventy-acre farm in Maury County Saturday morning, stopped by the *Banner* for a photograph, and started merrily on their way for their first real vacation away from the cows and chickens and crops.

The Ford, affectionately referred to by the family as "Elizabeth T.," was slightly overloaded at the start, for Mrs. Knox doesn't intend to let the family starve while she pecks the trusty portable. Mrs. Knox is a Class A farmer's wife as well as a writer of farm and household articles for leading farm journals, and she is carrying along in the "kitchen" a well-stocked cupboard of fruits, vegetables, and chicken which she has canned, sufficient for three balanced "squares" a day for the two weeks they plan to be gone. Of course there's a stove along and all necessary equipment and the family will set up kitchen whenever they feel the urge to eat. There won't be any regular hours for anything, for they don't even carry a watch. They are all set to furnish a simple bedroom in the great open spaces if they so desire, carrying pads and quilts rolled up in a bed-ticking, but they plan to put up for the night at tourist homes and camps when they feel like it.

Margaret and Jack, joy radiating from every one of their several thousand healthy freckles, have never before been out of Tennessee and Alabama. What the wonders of the magic trip will mean to them will be told by their versatile mother.

Mrs. Knox has lived in Columbia all her life but did not take to farming until she married. She attended Peabody College here and taught in the city schools of Columbia for several years before settling down to the intricacies of farm life. Overflowing with health, optimism, and humor, Mrs. Knox will describe in her own inimitable way what will interest her family or any other farm family on the way to and at the great Century of Progress Exposition. Her articles will be sometimes informative but they won't be dry.

EXPERIENCED WRITER

Mrs. Knox has been writing a daily garden article for the *Daily Herald* of Columbia for the past three months. Several years ago she wrote for the woman's page of the *Maury*

Democrat. She has had articles published in *Farmer's Wife*, *Southern Agriculturist*, *Progressive Farmer-Ruralist*, and *Country Gentleman.*

Of an inquiring mind, Mrs. Knox wants her family to see and know as much about the world at large as she learned about her native state several years ago when she was the only woman semifinalist in the *Banner*'s "Know Tennessee" contest.

Mr. Knox is a real dirt farmer. He claims the distinction of being one of "Old Sawney's" boys, having attended the famous Webb School at Bell Buckle, his former home.

Jack carries his belongings in a little wooden box in the back of "Elizabeth T." Margaret's wardrobe is likewise self-made, consisting of a cardboard box lined inside and out with *Banner* Sunday comic sheets. They plan to ride three in the front seat and one in the rear. Just where, it would be difficult to explain. But if grit, perseverance, ingenuity and a sense of humor count for anything in this world, as the orators claim they do, then the Knox family, Dixie's farmers turned gypsies, will come back to the "Dimple of the Universe" a wiser and a happier lot.

THE DAILY HERALD
COLUMBIA, TENNESSEE
MONDAY, JULY 17, 1933

Knoxes Back From Fair, Had Enjoyable Trip

Maury Farm Family Makes 'Century of Progress' In Auto, Sees Many Sights Besides

A trip to the World's Fair which took them everywhere from Governor's mansions to bootlegging joints was completed when Mr. and Mrs. Alex Knox and their children, Margaret and Jack, returned to their home at McCains, Tennessee, yesterday morning in "Elizabeth T," the family Ford.

In spite of the venerable condition of the family car, there were no flats or punctures along the whole of the journey, during which they visited, in addition to the Fair, nearly every worthwhile and interesting place between here and Chicago. With them they brought back four fine Leghorn roosters, who claim the World's Fair as their birthplace and who have been named Century, Progress, Chicago, and Illinois. Jack Knox also brought home with him a kitten given him by former Governor Warren T. McCray of Indiana.

Places visited by the Knoxes en route to and from the fair included the cave section of Kentucky, including Mammoth Cave and Sand Cave, where Floyd Collins met his death; the

Lincoln Memorial and his birthplace and boyhood home at Hodgenville, Ky.; the grave of President Lincoln's mother at Lincoln City, Ind.; the house at Bardstown, Ky., where Stephen Foster wrote "My Old Kentucky Home;" James Whitcomb Riley's birthplace and boyhood home in Greenfield, Ind., where the Knox family went in swimming in the "ole swimming hole," which Riley immortalized; Newcastle. Ind., "the rose city," where the American Beauty rose was originated; the Ball Bros.' glass factory and a Muncie, Ind., millionaire's dairy farm, on which the cows are kept in glass houses and fed yeast to produce Vitamin D milk; Governor McCray's 2,101-acre farm at Kentland, Ind., where 1,000 acres are planted in corn and where one of Governor McCray's 22 cats was given to young Jack; the home of George Ade, the famous humorist, whom the Knoxes met in person and had an interesting talk with; Purdue University, the study of Lew Wallace, who wrote *Ben Hur*, the original manuscript of which is in his study; the Crawfordville, Ind., home of Colonel Lane, who nominated Lincoln for the Presidency.

The apartment in which the Knoxes stayed in Chicago was only one block from that of Amos 'n' Andy, famous radio team.

During their trip, they covered 1,100 miles on 78 gallons of gas and no beer—they say their trip to the bootlegging joint was purely accidental, the Tennessee family going there by mistake when directions as to reaching a tourists' home led them astray.

THE NASHVILLE BANNER
SATURDAY, JULY 29, 1933

A Farmer's Family Flivvers to Fair

"A Farmer's Family Flivvers to the Fair," a series of humorous articles describing the adventures of Mr. and Mrs. Alex Knox, their children Margaret and Jack and their automobile, "Elizabeth T" all hailing from "Knoxdale," seventy-acre farm near Columbia, Tenn., in the very "Dimple of the Universe," will start in the *Banner* Sunday. The articles are being written by Mrs. Knox (Lera Knox), who is already known to readers of several farm journals through her articles on gardening and kindred subjects.

The eight-day trip to Chicago, in the Model T Ford, in which they visited Mammoth Cave, and other Kentucky caves; Abraham Lincoln's birthplace; "My Old Kentucky Home;" the home of James Whitcomb Riley, where they "went in a-washing" in the "Old Swimmin' Hole;" the farm of Indiana's former Gov. Warren McCray, who presented Margaret with a pigeon and Jack with a kitten which somehow found a place in the already over-loaded lap of "Elizabeth T;" and a visit to George Ade, famous humorist, and to Frank M. Cary and his thousands of "adopted" orphans at LaFayette, as well as to Purdue University, are but a few of the things this enterprising farm family did before it ever got to the Century of Progress. The trip up will be described in the first article in Sunday's *Banner*.

THE NASHVILLE BANNER
SUNDAY, JULY 30, 1933

Farm Family from Tennessee Flivvers to Fair

Knoxes from Knoxdale Get aboard 'Elizabeth T' and 'Light Out' for Chicago

Take Their Own 'Grub'

Family of Four Spend Two Weeks and Less Than $60

BY LERA KNOX

After fifteen years with the pigs, cows, and chickens, we decided we had to have a vacation. We wanted to go to the Chicago Fair, but we knew we couldn't afford it because we had been farming for a living and trying to pay off an inflated mortgage with deflated farm prices. When we bought "Knoxdale" back in war times, we stretched our credit so far that it sprang back and has been choking us ever since. We've been working, scheming, stinting, stingying, trying to keep the interest up and the mortgage down, but in spite of it all, debts kept swelling and our dollars kept shrinking until they were the size of dimes.

You people who have howled "depression" for the last two or three years don't realize that farm depression was old enough to enter high school before world depression had cut its eyeteeth.

Here are the Knoxes making camp along the road on their trip to the Century of Progress Exposition. Mrs. Knox, the writer of the accompanying article, is seen on the running board of "Elizabeth T," pounding out the story on her portable. Margaret, in the foreground is warming up some of that good home-canned chicken and vegetables, and Jack and "Daddy" are unpacking some of the baggage from the Model T.

Finally we decided we had two perfectly good excuses for going to the Fair, just as we had always had excuses for going to the circus—our boy and our girl. On their account we felt that we couldn't afford to miss the fair, farm or no farm. But where would we get the money? The farm couldn't produce it, with corn $1.25 a barrel; Jack decided to raise gourds, Margaret thought she could sell cabbage plants and they pooled their interests, and raised ducks. I was counting on flowers and broilers and Daddy tried potatoes. But gourds are slow growers and the cabbage plants died of drought and ducks dropped to 3 cents a pound; flowers hit a glutted market; broilers dropped to a baby chick price level and potatoes couldn't make their seed back. The little pile of vacation money under the living-room rug dwindled more than it grew. I wrote some magazine articles and sent them off but they came back with "regrets," of all sad words.

But finally Daddy put forth an idea. "Why don't you try the *Banner*?" I hardly dared hope that a big city newspaper like the *Banner* would be interested in what we country folks have to say, but it was a straw and I reached for it. Rather I reached for my typewriter and pecked off a letter, asking if the *Banner* could use a series of articles about a farm family going to the fair, expecting another "regret;" nevertheless, we watched eagerly for the mails. When the letter came, I didn't have the heart to open it. "Read it, Daddy," I said, resignedly. He opened it and began to read: "The *Banner* will be glad to take your series of short articles about the trip to the Century of Progress." I knew he was kidding but it sounded refreshing anyway. "Oh, Daddy, read it like it is. I can stand it." But he said, "That's what it says," but still I knew better and took the letter in hand to read what I was prepared to receive. And there it was in blue and white: "The *Banner* will be glad, etc.," and I was glad and still gladder when I read further on that they would pay me "by the inch" for such articles as they could use. "Oh, kiddies," I yelled, "we are going to the fair." We had a real celebration and then we began to get ready before the *Banner* could have a chance to change its mind.

All hands to the wash tub, then to the ironing. It was so hot we had to take the thermometer out of the kitchen to prevent breakage. Then came darning and patching, sorting and packing of our pre-depression wardrobe. We had no new clothes, for try as you may, you can't grow dresses on corn stalks, hats on cabbage heads, suits on bean poles, nor shoes on potato vines—not in dry weather, anyway. Our combined wardrobe was just about one jump ahead of the scarecrow. If the gangsters got our trunks, what a joke we'd have on the gangsters!

To celebrate the fact that President Roosevelt had promised to prop up the farm income to where it could look the farm outgo in the face, and to officially mark the end of the depression and join in the national recovery program, I re-covered myself with an 88-cent dress, a 79-cent hat, 48-cent pair of hose, which I later snagged when I ran across an Indiana wheatfield to snap a picture of the first combine we ever saw. Margaret made herself a new print dress and a pair of pajamas out of a bargain day remnant, but the men folks had to struggle along as best they could with reinforced left-overs.

If we could make our mileage out of the *Banner*'s inches, the farm ought to furnish the food. That was one thing we had plenty of, but how to take it along? I fell back on my old standby, canning, figuring as best I could how much it would take to give us a protein, a starch, a fruit, and two green vegetables each day for two weeks, with normal appetites.

Into our "kitchenette" we packed home-canned chicken and sausage, asparagus, peas, carrots, beets, kraut, strawberries, grapes, rhubarb, and apple sauce; ham and eggs, flour, sugar, meal, coffee and cocoa; fresh cabbage, tomatoes and onions; canned milk, cereal, sandwich spread, salt, pepper, and vinegar, matches, cup towels, dishrags, soap and washing powders. The only thing we would have to buy would be fresh bread and milk along the road. Weren't we independent? Dishes for four and kitchen utensils completely filled the "Elizabethan Apartment's Efficiency Kitchenette." We even remembered to pack in baling wire, pink pills, and paregoric.

We had $3.81 under the rug; we sold thirty broilers for $5, seventeen fat hens for $4.88; borrowed $25 from the bank and sold enough farm and garden products to make a total of $59.50. We went to the fair, stayed two weeks, traveled 1,400 miles on seventy-eight gallons of gas and no beer, saw geography that's not on the maps, history that hasn't been reported, people not listed in *Who's Who*, and returned with 50 cents in our pin-checks and five gallons of gas in our tank. We will tell in the forthcoming articles how much brass we had to mix with our silver in order to see it all and get home again.

THE NASHVILLE BANNER
AUGUST 1, 1933

Fair Bound Farm Family Gets Liberal Education in Kentucky and Indiana

Elizabeth T Makes Trip With No Punctures and 25 Cents for Repairs

Sightseeing Takes Week

Stops Made at Old Kentucky Home, Lincoln Birthplace

At some time in her youth, "Elizabeth T" must have been a latest model; doubtless she was then a "glass of fashion and a mold of form." But after many winters of taking the children to school, and many summers of taking farm products to market, she is beginning to show her age, although apparently she doesn't feel it yet. Her faithful old engine is still hitting on four.

Although Elizabeth is old enough now to go to school, and her youngest tire is old enough to walk, we believed she could take us to the Fair and bring us back. She did—without a puncture. We went several hundred miles off our charted concrete path, too, in order to see some places of special interest, but the old Ford didn't complain.

"We cleaned Elizabeth T's spark plugs twice, shifted her coils once, replaced her timer brush with another old one."

We cleaned her spark plugs twice, shifted her coils once, replaced her timer brush with another old one, and she rattled cheerily on. Her total repair bill on the 1,400 mile trip was 25 cents. The only other attention she required was her regular diet of gas, an occasional dose of oil, and plenty of cool water.

Elizabeth was and is faithful. We are all fond of her, but after each particularly hard stretch of road Jack wanted to get out and pat her on the hood. Daddy said that was too much "mushing."

OUT AFTER "RECORD"

Most people who go from Tennessee to Century of Progress leave home early in the morning; eat breakfast at Springfield or Hopkinsville; dinner at Vincennes or Terry Haute, and supper in Chicago. One man claims to have driven it in nine hours. But we determined to "smash all previous records," and I believe we did. We left Columbia at 7:45 o'clock Saturday morning, and arrived in Chicago at 2:45 o'clock Saturday afternoon—a week later. Whereas others ate two meals on the road, we ate twenty-eight.

About all we knew about geography when we left home was what we could see from our kitchen window; what we learned from the atlas on the school teacher's desk; and what we could interpret from the road maps. Jack summed up what we learned on the trip by saying, when we returned, "If the world is as big back the other way as it is the way we went, it certainly is a whopper."

Our first adventure was in Nashville. We rolled into town on a busy Saturday morning; the traffic lights all turned green when they saw us coming. We didn't know whether this color was caused by envy, or whether it was for Irish good luck, or whether they wished us to "go on and be gone." But go we did, that is as far as we could, for soon we got into a traffic jam, or rather a mush, and it was a hot mush, so thick it would hardly pour through the street.

I was driving, and Elizabeth got nervous. I bade her keep a cool head but we both got hot. Finally we found out what was the trouble. Nashville had opened up a street. I don't know whether it was to adjust its ribs or just to show us some traffic before we got to Chicago, but we dived like a frightened rabbit into the first alley that didn't say "No Left Turn." There we cooled our engine and powdered our noses and got ready to drive down on Commerce to have our picture made at the *Banner* office. Anyone who saw us that morning and didn't laugh must have been without a certain useful bone.

Pictures made, we started toward Kentucky.

We stopped at the Kentucky caves, for the children wanted to see "any hole in the ground that was bigger than our cellar at home." We visited the cabin where Lincoln was born; the farm where he spent his childhood; the trees he played under; the creek he waded in; and the fields where he "on Saturday afternoon dropped pumpkin seeds, two in every other hill of every other row. The next Sunday morning there came a rain … and washed ground, corn, pumpkin seeds, and all clear off the field." [1] Yes, Abraham Lincoln had some real farm experience.

We saw for ourselves how "the sun shines bright on the old Kentucky home," where Stephen Foster wrote that immortal song. There "Old Massa's in the Cold, Cold Ground" and Old Uncle Ned "hung up de fiddle an' de bow"; and Old Black

---

[1] Abraham Lincoln, recalling his childhood

Joe heard "the gentle voices calling." "The corn-top was ripe and the meadow was in the bloom," but "My Old Kentucky Home, Good night," I'll have to hurry on.

Other celebrities who had been there before us were LaFayette, Monroe, Clay, Buchanan, Polk, and Queen Marie of Roumania. The Governor of Kentucky gave a luncheon for Queen Marie when she visited there. I copied the menu so that if we ever have a queen for dinner, I would know what to serve. Governor Laffoon just did miss seeing us by one day; he was to attend a celebration there the next day, but we had to go, we couldn't wait for him.

ST. JOSEPH'S CATHEDRAL

At Bardstown we visited famous old St. Joseph's Cathedral and stood in reverence before those old masterpieces which were painted 600 years ago by such artists as Van Dyke, Murillo, and Rubens. We were told that these and other treasures were presented to the Bishop and the Cathedral by Louis Phillippe, an exiled king of France who visited there and was kindly treated.

We saw the grave of John Fitch, who "was carrying passengers for hire in a steamboat of his own invention nearly twenty years before Robert Fulton invented the *Clermont*." Now you see that copy books can be mistaken.

We liked Louisville and Indianapolis and all the places and all the people we saw in both cities, and between them.

Louisville, like Bowling Green and Nashville, turned on its green lights and opened up a street for us (or somebody); but Indianapolis just tore up a sidewalk.

On this stretch of road Jack, being our tree-lover, was especially interested in the State Forest Nursery, where ten million baby trees were growing in long narrow beds.

In Indianapolis we went to the Lockerbie Street house where James Whitcomb Riley spent his later years, but it was closed for repairs; so we decided to go out to Greenfield, twenty miles away where he lived as a boy.

There we had a pleasant visit with members of the Riley family who still live there. Mrs. John Riley, the wife of the favorite brother "Jonty" to whom many of the poems were dedicated, is just the age that "Brer Jim," the poet, would have been now. "Jimmy Riley," her enormous Persian cat, had his foot dipped in a bottle of ink and put his "autograph" on a book of poems we got there.

This is the home where:

> Little Orphant Annie's come to our house to stay,
>
> An' wash the cups an' saucers up, an' brush the crumbs away,
>
> An' shoo the chickens off the porch, an' dust the hearth and sweep,
>
> An' make the fire, an' bake the bread, an' earn her board-an'-keep. [2]

---

[2] "Little Orphant Annie" by James Whitcomb Riley

We remembered the "little boy 'at wouldn't say his prayers... An' seeked him in the rafter-room, an' cubbyhole an' press. An' seeked him up the chimbly-flue, an' ever'wheres, I guess." All these places are right there in the old kitchen, now used as the dining-room "when they wuz company," but out to "Old Aunt Mary's," (as we called Mrs. Riley), "we et out on the porch." [3]

We went to the "old swimmin' hole, where the crick so still and deep looked like a baby river that was laying half asleep." Not content with being sole owner of the old swimmin' hole, Greenfield, a town much smaller than Columbia, has built a $40,000 new swimming pool; and if you think it is not a beauty, guess again. We like Greenfield and its people. To us it will always be like "Griggsby's Station," of which Riley wrote:

Le's go a-visitin' back to Griggsby's Station
Back where the latch-string's a-hangin' from the door
And ever' neighbor 'round the place is dear as a relation
Back where we ust to be so happy and so pore! [4]

When we left, dear old Mrs. Riley said, "I'll tell you now, like Jim used to tell the soldiers when they went by to war—he was just a kid then—Good-bye—when you die—send me a piece o' pumpkin-pie."

---

3 Ibid.

4 "Riley Farm-Rhymes" by James Whitcomb Riley

THE NASHVILLE BANNER
WEDNESDAY, AUGUST 2, 1933

Farm Family Flivvers to World Fair

Qualify as 'World's Worst' Camp-Finders and Decide To Spend Night in Open

See Sights Along Way

Visit Fruit Jar City and Home of 'American Beauty'

Editor's Note: This is the third article of a series by a Maury County farm woman, describing how she and her family took a two weeks' trip to the Century of Progress Exposition at a total cost of $59.

BY LERA KNOX

After two nights on the road we were ready to apply for medals as the "World's Worst Camp Finders," for we experienced all the evils that tourist flesh is heir to. On the first night it seemed that our room had a full combination of both steam heat and furnace heat. On one side of us a Saturday night party was being enjoyed by all; on the other side a beer garden flourished; and upstairs a dance hall was in full swing. You'd never believe how many fence-jumping sheep we counted that night. If we got any sleep at all, "it rested," as Bob Taylor would have said, "mighty lightly on our constitutions."

The Knoxes thought of stopping fifty miles out of Chicago so "Elizabeth T" might get over her nervousness before getting into traffic, but found themselves in the city's "front yard" before they realized it.

The second night we decided to sleep in the cool, quiet, open spaces; but the ground was as hard as marble. Those mosquitoes must have been as big as buzzards; they could sing like airplanes, and sting like hornets. We covered up heads, ears, arms, and legs, but even then those rascals would find a way to nab us in that unscratchable spot between the shoulder blades. If Kentucky's bears were ever as ferocious as those mosquitoes, our respect for D. Boone is increased.

We made a burnt offering of our extra clothing and our dishrags, and dozed off to awaken a few minutes later with a hard rain coming down in a hurry. All tourists do not get shower-bath accommodations, but we did that night.

We visited the Indiana Soldiers' and Sailors' Children's Home near Kingstown, where nearly a thousand orphans show by happy faces, rosy cheeks, and good behavior that they are being well cared for.

Newcastle is proud of being the "Rose City," the home of the American Beauty rose, and the birthplace of Wilbur Wright. The five-acre municipal rose garden promises to be another American beauty when it is completed.

Ever since I have been big enough to wash fruit jars, I have known that they were made by "Ball," but what I didn't know was that the Ball family had also made a city. Muncie is called "the town that Ball built." Nearly sixty years ago the sons of a farmer's widow began making glass bottles for vinegar and oil. Now the factory covers seventy acres, and turns out 600 jars a minute. Two of the brothers are still at the head of the business and are the hardest working members of the "clan." Among the thousands of worthy causes which they have sponsored is the famous Ball Teachers' College, at Muncie.

We saw a dairy farm where fat cows are kept in glass houses and fed "irradiated" yeast—that word means suntanned, I think—so that they can manufacture Vitamin D milk for babies with rickets.

For curiosity we stopped at a Boy Scout camp, near LaFayette, and just as we were learning how the boys take two whole days to cook "bean-pole beans," and as we were making off with the scout executive's raspberry pie for our lunch, we met Frank M. Cary, the man who had given this $11,000 camp to the boys. Our outfit and our curiosity seemed to interest Mr. Cary, so he took us all about LaFayette to "see the sights." He is a retired business man who, "having no children of his own, has adopted thousands." We saw his Children's Home where the smaller children are cared for, the scout camp and Cary Hall at Purdue, which when completed will house probably 1,500 students.

Kind and friendly "Tommy" Johnson, publicity director of Purdue, showed us over the university from President Elliott's office to the ice cream parlor. We liked it all, but Jack and Margaret were interested in the fact that Purdue has its own airport. They exclaimed: "Why mother, we can come to school here from home by airplane." And who knows but that they may some day?

We saw our old friend, Prof. "Red" McClintock, hard at work in the research laboratory. He was formerly horticulturist with U. T. He was much interested in happenings at home, and sent regards to his friends in Tennessee.

One thing that especially interested me at Purdue was a cheap and simple source of electric power. An airplane propeller was mounted on a windmill tower; when the wind blows this simple mechanism generates enough electricity to operate ordinary farm and home appliances. I figured that if I could fasten one of Jack's "windmills" to a clothes line post, and get the wires hitched up right, the wind would light our house, toast our bread, perc our coffee, curl my hair, milk our cows, churn our cream, and launder our clothes. Mr. Johnson said that Purdue would tell me how to tie up the wires and batteries, so I have concluded that perhaps there is something useful in boys, windmills, and universities after all.

Kentland we will always remember because of the genial hospitality of Indiana's Governor, Warren T. McCray, and his family, the beauty of their "Orchard Lake Farm," and the clever wit of fabulist George Ade. Governor McCray is a real dirt-farmer. He has more than 500 head of registered cattle, nearly 600 white-belted pigs, twenty-two cats, and cornfields a mile long. He gave Margaret a pigeon and Jack a cat. The pigeon was murdered by a Chicago gangster-alley-cat; the kitten we still have, but have named it Depression because it looks as though it won't last much longer. If it recovers it will be called Nira.

Mr. Ade took us into his study where he is trying to out-write the hard times. He offered me a seat in his trick electric-chair, but I didn't happen to touch the right button so the joke was all off. He said he had a poem which he couldn't sell so he gave it to us with his autograph for our souvenir box. Before we left he posed for a picture with Elizabeth T, and his favorite walking cane, which he carefully selected from a collection of several hundred.

On from Kentland to Chicago.

We thought we knew Chicago. Why, we have read about it in the newspapers; looked it up in the encyclopedia; and heard about it all our lives; but after staying there a week, we decided that Chicago is the worst advertised place in America. We didn't see a gangster anywhere.

We had planned to stop out about fifty miles this side of the city limits, so Elizabeth T wouldn't get nervous in the traffic. We thought it would be easier to go in on train or bus or whatever they had. But the nearer we got, the bolder we became; and the first thing we knew we were right beside Chicago's front yard, Grant Park; right on her front pavement. Michigan Avenue, and cars, real automobiles, were passing us on both sides, and still we weren't scared; that is, not much. We saw the lake, and the river which Chicago turned around. I thought it looked rather sulky.

We had heard monstrous tales of the famous "Loop," a place "not more than a quarter of a square mile in area," where a million and a half of people congregate daily to work, to shop, to transact business, or just to "see the sights." But we were not interested in the Loop, we dared not get near that. We drove around and around looking for a Sign that said "Post Office." We wanted an armful of mail from home and some *Banners*.

We finally found the office and as a reward got a postal card from our hired man's wife. That's all.

After that we found "Visitors' Tourist Service," met a girl from Middle Tennessee, first thing, selected our apartment from several listed; located it, and liked it, ate supper, and went to bed. Later we asked where the Loop was, and learned that we had spent half of Saturday afternoon driving around in it looking for that Post Office. Wasn't that a "let down!" And the traffic hadn't been as frightful as that in Columbia on First Monday. No, we don't know Chicago. But it is badly advertised.

THE NASHVILLE BANNER
THURSDAY, AUGUST 3, 1933

World's Fair Is One Place Where 50 Cents Buys More Than One Can See in Weeks

Some Helpful Hints for Those Who Contemplate a Visit to the Exposition

Color, Light, Culture

Enchanted Island Looked Like Santa Had Just Left

Editor's Note: This is the fourth article of a series by a Maury County farm woman, describing how she and her family took a two weeks' trip to the Century of Progress Exposition at a total cost of $59.

BY LERA KNOX

If we were to give our impressions of the fair in a few words, they would probably be: color and light, culture and courtesy, information and inspiration, tired people and sore feet.

Visitors may or may not find what they are looking for at the Century of Progress. A friend of ours went up there, and, to use his own language, "found out that the thing was over three miles long, walked all up and down it twice, and never did see anything." On the other hand, we saw enough sights in five

The author takes "time out" to make a few notations on the trip, and have a peek at the official guide book in order to get her bearings.

days to dream about for a lifetime, and if we could have stayed five months longer, we would not have seen all that we wanted to see. The difference is in the folks, not the fair.

Century of Progress is one place where 50 cents, paid for general admission, will buy more sights than you can look at in the longest day and the longest night, if you know how and where to look. Our advice to anyone interested would be to order an official guide book and to study it through and through, so that you may know what it is all about, and know where to find what interests you most. When you arrive at the fair grounds, go to some high point and get a view of the entire park. There you can readily get your bearings; otherwise you may wander around for days and miss the best things to see.

NEED NOT APOLOGIZE

The farmer needs to apologize to no one at the Century of Progress. The officials themselves, even those of highest rank, are indebted to him for the roof over their heads: the roof insulation of the Administration Building is made of processed cornstalks.

Space will not allow me to tell you of all the buildings, but I can give you some idea about how the others are built by describing this, the first building we entered. The building, like most of the others is erected for temporary use; therefore it is built of asbestos cement boards so that it can easily be salvaged at the close of the fair. It is said that these walls, although they are scarcely more than three inches thick, have insulating qualities equal to those of a thirteen inch brick wall. That's progress.

The building is laid out in the shape of a large E. The colors used on it are ultra-marine blue, yellow, and silver; and unique landscaping adds to its attractiveness.

You may think upon hearing of the freakish, flaring colors used on those great buildings, that you would not like them at all; and indeed at first sight you may not, but after a day or so, you really like, not only all the peculiar colors and their unusual blendings, but the modernistic or futuristic (or what-ever-it-is) shapes of the buildings. The effect becomes more and more pleasing as you gradually get used to it. And the beauty of the lights shining through and on the colors at night is indescribable. The first glimpse of the lighting of Chicago and of the exposition grounds as seen from the Tower at night almost took our breath. The long ribbons of light, which were cars coming and going on the boulevards, and the great beacon lights playing over all, seemed like a dream of fairyland to us country folk who, at home, use nothing stronger than one mantled reading lamp, an oil burner, if you please.

CENTURY OF PROGRESS

You may think that to have progressed like the past century has, it must have arisen very early in the dawn of civilization, but really, this precocious century is, they claim, just a hundred years old. When it began, Chicago was merely a cluster of log cabins huddling in the muddy marsh around Old Fort Dearborn, asking protection from savage Indians; now she is the second largest city in America. Her population of 4,000,000 is growing at the rate of 70,000 a year. She is all too big for my vocabulary; you'll have to see for yourself to appreciate or even guess at her size. Daddy says he won't argue with anyone who declares she's larger than Columbia.

On our first day at the fair, we tried to see the main features around the north entrance (Twelfth Street) and some of the island. We visited Field Museum, the $6,000,000 marble home of some of the most aristocratic stuffed animals in the world. Along with the animals are rocks, plants, skeletons, and so many relics and curios of present and forgotten ages from all parts of the earth, and some of the planets, that it would take days to see it all, and many columns to tell of it.

From the museum we went to that great home of fishes, the Shedd Aquarium. Swimming there in glass enclosed pools, all around the walls and on each side of the several halls (which are arranged somewhat like the spokes of a wheel around the central hub, a beautiful circular pool) are thousands of big and little fishes; all shapes, sizes, colors, and combinations of shapes, sizes, and colors. There were sharks from oceans, and guppies from tropical seas, and Arctic inhabitants that have to be kept in ice water. You will not be surprised that we do not remember the names of all of them when you have read and pronounced this one name, which belonged to one of the smaller fry; it is spelled "Humuhumunukunukuapuaa." This fish hails from Hawaii. I suppose its post office address would be Honolulu, R.F.D., if you want to know the rest of its name, write there. So much for fish; but we noticed that unusually large and interested crowds visited the aquarium. It is evidently very popular.

ABOUT THE BUILDINGS

Now a few words about the buildings on the island which we visited first. They are directly across the lagoon from the Administration Building, Sears-Roebuck Building, Illinois Host Building, Hall of Science, General Exhibits Building, Havoline Thermometer, and Firestone Building. The island extends from a bridge at the Twelfth Street entrance to another bridge at the Twenty-third Street entrance, so you can judge by counting the blocks how long it is, but you cannot imagine how beautiful. We crossed from the mainland on the Sky-Ride and went up into one of the 628-foot steel towers. Looking down on the island from this great height we could not but think that Santa Claus had come and brought all of toyland to spread out at our feet.

To the north we could see the dark granite dome of the Planetarium; the white and silver Dairy Building; the black and blue and orange and silver Agricultural Building; the tricolored United States Government Building with its three stately towers signifying the three branches of government: legislative, judicial, and executive; the V-shaped court of states adjacent to this building; and between all the buildings and the lagoon lay the beautifully landscaped Florida Gardens, while on the other side lay the lake, fringed by beautiful Jantzer Beach.

Looking southward from the tower we could see just below us the Boy Scout camp; the Hall of Social Science; Radio and Communications Building; Columbus and Edison Memorials; Electrical Building; the beautiful gardens surrounding the Horticultural Building and that building itself; the Enchanted Island, looking like fairyland itself, and the beautiful fountains at the foot of the lagoon. Dotted all among the larger buildings and larger areas of bright colors were smaller buildings set like gay little jewels among larger precious stones. Across the lagoon could be seen the Avenue of Flags bordered by other beautiful buildings and as far down the lake as we could see were colors, colors, colors, with silver birds of aircraft sailing over all.

THE NASHVILLE BANNER
FRIDAY, AUGUST 4, 1933

Farm Family Begins Inspection of Various Buildings at World's Fair

Artificial Cow That 'Moos' and Gives Milk Proves Unusually Interesting

No Tennessee Exhibit

Search for the 'Reason' Dry Fountain 'Spurts'

Editor's Note: This is the fifth article of a series by a Maury County farm woman, describing how she and her family took a two weeks' trip to the Century of Progress Exposition at a total cost of $59.

BY LERA KNOX

Coming down to earth again after getting a bird's-eye view of the beautiful panorama of Northerly Island from the Tower, we began to get some close-up views of the contents of some of the buildings. The outstanding feature of the Dairy Building is the color Organ, designed to play with colors as musical instruments play with sounds. With the accompaniment of music, colors, pictures, and an explanatory voice, the story is told in the pageant of "Man's Dependence Upon the Cow, His Foster Mother."

What a thrill! The *Banner* announces that the story of the "Farm Family Flivvering to the Fair" will be published in installments. Of course, there is lots of other news, but that item takes the eye of the whole family.

The Dairy Building is like a gigantic snail shell full of interesting things to see. This snail-shell shape makes it easier to follow one-way traffic through the halls, without retracing, overlooking, or getting lost. The prime object of the entire building is to persuade the public to "drink more milk."

In the Agricultural buildings nearby, moving exhibits attract many spectators. Newest improved farm machinery is being exhibited by the side of the old devices used throughout the past century. An example: with one piece of machinery, the manufacturer declares that "two men can do more and better work in ten hours than they could do in three months with old machinery and hand labor." It looked as though the farmer who bought one of those machines was due to be unemployed for eighty-nine days (and probably in debt for it longer).

One machine cuts, threshes, and cleans the grain (does all except grind it and make the biscuits) while you stand there and look at it.

THE "MOO" COW

The machinery exhibits included, also, corn harvesters, cotton-pickers, four-row cultivators, trucks, tractors, farm engines, feed grinders, and milking equipment operating automatically on an old cow who chewed her cud and looked so natural that she had to be sprayed to keep the flies off of her.

She would obligingly turn around and "moo" when the bucket got full: all that the lazy farmer had to do was turn off the switch and sell his milk. (If we hadn't already known better we might have been persuaded to go into the dairy business here.)

After the machinery, we saw some interesting fertilizer exhibits, and dozens of others showing the processes used to manufacture farm products into various nationally advertised foodstuffs. It seemed to be more of a display of manufactured goods than it did of farm products. If you go to the fair expecting to see big pumpkins, tall corn, and fine tobacco, or big hogs and fat cattle in the Agricultural Building, you are due to be disappointed. The manufacturers have the day, because, I suppose, they have the money. At any rate, the farmers haven't much.

If one is very much interested in flowers and gardens he may find it worthwhile to pay a nominal admission fee to get into the Horticultural Building. This is a large L-shaped building beside the lake, inclosing within its L a four-acre plot planted in model gardens of many different types. There are formal, informal, colonial, and modern, summer, spring, fall, winter, and rock gardens, rose gardens, Italian and other foreign gardens, and more kinds than I can tell you about here.

Inside the building, too, there are models of gardens and landscapes. But one thing that made me chuckle was what was represented to be the famous old Southern "Maxwell House." There it stood, a two-story Colonial residence with a magnolia tree draped in Spanish moss hovering over the doorway. Think of that, you folks who know the Maxwell House as it is today. Chicago is not the only place that needs accurate advertising.

TIP TO PARENTS

I could write pages about the Enchanted Island, but because of limited space will have to sum it all up by saying it is just the kind of place I would like to stay in if I had ten years and plenty of dimes to my credit. There are giants and fairies, a real-like castle, and mountains to slide down, and merry-go-rounds, and pop-the-whips, and story-telling ladies, and a marble house and a candy land, and a pop corn man, and a miniature train with a Boy Scout engineer, a theater, and a marionette show. In fact it is a World's Fair for children all in itself. (Tip to parents: a good place to leave the kiddies while you see the grown-up's fair).

In the great Electrical Building, curved like a C around a huge court and fountain, twenty companies with hundreds of educational exhibits depict the most interesting features and uses of "juice." The smallest incandescent light, one the size of a grain of wheat, is shown; in contrast there is a fifty-kilowatt light, the world's largest incandescent. Electricity is shown as an aid to farmers in all work from killing bugs to filling silos. When a farmer is ready to have his plowing done, he turns on his radio that starts a tractor to work. We saw so much electricity in that building that we felt almost "illuminated" when we came out.

The Radio and Communication Building lies between the Hall of Social Science and the Electrical Building. In it there are many exhibits explaining such things as the intricacies of dial telephones, radio telephones, scrambled speech, and an oscilloscope (Don't ask me what that is. Century of Progress will show you). The four gigantic bluegreen towers of this building can be seen from a great distance. They represent the four great means of communication—you guess what they are. Another important building on the island is the United

States Government Building. In it every department of our Government tells the story of its activities and achievements.

TENNESSEE MISSING

In the Parade of States, a V-shaped court where many states had interesting exhibits, we were "rebarrassed" as Jack said because Tennessee was not represented. We supposed however that it was for financial reasons that our State was left out—seems like we remembered hearing or reading something somewhere about Tennessee being in debt.

But some of the states were certainly "telling the world" about their great domains, their resources, and potentialities. Florida, for example, was on a great boom. Missouri, the 'show-me' State, really was showing the world a great exhibit. Other exhibits that we especially liked were California, Georgia, Illinois, and Wisconsin. Puerto Rico, too, had a creditable display and Washington had sent in some of the biggest strawberries that the world has ever seen, (I suppose). They were huge, anyway, and were in magnifying glass jars.

Now we must leave the island although we have not seen nearly all of it. But I want to take you up to the Sears-Roebuck Building to get a drink. A sign over a perfectly dry fountain says, "Cold Spot, Take a Drink, Just Bend Over." It may take a lot of faith to bend over and expect the water to come up and meet you, but if you bend the water comes. No, you can't guess why. We 'hicks' almost overflowed our capacities trying to find out why, and wherefore and where from until we discovered the "electric eye." It is a shiny piece of metal with a small light shining down on it from above; when the light is intercepted by your shadow, the water flows. That's all. Isn't it simple? I wished hard that every farm woman in the country had such an "electric eye" in her kitchen; bending over a fountain like that is a lot easier than bending over a well or spring away down the hill from the house. Sears also showed how to modernize completely kitchen, laundry, furnace room, and bath with but the touch of a button, but I wasn't able to get a special kind of button like that.

To the *Banner*:

Am pleased with your series of articles about the Knox family's trip to Chicago. It sure is good. She brings out her heartfelt anxieties and feelings in a way few if any others will turn loose and do.

That is what made Mark Twain, and Will Rogers catch the public. They told what they saw as they saw it.

Respectfully yours,
JNO. J. WILSON,
A *Banner* reader for thirty years.

THE NASHVILLE BANNER
SUNDAY, AUGUST 6, 1933

Two-Story, Nine-Acre Hall of Science Is 'Heart' of Century of Progress

One Might Spend Days in It And Learn Something New Every Hour of His Stay

All 93 Elements Shown

Suggests Visitors Flop Down On Every Bench Seen

Editor's Note: This is the sixth article of a series by a Maury county farm woman, describing how she and her family took a two weeks' trip to the Century of Progress Exposition at a total coast of $59.

BY LERA KNOX

The Hall of Science is the heart of the Exposition. In that one building a person with enough intelligence to understand it can spend days and days and be learning something new every hour. He can learn things worth while, too, and things that he will not easily forget, for they are depicted most clearly and vividly. We regretted that we had only a day to devote to this great hall. Trying to see it in a day is like trying to get a B.S. degree overnight.

The author, seated on the running board of "Elizabeth T" with her trusty portable in her lap, taps out the story of the farm family that flivvered to the fair.

In this two-story, nine-acre building are depicted the greatest steps gained in the study of the basic sciences within a century. Can you imagine from that statement how much there is to learn there? And the facts are shown, as many as possible, by moving exhibits which explain the processes and operations. The sciences to which this great hall is devoted are: chemistry, physics, mathematics, geology, biology, and medicine.

How chemists work, how elements are combined, how substances are analyzed, and how they are changed—even all of the ninety-three elements that are used in this old world's make-up are shown. It is in these chemical exhibits that you see a lot of things you can't believe, yet you know they are true; a teakettle boiling on a cake of ice, for example, it contains liquid air you know, and yet it puzzles you; a ribbon of iron burns like paper in a jet of oxygen; potassium bursting into flames when it is dropped into water; an electric furnace with a temperature of 3,400 degrees centigrade, think of that.

BELIEVE IT OR NOT

If I told you even the smallest things that the Hall of Science showed us, you would declare that we had confused that great building with Ripley's Believe-it-or-not Odditorium, but we didn't—we saw that, too. Now I am going to tell you something that will be hard for you to believe. I put my hand into a furnace that was heating a bar of iron to melting point, and didn't even get a blister, not the tiniest burn. (I am a Sunday school teacher, and I tell that for a fact.) Of course you want to know why? Well it was an electric furnace and it heated only metals or things that could be affected by electricity. My hand isn't metal, so I didn't feel the electricity, but if I had been wearing a ring it would doubtless have melted like wax and dropped off my finger (Moral: leave off your jewelry when you go into an electric furnace). Do you think that the fiery furnace of the Hebrew children could have been electrical?

From one extreme to another. We saw liquid air (which is just plain ordinary air that has been squeezed or compressed at 3,000 pounds to the square inch or until it is chilled to a temperature of 317 degrees below zero). We dipped the stem and leaves of a rose into that stuff and when we took them out they were frozen so stiff that they broke like glass.

I think I have found a way for Tennessee to solve her school teacher problem. They were using giant, talking, gesturing robots (the children called them iron men) at the fair to tell you what you needed to know about some of the exhibits. If we don't make better arrangements about paying our school teachers, we may have to install robots in our schools; they can be operated on school-teacher pay when Muscle Shoals puts out free electric power. Don't you think?

PHYSICS SECTION

In the Physics section a series of ninety exhibits shows the generation and control of power. There is a steam engine with glass cylinders that shows the operation of the steam within them. Fundamental principles of electric dynamos are shown, as also are interesting, if complicated, facts about X-rays and other lights and rays. It was all too big for me to comprehend in a short time. One ought to visit the Hall of Science alone, take his time, and study things out for himself. It is no place to appreciate with a fun seeking crowd if one is searching for information.

Mathematics and geology as they were shown there were unusually interesting, but a little too deep to be skimmed over in the short time we had for that building. Biology was especially interesting to us for we knew more about that to start with. (The idea is, the more you know already about a subject the more you can learn about it and the better you can understand it there.)

The department of medicine is wonderful. We learned just where all our internal organs are located, how they operate, what is and is not favorable to their operation; how to avoid and how to prevent some too-common diseases, and how pink pills are molded. We saw a huge malaria-laden mosquito bite a hideous looking skeleton and give him such a chill that his bones rattled shockingly; then his fever went up as high as the thermometer could carry it; and he must have had a splitting headache for the top of his skull turned back like the lid of a box. Needless to say we don't like mosquitoes after seeing that skeleton have malaria.

HALL OF RELIGION

Ranking in popularity with the fish farm machinery, and the Hall of Science, is the Hall of Religion. In this building the religions of many peoples are represented. Above the door is the inscription, "Righteousness exalted a nation." Beautiful strains of organ music greet the visitor, and he can hardly pass the inviting little chapel without stopping there for period of meditation and prayer. Many denominations and religious welfare organizations have exhibits in the building. Some give the past history of their faith; some tell of the accomplishments of their organizations, others explain more fully the reasons for their belief.

In this building may be seen the smallest Bible in the world, one smaller than a postage stamp—it is shown under a magnifying glass. There, also, is the famous Chalice of Antioch, one of the rarest relics of Christianity.

In the Firestone Building we saw tires being turned out like huge fat black doughnuts. Near the door a great machine was chewing, and rolling, and popping crude rubber as a flapper does her chewing gum. The rubber was joined to the fabric, gum-dipped, molded, and baked into a tire right before our eyes, and finally wrapped for shipment.

In another building we saw cars completely made with everything except the license tag and the gas and oil, all on one floor as we looked on from the balcony just above. The cars were Chevrolets with body by Fisher, for the men who worked on the body wore the name Fisher across the shoulders of their work suits, and the men who assembled the other parts were stamped "Chevrolet," so I know that they were not making Ford cars.

Time and *Fortune* offer a cool and pleasant place to rest and read, if you have time to read. We didn't. But we did take advantage of numbers of places to rest. One of the most important rules in seeing the Fair is drop on every bench and comfortable-looking chair that you see, and relax for just a few minutes.

THE NASHVILLE BANNER
MONDAY, AUGUST 7, 1933

Maury County Farm Family's Interest Is Held by International Egg-Laying Derby

Some of the Hens Are Kept In White Cottages, Others Are in Apartment Houses

Model Homes Inspected

Chicago Living Costs About In Line With Tennessee's

Editor's Note: This is the seventh article of a series by a Maury county farm woman, describing how she and her family took a two weeks' trip to the Century of Progress Exposition at a total cost of $59.

BY LERA KNOX

Trying to tell in a few short articles the many interesting things we saw, heard, and experienced on our trip is like trying to put a whole toy shop into the littlest baby's Christmas stocking.

After three days at the northern end of the fair grounds, we headed for the south end. We wanted to see that great "International Egg-Laying Derby." Now don't misunderstand—that's not a Plymouth Rock Hat, nor even a Leghorn. It is a contest in which 1,600 hens of twenty-four breeds from twenty-six states and four foreign countries are trying to see who can lay the most eggs. By the way, I learned this too: most here doesn't mean "many-est"; it means "heaviest." The eggs are weighed rather than counted, or that is the way I understood it. Some of the hens are kept in neat white cottages; others in "apartment houses." That is the only way I can explain it (after being in Chicago a few days I think in Chicago terms). If I had seen them on the farm I should have said "in wire coops, one on top of the other."

BABY CHICKS SOLD

The eggs laid in the contest are placed in mammoth incubators and given a chance to hatch. The baby chicks are sold or put into battery brooders, which might be called apartments for orphan chicks. The little fellows have just room enough to put their heads out to eat—but they thrive. Of 3,400 which were three weeks old, only 83 had died. I bought four little white Leghorn roosters at 15 cents each, the four weighing 1 1/2 pounds, so you may guess that they were large for their age. I don't know whether or not they were Sons of Lady Dixiana, the 342-egg hen from Georgia, who carries a life insurance policy of $10,000. Anyway, I don't think her policy is made out to her children. We named them Century, Progress, Chicago, and Illinois. These, with the cat and ourselves, made nine passengers for Elizabeth's homeward trip.

Within the grounds you may ride by bus, air, or water. We had been there three days before we discovered that a bus would give you a three mile ride through the grounds for a dime. That's service, if your feet hurt, and they will, don't worry. That's "about the feet-hurting-est place they is," as William Greenhill might have said. The pass-word, watch-word, byword, and cuss-word is "Oh, my feet." It's a great location for a corn doctor. I suppose it must be the concrete streets, and the great distances, and the fact that most of us have forgotten how to use our feet since autos were invented.

NO GONDOLAS, PLEASE

We rode by bus and by water, but not by air. "He that goeth not up, falleth not down"; that's our creed. Neither did we ride in the little gondolas. They are picturesque, I'll admit, but it looks like too much water and too little man. If the fellow who stands up and paddles the thing along should lose his balance—well it would be too bad, we thought.

One attraction of the gondolas is pointed out; it is that as the gondolier flows, he sings to you—so do the angels. But I don't have much appreciation for that kind of music, just yet. We stayed on dry land except for a spin in a gasoline launch, and I saw to it that I was sitting on a life preserver before I was ready for that to pull away from the dock. (I guess those are correct terms. I'm not a sailor.)

We spent very little time in Midway, not that it was not clean and creditable, but because time was limited and we were looking for education more than entertainment. We did stop at the Midget Village to chat with Homer Park, our own Maury County boy; he is just seven feet tall, and to see him with those two-and-a-half foot Midgets makes you almost believe in Gulliver. Homer is a great old boy; we learned that he had just had a letter from his mother telling of the good rain that has come in Tennessee. Daddy began to get homesick at once.

The buildings of foreign nations interested us very little; they appeared to be just places to sell souvenirs. There are plenty of restaurants, cafes, lunch and cold drink stands about the grounds. Sandwiches and drinks were priced at 10 and 15 cents each, but having a hungry crowd and a thin purse, I almost always prepared a picnic snack and carried it along with us.

We enjoyed looking through the eleven model homes. They are not so peculiar-looking face to face as they seem in their pictures. The colors used in them are so soft and pleasing that you can not even remember what they were after you leave the houses.

It is the color, though, rather than the lines of architecture that make them attractive. That is the reason they must be seen to be appreciated.

WHAT TO WEAR

Now I wonder what I can say in the few inches left of this article that will tell you what you want to know about the fair. For one thing, I imagine that the women will want to know what other women are wearing there. Margaret was the style-specialist of the expedition. She reports that they were wearing more silk suits; that is, one-piece dresses with three-quarter length coats, than anything else. We saw hundreds of these in all colors from pastels to dark shades. Besides those ensembles, we noticed many linen suits. But the apparently washable two piece silks seemed better suited to the fair than anything else. We may have had an unusual week of weather for our trip, but every night and early morning after we crossed the Ohio, coats were welcome.

Now you may ask where you can stay if you go to the fair. Hotel rooms seem plentiful at $1.50 to $5 per room. Rooming houses offer accommodations at from 50 cents to $1.50 per person per night, and tourist camp prices run about the same.

We were thoroughly pleased with our little apartment. We were in a good neighborhood, out in North Chicago. One block from Lincoln Park, and a few doors from the home of Amos 'n' Andy (I think it must have been their Fresh Air Taxicab that parked between their apartment house and ours every night by the side of Elizabeth T). In this section apartments range in price from $7 for a single day to $20 a week. For from $10 to $15, a party of four can get comfortable rooms, that is living-room, two bedrooms, bath, and kitchenette, with modern conveniences and everything furnished except food.

Food ranges in price just about like it does in Nashville and Columbia. If you buy from a delicatessen you pay more, if at a grocery you pay less. But you won't like the milk, and you won't have any hoe-cakes. Sad but true.

THE NASHVILLE BANNER
TUESDAY, AUGUST 8, 1933

Farm Wife Decides Yankees Didn't Kill Her Frying-Size Chickens After All

If the Fair Had Been Held First, There Would Have Been No Civil War, She Says

Finds Use for Collegians

Family Admires Any City That Can Turn River Around

Editor's Note: This is the eighth article of a series by a Maury County farm woman, describing how she and her family took a two weeks' trip to the Century of Progress Exposition at a total cost of $59.

BY LERA KNOX

Because Yankee soldiers killed my great-grandmother's frying-size chickens, I inherited a bad taste in my mouth toward anything "Northern"; and because, try as I do, I can't overlook the headlines of the terrible crimes, murders, and kidnapings that are advertised freely on front pages of newspapers, I believed that north of the line is "where the wicked dwell."

So after we crossed that mile-long bridge at Louisville, I said to my outfit, "From here on we must be very dignified; don't talk to strangers and be very careful what you say to anybody; you are 'over the line' now and you are likely to meet a Yankee or a gangster any time."

Well sir, you could have knocked us down with a feather duster. The first filling station operator we saw on that side of the river was every bit as nice as the last one we saw on the other side. But we all admitted maybe he was an exception. Just a bait, perhaps, but we did like the kind of bait they used.

IT ISN'T SO

This is what we thought about Chicago before we got there:

Hold your hat! Hold your purse!
Hide your money in your shoe!
Trust Nobody!
You're in Chicago now.

Lock your trunk! Bolt your door!
Tie your key about your neck!
Trust Nobody!
You're in Chicago now.

You'll be disappointed in Chicago if you are addicted to newspaper reading. Don't go up there expecting the gangsters to put on a special display for you—murder you or kidnap you or shoot off a machine gun in your honor. They simply don't do that for ordinary people. You won't be "taken for a ride" either, unless you pay for it—7 cents on the street car and 10 cents on the bus.

Now I am going to tell you a dark and family secret. Don't tell it, for if you do I may get in bad with the newspapers for libel or something like that. But it's this: I don't believe in gangsters! I think they have been invented to fill in whatever newspaper space the advertisers won't buy. They are like fairies, and giants and gnomes, just made up to make fairy tales out of.

Now I may be wrong. I just know we didn't see them. They may have been away on vacation, of course; or they may have been in the "underworld"; I suppose that is where the subways take you. We didn't ride them, too much to see on top of the ground. The only troubles we found in Chicago were too much chlorine in the water, too little cream in the milk—and the fact that the people there are hard of hearing or can't understand plain Tennessee English. I know I talk distinctly, but every time I said anything to anybody I had to say it over and over again.

TALK "FEST!"

People there said that they didn't need to see our Tennessee car license to know we were from the South; we didn't know whether they meant that to be complimentary or vice versa. The nearest I came to getting an insult, was when I went into a store to get bread, cheese, milk, and peanut butter, and that grocer couldn't understand such simple words as that. He couldn't talk plain himself, but I managed to understand that he was trying to ask me why I didn't "talk fest." Well I never did see much need of being in all that hurry.

I never was as busy and as rushed as Chicagoans are—but they do have a lot to do I know. Why they even turned their river around and made it go back the other way. They didn't want all the dirty Illinois water in their pretty blue lake, and I don't blame them. But they load all their filth into the river and send it back somewhere into Illinois; at least that is the way I understood their sewage system. At any rate, I do know that the river looks sulky and pouty about something, and I supposed that was what the trouble was.

But as I was going to say, and this will surprise you if you ever heard of the Civil War, those Yankees are not nearly so bad as they are advertised. They are just the same sort of folks we are. Now of course I wouldn't go so far as to say that they are all angels, they couldn't be. There'd never be enough wings to go around, but they certainly are nice to you, or they were to us.

We made up our minds to be nice to them but everybody we met was a little nicer to us than we could be to them. The harder we tried, the harder they tried, until at last it all resolved itself into a "Being Nice Contest," and they won—but they were on their own ground.

USE FOR COLLEGE STUDENTS

We learned why college students were invented. Guess. No you can't. It is to show people around over Chicago and to give information to visitors and to roll those fat women with tired feet and plump purses around the fair grounds in baby buggies for a dollar an hour. Now you people who think all college boys swear and drink and wear coonskin coats will have to guess again, the ones we saw didn't have on coonskin coats nor much else, especially the boys who pull the Jin-rick-shas. Visitors can see the fair that way, too. There is a transportation for every purse and a college boy for every wheel chair. And they are all nice.

I cannot close this article without a tribute to the "boy's in gray." Don't misunderstand again. I mean the fine, upstanding, soldier-like young men who stood all day on feet that must have been aching and burning, and sweltered in hot blue-gray uniforms with bright red trimmings, and guarded the exhibits and gave in the kindest way the very information that you wanted. If you were tired and cross about anything they knew how to smooth down your ruffled temper just as a doctor does. They are wonders, those boys in gray, and as necessary to the Fair as President Dawes himself. They are, too, by the way, young college men who have been trained for this particular work.

And the people who attend the fair! You would never imagine that there are so many high class, refined, intelligent, cultured people in all the world. This fair seems to attract the "cream" of the country, no trash did we see anywhere; they were all nice people. And I think that any country that can produce as much "cream" as is attending the Century of Progress Exposition, is rich indeed, and we are gladder and prouder than ever that we are Americans, not merely Tennesseans. I don't believe that the Civil War could ever have been fought if they had had this Fair first. And I doubt if it was Yankees that killed my grandmother's chickens after all.

THE NASHVILLE BANNER
WEDNESDAY, AUGUST 9, 1933

Fair Exhibits Put Life in Fossilized Historical Facts for Maury Family

Replica of Fort Dearborn Recalls Stories of the Frontier Indian Battles

Antiques Are Plentiful

Chief A. Roi Clearwater Poses with Jack Knox

Editor's Note: This is the ninth article of a series by a Maury County farm woman, describing her family's two weeks' trip to the Century of Progress Exposition, which was made at a total cost of $59.

BY LERA KNOX

Henry Ford is credited—or discredited—with saying, "History is the bunk." Perhaps it is, when it consists of dry, fossilized faces which are cut on the bias to "suit the consumer," or of dates that can't be remembered after the examination papers are handed in. But when we met history face to face on its own old "stamping ground," we liked "the bunk," especially, as Jack said, when nobody had to hand in written work except mother. To see an historical place, or anything else at its best, we think it necessary to let the spot light of imagination play over it a little, anyway.

We tried to remember. Did Chicago used to be in Louisiana? Did Marquette and Joliet discover this territory? Or was it La Salle? And who named the land from the Gulf to the Lakes, "Louisiana" for a French king? Was Chicago included in the Louisiana Purchase? Now brush the dust off your history book and find out. I know, now, but I won't tell.

In 1803, it seems, Capt. John Whistler, grandfather of the artist who painted "Mother," led a troop of soldiers to the mouth of the Chicago River and built a fort, which was called Fort Dearborn. This was the farthest outpost of the United States at that time.

Nine years later in an Indian attack fifty soldiers and settlers were killed and fifty others wounded, and the fort was burned. It was rebuilt, however, in 1816, and remained intact until 1857. A replica of the old fort has been built to show the visitors to Century of Progress what Chicago used to look like.

There are seven buildings within the stockade, a tall fence built of logs sharpened and driven into the ground, and sharpened on top, too, to keep the Indians from climbing over. There are double rows of these palings. The fort at the fair is built according to the plans and specifications used by Captain Whistler in building the original fort. They were obtained by Chicago Historical Society and Century of Progress from the War Department.

At the northeast and southwest corners of the large fenced-in enclosure there are taller buildings called towers or block houses from which the soldiers could watch for enemies and use their guns. The second story of each block house extends out over the fence.

Inside the big square enclosure of the fort is the soldiers' parade ground. A flag pole stands in the center. Someone called our attention to the fact later that the flag had fifteen stars and fifteen stripes, representing the number of states at that time. I thought that there should have been seventeen stars but I didn't argue. I suppose news traveled so slowly back in those days that up to 1812 Chicago people hadn't heard that Tennessee entered the Union in 1796 and Ohio in 1803; they just recognized Vermont, 1791, and Kentucky, 1792.

A stone building inside the enclosure was built to hold powder and ammunition. Guides in and about the premises, dressed in the uniforms of that era made us think that the soldiers were still there.

ANTIQUES

The contents of the rooms of the old fort will make an antique collector clap her hands with delight. There are four-posters, trundle-beds, corner-cupboards, rocking-chairs, hand-hewn benches, antique lanterns, grease lamps, candle holders, pewter dishes, and irons in ancient fireplaces, long-handled frying pans, spits for roasting fowl and game, huge iron, brass, and copper kettles, a large maple churn, a wooden mill for grinding meat, a dough tray large enough to serve as a baby cradle in its leisure moments, and even warming pans to slip between those rough home-spun hand-woven sheets to make them "comfy" on cold wintry nights. Yes, those old settlers had their luxuries.

In the upstairs rooms of the block houses there were benches to stand on so one could rest one's gun on the edge on the long narrow opening—one log wide—and shoot at the Indians. There were two brass cannons brought to the original fort in 1804, and two others made in Paris in 1793, and plenty of rifles and other guns. If the soldiers and settlers had stayed in the fort one August 15, 1812, they might have protected themselves, but they were out on the lake edge, going somewhere else when they were attacked, and the fort was burned the next day. The orders given to Captain Heald by General Hull to evacuate the fort are shown in facsimile in the fort, as are many other interesting documents.

LAND CHEAP

A treaty between the United States and tribes of the Fox and Sac Indians shows that the land in Northern Illinois was bought for 3 cents an acre in 1832. I wondered when I read that how much an acre of Grant Park, fronting on Michigan Avenue would be worth now.

We met a "friendly" Indian at the Trading Post, one of the buildings of old Fort Dearborn. That is he was friendly when we approached him and told him we were a farm family from Tennessee looking for interesting things to tell the people back home—the *Banner* readers.

He said that he, too, had been in Tennessee, had read the *Banner*, and that he, too, was aspiring to learn to write. He confessed, as he pulled a notebook from under the counter, that he had been writing down some of the questions asked him by the "so-called civilized white people, who look upon the Indian as unintelligent."

I suppose Chief A. Roi Clearwater thought we looked enough like "pioneers" that he could trust us with his private jokes, for I noticed that he is vary reticent with most of the people who come into the Fort, especially with the regular run of newspaper representatives. He said he was "afraid of them." Imagine my surprise when I looked up from his "diary" to find a battery of cameras turned on the chief and myself. He saw them too, and stepped quickly into the shadow, leaving me in the lime light alone. I don't think, however, anyone could have mistaken the woman in the picture for Pocahontas, although there was no doubting Chief Clearwater's reality. He willingly posed for a picture with Jack. He did this, I think, because Jack has a habit of "liking" folks, and he repeatedly told us all, "I like that Indian."

THE NASHVILLE BANNER
THURSDAY, AUGUST 10, 1933

Farm Family Is Thrilled by the Home And Study of the Author of 'Ben Hur'

Gen. Lewis Wallace's Garden Found Maintained as He Had Arranged It in Past

Valuable Objects Seen

Case Contains Original Copies of Famous Volumes

Editor's Note: This is the tenth article of a series by a Maury County farm woman, describing her family's two weeks' trip to the Century of Progress Exposition which was made at a total cost of $59.

BY LERA KNOX

If you have read *Ben Hur*, *Prince of India*, *The Fair God*, or *The Life of Gen. Benjamin Harrison*; if you have heard how their author, Gen. Lewis Wallace, commanded a division at the capture of Fort Donelson, led the attack in the second day's fight in the battle of Shiloh, prevented our own Gen. E. Kirby Smith from capturing Cincinnati, and General Early from capturing Baltimore and Washington, served as a member of the commission that tried the assassins of President Lincoln, and served as Governor of New Mexico and Minister to Turkey, you will know why we were delighted to know that his home and his very peculiar "study" were located at Crawfordville, Ind.

You will not be surprised either that after the Riley family had told us many interesting things about General Wallace of his friendship with "Brer Jim," the Hoosier poet, and had given us a very kind and much appreciated letter to the custodian of the Wallace property, we were determined to go to Crawfordville.

We did not know before that it was an argument with Bob Ingersol, the noted infidel, that caused Lew Wallace to write *Ben Hur, a Tale of Christ*. Mr. Ingersol undoubtedly did more good than he knew. We passed near the station where Wallace got off the train after this argument, and determined to write a religious story as Ingersol had sarcastically challenged him to do.

From the minute we saw the gate of the park that surrounds the study we knew we were in for an interesting visit, perhaps a series of thrills. I can't explain that gate, it just does something to you that makes you feel thrilly inside. I learned later that it is modeled after an old Abbey gate of the Eleventh Century in France.

THE STUDY

That study! In front of it stands a monument, a bronze statue of the General, cast from a model of the marble statue which is in the Hall of Fame at Washington. This statue marks the spot where the old "Ben-Hur Beech"—one of the noblest of its kind—offered its protection to General Wallace as he wrote with his "lap-board" on his knees. The study is a large brick building, with few windows in the sides. All the light comes from the skylight. The frieze is sculptured to represent the characters in his books.

The garden around the study is as it was made by the General. I am glad he made that garden, glad to know that he was that kind of man. It is a lovely place owned and maintained by the Wallace family, and carefully watched over by Col. Walter D. Elliott, who thirty-one years ago was selected by General Wallace to be its custodian.

All within the study is associated with General Wallace and his family. Beside the fireplace is his favorite chair, rug, taboret, lap-board, and other paraphernalia that he used in writing. On a bench nearby lay his violin and Mrs. Wallace's guitar. They are now tied together with a scrap from her wedding dress, worn in May 1852. There is also an unfinished violin—he was a violin maker. A real Stradivarius hangs on the wall above (that is one reason for the locked doors and gates and the reason Mr. Elliott is never without his big gun.) About the room are pictures and sketches that General Wallace made, and some specimens of molding and sculpturing. He must have been really a genius in many ways. There are also poems and songs that Mrs. Wallace wrote. So there must have been more than one gifted member of the family.

In the center of the room, right under the peculiarly shaped dome that lights the room, is a case containing the original copies of *Ben-Hur*, *Prince of India*, and *The Fair God*. *Ben-Hur* is written in pencil in the neatest, most legible handwriting I have ever seen. One of the other books was written with pencil, but the other was a printer's copy written in ink. Besides these there are more than 100 other valuables in the room.

There were letters from Abraham Lincoln; from General Dix, famous for the order "If anyone attempts to haul down the American Flag, shoot him on the spot;" from W. H. Bonney, desperate outlaw known as "Billy the Kid," who at that time had twenty-one murders proved against him; from Richard Gatling, inventor of the first rapid fire gun, rejected by United States but accepted by France; an inquiry from the Sultan of Turkey asking if there were any position or compensation in the gift of His Majesty that would induce General Wallace to return to Constantinople after a six years' absence. This, we were told, was probably the greatest compliment ever paid the General.

I looked about the room for things that would give me an idea of the character of the noted man who had lived there. Undoubtedly he loved the people of his books. Hand painted pictures and sculptured models of them were all about. He loved music, art, and flowers.

I wondered then, what those who knew him thought of him and I found this inscription on a loving cup: "A Token of Respectful Admiration and Affection from His Hoosier Friends. Thro' all this tract of years wearing the white flower of a blameless life!" Thomas Buchanan Read pays this tribute, "I have fallen in love with many a woman, never with but one man—Lew Wallace."

While at Crawfordville we were not very far from the home of the famous Abe Martin. How we should have liked to visit that! And we would have liked also to have seen Gene Stratton Porter's Limberlost Cabin in a nearby county, but we were headed for home and, well, you know how we felt.

THE NASHVILLE BANNER
FRIDAY, AUGUST 11, 1933

Maury County Farm Family Pays Tribute to Lincoln

Writer Wonders Why Some of Money for Temple Covering Cabin Couldn't Have Gone for Conveniences in Cabins of Other 'Nancies'

Editor's Note: This is the eleventh article of a series by a Maury County farm woman describing her family's two weeks' trip to the Century of Progress Exposition, which was made at a total cost of $59.

BY LERA KNOX

"It is fitting indeed," say the officials of Chicago's 1933 World's Fair, "that in an exposition of the progress of a century, the most important man of that century should hold a high and important position. Lincoln holds that place by right and by acclamation." For this reason the story of his life and memorable actions is told in a series of excellent exhibits at the fair.

We were not interested in Lincoln as President, or in Lincoln as the Great Emancipator (anyone could sign a "scrap of paper"), but we are intensely interested in Lincoln as a man—a man who because he struggled through poverty, handicaps, hardships and tragedy, came out with a "soul."

The fact that "Lincoln's great heart and brain sprang from poor unlettered ancestry and were nourished in the sterile soil of backwoods life" has inspired millions and will continue to inspire other millions.

The tragedy of Lincoln was not only in his assassination, it was woven into every inch of the fabric of his life, yet he could humorously say—not of life, but of one of its incidents—he "was like the boy who stumped his toe, it hurt too bad to laugh and he was too big to cry."

SUFFERING TAUGHT SYMPATHY

Suffering taught him sympathy, hardships taught him humility, deprivation taught him appreciation; experience taught him to say and to practice: "Stand with anybody that stands right. Stand with him while he is right, and part with him when he goes wrong."

Life itself inspired him to exhort, "Let us have faith that right makes might, and in that faith let us to the end dare to do our duty." In spite of deepest sorrows, of unjust prejudices, and unsympathetic friends he was able to live and die "with malice towards none, with charity for all."

These are the reasons we visited the places connected so intimately with his life, why we paid reverent homage to Lincoln—not because he was a President but because he was a man.

In a marble temple, erected at a cost of $250,000, is reverently preserved the weatherworn log cabin of Thomas and Nancy Lincoln where Abraham was born. Perhaps, I am irreverent and iconoclastical but I thought as I looked at that memorial edifice, "What a pity some of the money spent to put that building around the outside of that cabin could not have been spent to put running water and other modern conveniences into the cabins of other "Nancy Lincolns."

The Lincoln family, so Abraham said, "removed from Kentucky to what is now Spencer County, Indiana, in my eighth year. We reached our new home about the time the State came into the Union. It was a wild region, with many bears and other wild animals, still in the woods. There I grew up. There were some schools, so-called. There was absolutely nothing to excite ambition for education. Of course when I came of age I did not know much. Still, somehow, I could read, write, and cipher to the rule of three, but that was all. The little advance I now have upon this store of education, I have picked up from time to time under pressure."

A monument now marks the spot where the family built a rude shelter of un-hewn logs without a floor, and hung skins over the large opening for protection from the cold Indiana winter. Here Nancy Lincoln died and was buried on the hill nearby.

A monument, erected by a friend, marks the spot where a President's mother was buried in a rude coffin made by her husband, Thomas Lincoln, and their nine-year-old son, Abraham.

I wondered as I stood beside that lonely grave what kind of woman Nancy Hanks Lincoln could have been. How in the few short years that she was spared to her family, could she have inspired the boy Abraham to become the man, "Honest Abe"? Then I remembered this:

Nancy Hanks was inspired with the divine attitude of the fireside. Loved and honored for her wit, geniality, and intelligence, she justified an ancestry reaching beyond the seas...to her was entrusted the task of training a giant in whose childhood's memories she was hallowed. Of her he said: "My earliest recollections of my mother is sitting at her feet with my sister, drinking in the tales and legends that were read and related to us."

To him on her deathbed she said, "I am going away from you, Abraham, and I shall not return, I know you will be a good boy, that you will be kind to Sarah and your father. I want you to live as I have taught you to and to love your Heavenly Father."

"All that I am or hope to be I owe to my angel mother."

One of the "thrills" north of Midway is advertised as "The World a Million Years Ago." This stands near the Twenty-third street gate, on a hillside by the lagoon.

The building is globe-shaped and painted to represent the world. Around and above the entrance, mammoths and prehistoric animals are grunting and growling and gesturing. These are samples of what may be seen inside.

Strange though it may seem, our children were much more interested in the moving platform that carried us around to see the exhibits than they were in any of the replicas.

Stepping upon the platform, we were first carried by six dioramas which are like real, and yet like pictures. Well that's the way the dioramas looked. They represented "animals of the ice age, and man before the dawn of history." The huge, hideous creatures were moving, talking or grunting, and behaving and appearing in such a way that we congratulated ourselves—thankful that if they were any relatives of ours, the relation was happily "very distant."

The moving platform carried us on to see gigantic beasts and reptiles in a peculiarly lighted arena. There were hairy mammoths, giant gorillas, saber-toothed tigers, fighting ground sloths, and moving, noisy platybelodons, glyptodons, triceratops, pterodactyls, brontosaurus, and dinosaurs, and too many others with unspellable, unpronounceable names.

I don't think much of the appearance of the prehistoric men and women, but if they could pronounce the names of their domestic animals, they were more highly educated than I am.

THE NASHVILLE BANNER
SUNDAY, AUGUST 13, 1933

Four Farm Folks in a Ford Mistake Bootlegging Joint for Tourist Home

Decide to Go on in Rain Despite Appeals of Proprietor 'Feeling His Oats'

Experience Best Teacher

There Is No Place like Knoxdale After All

Editor's Note: This is the final article of a series by a Maury County farm woman, describing her family's two weeks' trip to the Century of Progress Exposition, which was made at a total cost of $59.

BY LERA KNOX

This is the article that chronicles the return of four farm folks in a Ford, or, if I may apologize to Mark Twain, of four "Ignorants A-Ford."

We were ignorant when we started and ignorant when we returned, and yet we had learned four headsful and two and a half notebooksful. Of it all I believe our last lesson was the greatest, "There's no place like home."

—BANNER Staff Photo

After all, there's no place like home, concludes the Maury County Farm family that went to the Century of Progress aboard "Elizabeth T." The family is shown as it arrived before the portals of Knoxdale.

But that next-to-last lesson, that was an experience, one that we won't soon forget.

We had gone far away from the regular route in order to see places where interesting events had happened, and to meet people who had done interesting things; night was coming down, aided by dark clouds that promised rain and storm. We were in a section of detours and mud, and few and shabby houses, no tourist camp or home could we hear of. After traveling hard all day, how we did want a "bath and a bottle of milk," a bed and a *Banner*. That cloud looked as though it would make us very grateful for a shelter also.

Then we came to a filling station. We loaded up with gas and asked about arrangements for the night. The nearest place had a beer garden. We had spent one noisy Saturday night near a beer garden so we asked, "Where is the next nearest nice place, I mean really nice place, you see we have our two children with us, and we don't want them to see or hear anything they shouldn't." That's how ignorant we were and are.

"THE VERY PLACE"

"Oh, I know the very place," said the operator. "It's eight miles down the road, off the highway a short distance and near the detour; a little hard to get to, but they are nice folks, just a man and his wife, and they will keep you, I know." Other complicated directions for reaching the place followed. We were to ask for Mr. A.'s place, in case we got lost.

It was dark then, and raining. Our curtains were under the seat. We had been in too much of a hurry to stop and eat supper, so you can guess how hungry we were as well as dead tired and sleepy.

We followed the directions and found the place. We asked the man who came to the door, "Is this Mr. A's place?"

"Yeah!"

"Are you Mr. A?"

"Naw, he ain't here, he done me dirty, an' I run him off."

Then what could we say? This is what we did say: "Well, we are looking for a nice place to spend the night, and Mr. C. told us to come here."

"That's funny. Funny he'd send you here, him an' me's at outs. He's a buddy of A's, but A ain't here. He's moved."

"Can you tell us then where we can spend the night?"

"Why, shore! Right here, if yer want ter. We got plenty of room—that is, wait till I ask the old lady."

Gone a few minutes, then back again. "She says OK if you can make it with one room. Our other room is 'bout full." Then apologetically, "You see, the old woman she's sorter mad at me today, and I never know what sort of humor she would be in about things."

"Aw nothing! Nothing! I ain't never got low down enough to charge folks fer spending the night at my house. Why I kept a man and his wife and six children and twelve chickens for a week and never charged them a cent.

I looked at Daddy and I suppose he looked at me, but it was too dark to "exchange glances." Meanwhile Mr. B was ushering Elizabeth T into a shed and wanting to help us unload.

"FEELING MY OATS"

I won't try to describe the "room" except that it was like the loft of a new barn. Mr. B went up to show us around and he talked more and faster every minute. Finally the "Missus" called to him and he said, "I know, I know," then turning to us he said, "I know I'm feeling my 'oats' a little tonight, but I've been 'under the weather' for two or three days, and just had to doctor up a bit." He staggered down stairs to get us a bucket of water. And we wondered. We wondered if that were "oats" or "corn" he was feeling, and how big a "crop" he had garnered.

We decided that I had better go down and talk to the "Missus." I told her I was sorry to come in on her that way, that we had been looking for Mr. A and as he had moved away we would go on and not inconvenience her that night. But to no avail, her hospitality was as generous as the "Mister's."

When I got back upstairs Mr. B had given some money to the rest of the family and had taken them in to show them his "stock in trade" in bottles and bottles piled up high in the "other room." We "yessed" everything he said until his wife called him downstairs, then we held a family council. To go, or not to go; and where; and how? That was the question. Margaret decided it for us. "Well. I'm tired and sleepy, but I won't go to bed here tonight." So said we all of us. But how? He might fight, or something.

I decided to go to the "Missus" and take a chance. "Will you not get mad if I tell you the truth?" I asked. "Our children have never seen a person who had been drinking and they are scared to death. They won't even go to bed. I'm sorry, and I hope you will understand, but we will have to go somewhere else.

"HE AIN'T TIGHT"

"Why he ain't tight," she exclaimed, surprised.

"I know," I said, "but we will have to go." She consented and I went back upstairs in a rush.

"Get ready, gather up everything, put his money on the dresser, and let's go quick." We went quick all right.

Mr. B went back to the garage with us, helped us load up Elizabeth, and as Daddy stepped on the starter, Mr. B humbly said, "I'm sorry you thought I was too drunk—but I wasn't going to charge you nothing." I'll say he was generous, show me any other business man who will give you the money with which to buy his wares.

I think even Elizabeth T was trembling more than usual as she pulled us out and through that mud of the detour; it was late and raining, and dark as Africa and still we had had no supper. We went on and on however until we did find a place where we could stay, even if beds were $8 per. They were worth it, and there was a bath tub, and rain water, and plenty of soap. How we did wash off that "tourist feeling" and how we slept!

Out we pulled next morning early, and headed toward home. We scarcely stopped for sight-seeing that day.

I remember saying, "I would like to stop and see Jeff Davis' birthplace." "Oh, I just want to see my birthplace," Margaret replied earnestly. Then mischievous Jack: "Well, if Daddy drives much faster, you may—being as it was a hospital."

So on we rattled toward our own birthplaces. When we got in to Knoxdale late in the night we were so tired that we probably would have gone to bed with our hats on if the hats had not become ashamed and dropped off.

When I opened my eyes next morning the place around me looked like something I was seeing in a dream. The figures on the wallpaper looked familiar, the dresser, the bed, the window-shades, even the old rug on the floor looked like home—I caught myself saying, "I wonder if this is really home or just a 'replica'!" (I had heard that word so much at historical places it seemed familiar enough for daily use.)

FAMILIAR NOISES

I realized well enough it was home when I heard those white leghorn roosters crowing, the ducks quacking, and the calves bawling, and pigs squealing, when Jack turned Buppo into the house for a romp. We always turn the pup in when there is a real celebration on hand. The little rascal was so happy to see us that I think I would not have scolded even if he had carried off one of my second best Sunday stockings.

And for breakfast we had real Jersey milk once more. While we were in Chicago we could probably have hugged any cow that looked like she would give Jersey milk.

And the water! Weren't we glad to get one more drink of water that wouldn't put a "coating" on our tongues. Lake Michigan is good to look at but terrible to taste.

The main business of the morning was baths, regular all-round Saturday-night-and-Sunday-morning combination soakings and scourings in plenty of hot, soapy cistern water. We took off at least that top layer of Tennessee, Kentucky, Indiana, and Illinois grime that had imbedded itself in our bodies. Now, after a few more Saturday night and Sunday morning exercises, and after resting from the first trip, we are eager to go back and see it all over again.

I promised to tell you how much "brass" we used with our $59 in travelers checks and silver in order to see it all and get home again. This is the truth. The only extra change we had were "Please" and "Thank you." They purchased courtesies that money alone could never have bought.

THE NASHVILLE BANNER
SUNDAY, AUGUST 20, 1933

Banner Feature Writer Is Called Fair's Most Resourceful Visitor

Chicago, Ill., Aug. 19—(Special)—Perhaps the fair's most resourceful visitor is Mrs. Lera Knox, sturdy farm woman of Maury County, Tenn. She and her husband and two children stayed in Chicago for sixteen days and saw everything time permitted, on their first trip to the Chicago World's Fair—A Century of Progress. The whole journey cost them $58.95. They ate foods from their farm, and Mrs. Knox was able to earn money by selling her well-written articles about the fair to the *Nashville Banner*. They are at the fair on their second trip now and have brought twelve neighbors with them.

A NOTE FROM THE TRAVELS EDITOR

After the flivver trip to Chicago Lera went back to Nashville to collect her pay. She was told that the series of articles had been so successful that the *Banner* was going to double the rate of pay that had been promised. The family turned around and went back to Chicago again.

After the Knox family made two trips to Chicago in 1933, we made a winter trip to Florida, and the next summer went to Washington, D.C. The impetus for the Washington trip was the fact that the organization, Country Women of the World, was meeting there that summer. Mrs. Roosevelt invited them to have tea with her on the White House lawn. She held a news conference in the White House on the morning before the tea.

Daddy drove Elizabeth T through the White House entrance and parked on the front driveway, under a large shade tree. He, Jack and I waited there for Mother to attend the conference. (To do such a thing in this post—9/11 era sounds almost unbelievable.)

At the press conference Mother said to Mrs. Roosevelt, "If a country woman from Tennessee were entertaining half as many guests as you are expecting this afternoon, she would have to borrow a lot of dishes from her neighbors."

Mrs. Roosevelt replied, "Well, fortunately here in Washington there are places where we can rent such things."

When the time came for the party Mrs. Roosevelt mingled with the crowd and shook hands with everyone. At one time she called attention of everyone to the fact that the President had come out on the family balcony and was waving from his wheelchair.

Margaret Knox Morgan

PART II

Westward, Ho!

PART II

Westward, Ho!

A NOTE FROM THE TRAVELS EDITOR

Shortly after we returned from Washington, D.C., Mr. Lynn, a family friend, asked if we would be interested in joining a group of neighbors on a camping trip to the West Coast. Daddy suggested Mother, my brother, and I go and he would stay home and care for the farm, since he had made that trip by train in his bachelor days.

Mr. Lynn, a mechanic, built a "camping trailer," and Mother checked with her editors. The editors were interested. Mr. Lynn's teenage son, my 13-year old brother Jack, and I, then fifteen, made up the younger contingent of the 15-member party. While

Mr. Lynn did the last minute tuning of the old Buick that would pull the trailer, the passengers wrote wisecracks on the trailer. Except for the fact that we created attention wherever we went, the trip out, along the southern route, was relatively uneventful. It included camping out at the Grand Canyon National Park. (Twenty years later on a train from Copenhagen to Germany, we encountered a woman who, with her family, had also sat around the campfire that night on the rim of the Canyon. We were not a group that was easily forgotten.)

The first real excitement came when we reached Hollywood. Mr. Lynn parked in front of a barbershop that just happened to be across the street from Paramount Studios. As men came out of the barbershop, we naive travelers asked each for an autograph. Mine was signed, "An Orchid to You, Bing Crosby." Bing was himself a newcomer to Hollywood in those days.

Mother called the Will Rogers home and came back to the car to say she had an appointment to interview Will Rogers the next day. Mr. Lynn replied, "We can't do that; we don't have the time." So Mother went into Paramount with her press pass and came back to say we had an appointment to watch a movie being made the next morning. It was *Mrs. Wiggs of the Cabbage Patch.* Not even Mr. Lynn could turn that down! Jane Wyman, then Mrs. Ronald Reagan, was playing the title role.

The little "Wiggs' kids" were running around the set and one of our hosts arranged for them to be photographed with us. One of the men, who seemed to be in charge, whispered to

Mother, "Do you see that guy coaching those two little kids? He's doing it to watch your son's reaction to see if it would be possible for you to stay over and let your son play a part in this picture." When mother brought it up with Mr. Lynn, he said, not unexpectedly, "We can't do that. We don't have time." When the movie came out, we knew it had not been a hoax. A small boy was featured who looked a lot like my brother, except that his freckles were larger.

We bid Hollywood, Will Rogers, and Paramount Studios farewell and headed for the northern route toward Chicago. In Salt Lake City a policeman directed us to the home of Brigham Young's oldest living daughter. She was 96, and she spent the morning telling us of the happiness she experienced as a part of a large family of siblings.

When we got to Yellowstone National Park, we stopped at the entrance beside a sign that said, "Do Not Feed the Bears." One buxom member of our party reached for a loaf of bread as she climbed out of the trailer. This was before the days of sliced bread and she pulled off chunks until she reached the bottom of the sack. With that, the bear she had been feeding reached for her ample bosom and scraped down her front, drawing blood. The Park ranger at the aid station was less than cordial.

We camped in the park that night. The next morning, Mr. Lynn's son, Bobby, decided he would not go on the tour the rest of us took. When he got up, he left his cot beside the camp stove while he made himself some pancakes. He stacked the pancakes on a plate on the cot until he thought he had about enough for his breakfast. Then he looked around to see a small bear sitting in the middle of the cot, swallowing the last of the pancakes.

We continued on our way, stopping by the 1934 Chicago World's Fair and eventually on to Tennessee. We never did learn what the rush was that caused Mr. Lynn to have to hurry so much.

The members of the party accompanying Mrs. Knox were:

Jack Knox, 13, Columbia
Margaret Knox, 15, Columbia
Florence Burkett, Columbia
Frances Mathews, Columbia
Gladys "Grandma" Wall, Columbia
Stella "Soupy" Campbell, Columbia
M. W. "Maw Green" Goodrum, Columbia
Edna "Brownie" Johnson, Dickson
Camilla "Stay-at-home lady" Manier, Chapel Hill
Bessie Anderson, Franklin
Henrietta "Tiny" Kearney, Columbia
J. Amos Watkins, Columbia
W. L. "Cap'n" Lynn, Columbia (driver/mechanic)
J. A. Lynn, 15, Columbia

Margaret Knox Morgan

THE NASHVILLE BANNER
TUESDAY, JUNE 19, 1934

Maury Farm Woman Leads Nomads on Long Trek; Will Write for Banner

With over 5,000 miles of sight-seeing and adventure ahead of them, fifteen temporary "nomads," most of them from Columbia or surrounding communities, answered the lure of the open road yesterday afternoon and headed for the California coast with visions of the Grand Canyon, Hollywood, and Yellowstone National Park spurring them on.

Among the group is the "Maury County Farm Woman," Mrs. Lera Knox, who will entertain *Banner* readers with accounts of the caravan's journey along the Western trail. Mrs. Knox is well known to *Banner* readers and especially remembered for her trip to the Chicago Fair in "Elizabeth T" last summer. Her journey to the West Coast this summer promises to be even more entertaining and to furnish some excellent vacation reading.

The spirit of the group is undoubtedly that of the pioneers, and their conveyance is a modern "covered wagon" with a high powered motor car substituting for long horned oxen. They

The 'Covered Wagon' Starts for California

—*Banner* Staff Photo

Shown above are fifteen California-bound travelers under the leadership of Mrs. Lera Knox, the Maury County Farm Woman, whose stories about her World's Fair trip and other adventures have interested *Banner* readers. The group was photographed just before the "covered wagon" started on the trans-continental trip. Mrs. Knox will send stories back. Left to right: W. L. Lynn, J. A. Watkins, Miss Stella Campbell (window), Mrs. Lera Knox (standing), Mrs. Max Goodrum (window), Jack Knox (window), Miss Gladys Wall, J. A. Lynn (window), Miss Frances Mathews, Miss Florence Burkett, Miss Bess Anderson, Miss Camilla Manier, Mrs. Henrietta Kearney, and Margaret Knox.

will camp, as their adventurous ancestors did, where night finds them, but won't have to depend on buffalo meat and venison for their provender—they hope.

If the party is able to keep within their prearranged schedule they will be exclaiming at the wonders' of the Grand Canyon sometime Sunday with memories of the Carlsbad Caverns and Arizona's famous Painted Desert behind them. Nine days, according to the driver W. L. Lynn, will see the end of the westward part of their journey, which will terminate in Los Angeles. There they will turn northward to Pasadena and begin the return trek by the Northern route. They will stop at Yellowstone National Park and climax the circuit with a visit to the World's Fair in Chicago.

With everything working smoothly and no long delays the little group of globe-trotters plans to pull into Nashville about six weeks from today with the 5,000-mile round trip completed at an estimated outlay of only $60 each.

The idea of a cooperative sightseeing trip across the continent and back was born in the minds of Mrs. Knox and Mr. Lynn some months ago after Mr. Lynn had successfully piloted such a party to the World's Fair in Chicago last summer. Friends of the "Maury County Farm Woman" encouraged the plan and finally fourteen of them signed an expense sharing agreement and started out for the California coast yesterday afternoon. [The article lists the members of the party. For their names, see the list on page 94 or the caption on page 96.]

THE DICKSON HERALD
DICKSON, TENNESSEE
TUESDAY, JUNE 19, 1934

Farm Lady to See Wonders Of West

Mrs. Lera Knox, Maury county "farm woman," who gained considerable prominence and notoriety last summer when she piloted her family in an "Elizabeth T-Model" to the World's Fair at Chicago at a meager cost and who interestingly related incidents of her trip enroute to and from the Exposition through the columns of the *Nashville Banner*, is the chronicler of another expedition, similar but more magnanimous.

Mrs. Knox and her party of some fifteen started on their first lap to the "Golden West" Monday, arriving in Dickson Monday afternoon, where they were pleasingly greeted by Mayor Dan Beasley and others. Mrs. Knox is a niece of Mrs. W. J. Johnson, this city, and this fact lent added interest to the adventurous Mrs. Knox. However, she is rather widely known for her interesting contributions to the *Nashville Banner* each Sunday, her writings in plain, everyday vernacular being titled, "The Scrap Bag." Her daily stories regarding the present expedition will appear in the *Banner* and will, no doubt, be quite interesting and educational, and will be read with eagerness by thousands of the Nashville daily's readers.

The party's conveyance is patterned similar to a modern "covered wagon," with a high-powered motor car substituting for oxen. They have a complete camping outfit and will camp enroute, as did the pioneers of long ago. They expect to finish the end of the western part of their journey in about nine days, which will terminate in Los Angeles. There they will turn northward to Pasadena and begin the return trek by the Northern route, stopping at the Yellowstone National Park, and climax the circuit with a visit to the World's Fair in Chicago. About six weeks will be spent on the entire trip, they plan.

This co-operating sight-seeing trip across the continent was the idea of Mr. Lynn and Mrs. Knox. They told friends of the plan and the same met with responsive encouragement, fourteen signing an expense sharing agreement. They have estimated the 5,000-mile round trip to require an outlay in expense of about $60 each.

While in Dickson, Mrs. Knox and her party added a fifteenth interesting passenger, Miss Edna Johnson, the daughter of Mr. and Mrs. W. J. Johnson. She had recently returned here for her vacation from teaching in Georgia, and the invitation extended by her relative provided a wonderful opportunity for her to "devour" and enjoy the picturesque "Golden West" during her vacation. An opportunity like this is to be coveted by many.

[The article lists the members of the party. For their names, see the list on page 94 or the caption on page 96.]

THE NASHVILLE BANNER
THURSDAY, JUNE 21, 1934

Maury Farm Group on Trek to Coast Find Camp Life Has Its Drawbacks

Snores in Arkansas Hills No More Soothing to Musical Ear Than Snores in Tennessee Hills, and Scrambled Eggs Without Pepper Not as 'Hot' as They Ought To Be

BY LERA KNOX

Hot Springs, Ark—Sometime in the night between Tuesday and Wednesday—

There are snores that make us giggle,
There are snores that make us sore.
There are snores that steal away our needed slumber
Like a rascal stealing from their "pore"
There are snores that make you want to throw a pail of water.
That the ears of those who snore can never hear.
But the snores that make us want to do a murder
Are the camp snores we have to bear.

SECOND NIGHT OUT—BENTON, ARK.

Well, folks you'd scarce expect an inspiration to find me where I am—sitting on the wash-room floor at Camp Joy—but after two days of travel without a decent bath until tonight, I just like to hang around where the water is. Besides this is the only place in camp where I can find enough light to read my notes, and this will have to be a "noted" story. I am too tired and sleepy to think of anything to say, so I'll just copy off some of Tuesday's notes in the raw, pure, and undefiled by any sober thought, any rhetoric, grammar, composition, unity, coherence, and emphasis.

THE TRIP BEGINS

Well, we have had some fun since we left Columbia Monday. We gathered there at 6 o'clock all ready to ride—that was the trouble—all were there—too many—nobody had backed out of the going as we expected they would. There were thirteen present and two more to be picked up at Franklin and Dickson—and the 1926 model Buick just groaned when we hitched her up to the load.

Word went out that we would have to have another car—and auto salesmen swarmed around like bees around spilled molasses. We finally completed a deal for the use of a larger car, and by the time we got it made over and ready to go, it was noon.

But don't think we were idle while waiting! We found a can of white paint and a brush and we "told the world" who we were and why and "how fore" all over the sides, top, front, and rear of our "traveling accommodation" trailer.

We had pork and beans and cole slaw for supper … the best ever … and the leavings from our picnic lunch. Supper over, everybody was ready to crawl in. Some slept in the tent; some in the trailer; some in the open; and some didn't sleep at all (they said), but we heard a lot of snoring from that direction.

We found out at about 10:30 p.m. that our camp was entirely too near the railroad track. When the train came by it sounded as though it was coming in on us. The highway was also too near for quietude, but we didn't think of moving it.

And then somebody yelled out "Ooooo-Ooooo! Git away dawg!" It was 4 o'clock in the morning, time to get up, and everybody ready. Everybody was hungry too, and how! A dishpan-full of scrambled eggs and a gallon and a half of coffee soon disappeared. Then packing up and ready to go again.

Some people recognized us and waved the *Banner* at us. The man on the bridge even gave us a fresh copy of Monday's *Banner* to read en route, and what a scramble it was for the comic strips. We found the crops looking better on the west side of the Tennessee River than on the east. A cotton patch near Bruceton was, I'll admit, even prettier than that mattress I am growing at home. The gardens all along the road, so far, are looking fine. The hollyhocks along the fences surely brighten the travelers' disposition.

Mayor Beasley of Dickson held an informal reception for us in the middle of Main Street. Many prominent citizens were present with wide-open grins. The acute traffic congestion behind us made us fear an invitation to visit the Judge. So we moved on Westward Ho! And now here we are in Arkansas.

After I had packed in the faithful and indispensable old "Pecky the Portable," and a dictionary of adjectives to be used on Western scenery, I did not have room for a grammar book. Sorry, but you'll have to take it without.

Even at that you are not the only one who is doing without. We had no black pepper for our scrambled eggs (they have to be scrambled) yesterday morning, and we will have none tomorrow morning, because nobody, it seems, can remember to buy pepper when we go through a town.

But that is not the worst yet. Yesterday morning I not only did without pepper, I did without eggs. We carry our salt in a mayonnaise jar with an improvised and inactive sprinkler top. I started to dust a little salt over my eggs and somebody had left the top unscrewed. My breakfast looked like a scrambled "sundae" with a salty sauce, or a yellow mountain with snow on top. I didn't choose to eat—not eggs, anyway.

The worst trouble about our eats is their vanishing qualities. "Maw Green" has such a delicate appetite that yesterday morning when we were packing up at Huntingdon after breakfast, she said, "Let's don't bother about stopping to eat lunch. Just a few cookies passed around will be all we care for. But when we stopped for a "cookie" at West Memphis at 1:15, her idea was "Why didn't you get four cans of "little hot doggies" as you call them, and six cans of pork and beans?"

By the time we stopped for supper nobody mentioned dieting nor reducing. Even "Tiny," who weighs 251 with her shoes on, postponed losing the fifty-one pounds until a later date.

But here come a few notes gathered here and there along the road—hot off the highway, and the highway was really hot—Stella, better known as "Soupy the Campbell Kid," has made a sun-burnt offering of her left arm to prove how hot that highway is. The opinion of the crowd is that the desert can be no hotter, but we are learning every day.

There seems to have been plenty of rain within the last few days all along the route.

Oh! Blackness ... Lights all gone out even in the washroom.

Good night! Turning in.

Notes will have to wait till next time.

We added a new sign right under our "Skule Teechers, Hill Billies, etc." It is "Bored of Education."

We named the car "Minnie" and the trailer "Ha Ha"—we are afraid to go by Reno for fear they will be separated.

THE ABILENE DAILY REPORTER
ABILENE, TEXAS
FRIDAY, JUNE 22, 1934

Tennesseans Are Chicago Bound At a Cost of $59 Each

Fifteen residents of Columbia, Tenn., passed through Abilene in a trailer-automobile combination late this morning, en route to the World's Fair at Chicago by way of sunny California. Combining resources for expenses of the journey, the tourists are estimating costs at exactly $59.25 each.

As the story is told by Mrs. Lera Knox, of the *Nashville Banner* and an organizer of the tour, things got pretty dull around Columbia, a town of about 10,000, with school out for the summer and the crops laid by. Deciding it would be cheaper and a lot more fun to travel, she promoted the tour idea; sold the proposition to 11 other women, one man, and two boys; had a trailer built for $100; and hired an automobile and driver, W. L. Lynn.

The party left Columbia last Monday, heading southwest and west along the Bankhead route. Spending last night at Cisco, the tourists have Pecos as their destination today. With a week at Chicago, sometime near the middle of July, the party will head back to Tennessee.

THE NASHVILLE BANNER
SUNDAY, JUNE 24, 1934

Maury Farm Woman Fails To Find Memphis Bluff

T.N.T. (Tennessee's Notorious Tourists) Have Trouble With Minnie in Arkansas but 'Cap'n' Waves Pliers and the Trip Is Continued

BY LERA KNOX

I had just started last night to give you some of the notes I have gathered as we ride along but the light went out. This is a continuation of that chapter:

Crop and weather report: Tennessee, Arkansas (what we have seen). Big rains west of Nashville. In White Bluff water was standing deep between corn rows. At Burns the ballpark looked like a swimming pool.

We liked the looks of gardens in Dickson, both flower and vegetable gardens. Cabbage and beans looking pretty good; corn only fair. Peas and peanuts were getting good start.

Cotton and corn were especially pretty around Bruceton. We saw our prettiest truck gardens near Jackson. Much of the land is well cared for, but the greater part is growing up in sassafras and persimmon sprouts. Weeds were tall and fence rows over-grown. I could not help comparing the slovenly, down-at-heel farms along our Tennessee highways (too many of them) with the neat, well-kept farms we saw in Indiana last summer.

I know they probably have better land than we do, but the main difference, I think, is in muscle-power and mowing blades.

The Stay-at-home Lady thought "'Willow Beach swimming pool" was Reel Foot Lake and she called the willows "birches."

One large West Tennessee family was so frightened at the sight of our gang rolling down the highway they took to their storm cellar.

To treats we brought from Columbia which were enjoyed for several miles were added a huge box of peaches from R. S. Hopkins, and a grown-up cowbell from Porter-Walker Hardware Company. Our music, mottoes, and general appearance are certainly spreading smiles over the faces of local population.

We went to see the zoo at Memphis and found all the animals at lunch. The biggest lion we ever saw was calmly gnawing a soup-bone. We didn't stay for lunch.

We drove up to the very front door of the *Commercial Appeal* and I walked in and invited all the "big folks" to come out and meet the T.N.T. gang. That means "Tennessee's Notorious Tourists."

People on the streets drove up and stopped and stared and grinned. If we do nothing else on this trip but let people laugh at our funny-looking rig, we will have done at least a little toward driving away Old Man Distression.

Of course I realize that Memphis must be a big city, but I don't see where they keep their "bluffs." All my life I have heard Memphis called "The Bluff City," but I couldn't find any more bluffs in Memphis than I could find gangsters in Chicago. They must be there or they wouldn't be so much in the papers, but what I saw were nothing to compare with the beautiful rugged bluffs on our own classic Duck River.

It all looks flat there to me, river, and all. The picture I could see from the long bridge across the river, looking back up at the city, made me think of Memphis as a maiden dipping her toes into a muddy stream.

In coming out of Memphis we had two thrills. We saw a mad-dog shot—at; and saw a mule put on four wheel brakes and pitch his rider across the road into the ditch. The Negro, a semi-nudist, climbed back on, and on they went with backward glances at us.

West of Memphis the cotton was growing luxuriantly. Women and children were chopping it, and men, many of them were fishing in the lakes, lagoons, swamps, mud puddles, or whatever the things are called.

Some of the men, of course, were plowing. In one field we counted forty-eight Negroes, thirteen were men plowing, and the others were women and children. And the mules on that side of the river are just as balky as the ones on the east side.

"Maw Green," the practical member of the party, wondered why all that beautiful land was not turned into dairy farms. But the Stay-at-home-lady answered. "From what you all say about mosquitoes in Arkansas, the mosquitoes would eat up the cows."

RICE FIELDS

Oh and we did see some rice fields! The first few we came to were so thick with white-top weeds we couldn't see the rice, but later we found some that were really pretty. Each large field had a tower of scantlings (is that what you call them?), and a pump and a house. The water was being pumped—out of a well, I suppose—in a stream as large around as a child's head. Oh, it did look good to us tired, thirsty nomads!

Just about the time we struck that hot flat rice country, "Minnie" the car began to cough and to sputter, finally choked down until she couldn't chug a chug. Trouble? We didn't worry. We had the "Cap'n" along and what that man doesn't know about the insides of automobiles! He got out and waved his wire pliers and wrenches over the business end of that auto, and when he got through she was willing enough to go on.

I have probably not explained the origin of that name "Minnie." You see we think a lot of our traveling accommodation and we wanted a romantic name for it like Pullman cars and things like that have. We decided to call the whole outfit "Minniehaha."

We divided the name, however, and call the car "Minnie," and the trailer "HaHa," and a merry ha ha it is.

We dislike going through Reno for fear the two will get separated.

Believe it or doubt, there is one place that had such modern conveniences as "hot and cold running water" before real estate agents and Chambers of Commerce were invented—even before Columbus went out sight seeing—that place is Hot Springs, Arkansas.

Yes, hot and cold running water are an old story to that town but they do have one very modern convenience, as live a Chamber of Commerce as any place could wish for. It is almost as live as our own in Columbia.

All the people think about there is "taking a bath." They are not satisfied with bath rooms, they must have bath houses, and not a few, but a whole street of them which they call Bath House Row.

So enthusiastic are those folks about this "washing" business that they even call their pet mountain range the "Wash-I-Taws"—only they spell it "Ouachita."

But Hot Springs certainly did give this bunch a warm welcome—if not a hot bath. The president of the Chamber of Commerce even gave us an "official welcome" and we got his picture in the act.

Little Rock, too, gave us a grand time: pictures in the paper—*Arkansas Gazette*—and a top-notch feature story.

THE NASHVILLE BANNER
MONDAY, JUNE 25, 1934

Hot Sun on Windswept Texas Plains Force Maury Group to Night Driving

But Everything Else, Including Those Queer Prairie Bugs Dozing in Shoes, Works for Enjoyment of Crowd Treking to West Coast and Back by World's Fair

Friday Morning, Daylight, Cisco, Texas—

I have been writing these squibs with a forward look, but I couldn't keep up with ourselves that way so this morning I am beginning where I am to tell you what we have left behind us. We drove from Fort Worth to this town of Cisco last night between suppertime and midnight. It is getting so hot we have to resort to night driving now. When we rolled in last night we were so tired we could have slept in a cactus bed. I think. We didn't bother about tents, just rolled up in blankets and dropped on cots, tent, prairie grass, or ground.

That was till morning. I could hardly pry my eyes open enough to see which shoe to put on. I looked twice to see if it was for the left foot. It was, and I knew it ought to go on. I looked in and saw something move. "It must be a rattlesnake I thought." But when I looked again and turned my shoe upside down with a shake, a vicious, whiskered, bright-eyed bug as big as a half-grown mouse told me good morning, and honest, I was too tired to return the salutation with a squeal. I scornfully ignored him, but that Argus-eyed 251-pound "Tiny" saw the performance and caught him in her handkerchief for a "souvenir."

Really this crowd hasn't tired of collecting souvenirs yet. They are planning to empty one of the trunks and put all their collections in to send back home ahead of us.

As I look back across the 951 (or more) miles we have traveled since Monday, one thing shines out above all the heat and discomfort—the hospitality and good will with which we have been received. Memphis, Little Rock, Texarkana, Dallas took us in with open—eyes and mouths—I started to say open arms, but the other words are more accurate. The way they stared and grinned at us, and clustered around "Minnie-Haha" was something to be remembered long.

HOT SPRINGS, ARKANSAS, AND SULPHUR SPRINGS, TEXAS

Hot Springs gave us the town. They even took it for a huge joke and a compliment when we parked our "accommodation" across the entrance to Uncle Sam's Department of Interior, or something, and instead of taking us to the calaboose, or hospital, or insane asylum, they took us to the magnificent Arlington Hotel where we had—tooth-picks for souvenirs!

At each town they have done everything they could for us to make us enjoy our few minutes there, and in almost every place of any size they have made pictures and put us in their papers, but the little town of Sulphur Springs, Texas, gave us about the most royal time we have had anywhere.

It is too bad that I have nothing else but words with which to tell you about the folks at Sulphur Springs, and most of the words are packed in the bottom of the trunk in the dictionary where I can't get to them. But it was somewhat this way:

We got held up behind an ice wagon in a bit of slow traffic, and in this slow parade we passed a newspaper office. By the time we had passed two more buildings a "bandit news-hound" had skipped out to the conveyance and held us up for "news." He insisted that we pull over to the curb and tell him what it was all about, in other words, explain ourselves.

Then he began to explain his town, and such a booster, you never heard—you may understand better if you know he came from Georgia. He soon had us believing that Sulphur Springs was simply ahead of anything else in the country, in spite of the fact that we were sitting looking at it.

He carried us into his newspaper building and all through it. Had the printer set each person's name up in type to take home as a souvenir—a small courtesy, but you have no idea what a kick we got out of having our names in such a shape that we could see them in print at any time we wanted to, and even more, could stamp them on anything we chose. I learned more about newspapers in the ten minutes he took to show us through and how and why than I learned in eleven and one-half months of writing pieces for the paper.

By that time, the Mayor and corporation and a large assembly of citizens had gathered around the outfit, and they proceeded to show us the town. They formed a parade with the Mayor's car in front and led us to the "finest curb market in the world," to see "the finest gardens in the States," and "the prettiest park in the country"—and made us believe it. They let us have some pictures of the "reception committee of 138"—more or less—right in the middle of market square, then when we told them we must move on, they took us to the bottling works and gave us cold drinks for refreshments. The milkman came along too and out of the goodness of his heart gave us a bottle of milk for the "baby"—that's Edna, our twenty-six-year-old teacher—she looks like a six-year-old in her traveling shorts, and gets by with it.

We put on a show for the town with some humorous readings and songs and after another drive through the park and another gift of ice for our tea at lunch, we left Sulphur Springs reluctantly—wondering if our home towns in Tennessee would take in strangers in such a way.

THE NASHVILLE BANNER
THURSDAY, JUNE 28, 1934

Maury County Farm Group Learns To Appreciate Plight of Lowly Arab

Cactus Pete and Alkali Ike Might Like It, But Out West Of Fort Worth, Everything That Crawls Stings, And Everything That Grows Sticks, Homefolks Advised

BY LERA KNOX

Some time last week, or something like a million years ago, it seems, I mailed you some articles from somewhere in Texas, but much dust has gone under our tires and into our eyes, ears, noses since then.

Somebody said, "Ship me somewhere east of Suez" and that may be all right, but don't let anybody ship you anywhere west of Fort Worth—not in dusty June.

The going would not have been so bad if we had stayed on the National coast-to-coast highway, "The Broadway of America." But adventurers that we are, we wanted to see Carlsbad Caverns and instead of abiding by map information, we tried a little man-information, and got a lot of bumping and dusting for our digression. Seventy-five miles of suffering in one stretch, then a short rest and fifty-seven miles more, and all across the alkali flats of West Texas and New Mexico, where "everything that crawls stings, and everything that grows sticks."

From 7 o'clock in the morning until half-past-noon we "spit cotton," and from 4 o'clock in the afternoon until 3 o'clock the next morning we inhaled sand.

And the water. Oh, that water! It tasted like a saturated solution of Epsom salts, concentrated lye, borax, alum, sulphur, salt petre, baking soda, arsenate of lead, and green persimmons—it was bad to the last slimy drop, but we drank it and liked it. Such is desert thirst.

And the heat that came across the fields and up from the highway, somebody said it was like, well, like seven purgatories stewed down to one—well, you know what they are building at Norris.

After those three days traveling through cowboy country I cannot blame the poor cowboy for being rough—they have to be rough to match their geography. And cussing? It is no wonder that they cuss; ordinary decent, ready-made, dictionary English is not adequate nor appropriate expression in such a country. And yet—I don't know what it is—but surely there is something remarkably attractive about the country. The people who live there think it is the best on the globe. Maybe it is, just because to them it is "home."

For the past three days and for the next several days we are going through climatic conditions that try men's soles—in case of a walk-in—and women's tempers, in any case. We have really had experience in studying human nature "in the raw" and cooked, or near about it.

Somebody prophesied when we left that we might start out as "Tennessee's Notorious Tourists," but before we had gone far "roughing it" we would be "Tennessee's Notorious Tomcats." But we are not, yet, anyway—the way the bunch has reacted under the most trying conditions has been a revelation to every one of us, perhaps the most remarkable feature of the expedition. They have managed to "keep sweet and keep smiling" and keep cheering one another even when they had to take off their stockings to make dust masks of them, and hold feather pillows over their faces. But the sense of humor that has come to the top of each disposition has carried us through in high glee in spite of tired, tired bodies, sleepy eyes, and sore muscles.

I'd like to tell you a lot of the ridiculously funny happenings and wise cracks that have been brought out, but some you would hardly believe and the others are just unprintable—of course, I mean by that they would lose their humorous value if repeated out of their original environment and all of that—you understand.

But don't think for a minute that hardships have made us sick of our trip. We surely are so far getting a huge "money's worth" every day.

Just the trip through Carlsbad Caverns was well worth all the dust and grime and bumping. Carlsbad is the newest

National Park, and, they claim, the most beautiful of discovered caverns.

We had our trouble getting to Carlsbad, not that the road was so very bad, but because of our heavy load we had to take it slowly and because on a dirt road "Minnie" the car kicks dust all over "HaHa" the trailer … and that is … well, too bad.

But after all our trouble and worry and slow driving in the heat, luck changed, and five miles from the cavern, superintendent of the park Col. Thomas Boles was coming to the cavern. He became interested in our gang, took some on up the hill, thus reducing our load.

We were too late to catch the party of between 300 and 400 who had gone down earlier, but Superintendent Boles helped us catch the elevator to make the down trip of 750 feet into the earth.

The main part of the cavern, the big room as it is called, is 4,000 feet long and 650 feet wide. It takes three hours to go through this part of the cavern.

As for the formations and the beauty and immensity of the caverns, they are, of course, too vast and marvelous for description.

Will Rogers described the cavern by saying it is "like the Grand Canyon with a roof over it."

Our party agreed that just the first room was worth all the desert traveling and all the discomfort, and worth even drinking alkali water to see.

THE NASHVILLE BANNER
SUNDAY, JULY 1, 1934

Maury County Farm Woman Helps Squaw Match Thread

The Indians Are Really Not So Bad, She Finds. In Fact She Was as Favorably Surprised as She Was at the Yankees on Last Summer's Trip

BY LERA KNOX

If you have any trouble interpreting this, imagine what I had to interpret in order to get this much to you.

We just stopped at an Indian Village in San Carlos Reservation: found as many Apaches hanging around the trading post as we would have seen of white folks around a country store on Saturday afternoon in Tennessee.

I went in to the mall and found some rather interesting new ideas. A woman with long hair hanging down over her shoulders, a loose bright-colored calico "dressing sack" for a blouse, and a skirt that must have measured ten yards at the lower edge, was buying enough gaudy, sleazy, electric-blue silk to make a dress. Just as I came in she told the merchant "eelo" and he brought the thread.

But the thread wouldn't match. I "butted in" and helped her select a shade that would, and told her in signs that I thought the silk was pretty, and so it was—for some purposes. But she was glad I liked her new dress, and from her I learned some other facts that may surprise you.

For instance, silk is "moskato"; thread is "eelo"; a watermelon is a "tchitka" (pronounced like a sudden sneeze); an Indian pottery vase in the window was a "toson"; a saddle is a "klivigil"; and a rug is a "zak."

My hat, she told me, was a "jar"—I confess I was a little surprised. I admit however it must seem a little shocking. You see, I lost my real hat somewhere west of Fort Worth, and I didn't care to cross the desert and alkali flats again for that hat or any other 98-cent Paris creation. What I am wearing is improvised. It is sometimes known as a bandana or a handkerchief—sometimes I tie it around my head like a turban, other times it is around my neck, and at other times it is around my nose bandit-wise to keep dust and sand out of my internals. But when I wear it on my head, it is a "jar" she said.

TRAVELING TROUSERS

My traveling trousers, the squaw said, are "lonostick"; they are also rather dusty and travel-worn, so I admitted she might be right. She called my shirt something that sounded like "glasses" but really it is just cheap blue chambray. And I learned that my rough shoes are "now-cat" when I had supposed they were good cowhide. My sox are "etches"; my camera a "badney"; that is the reason, perhaps, that none of the Indians will get in front of it unless they are well paid. And I can't afford to "pay."

I did however, manage to arouse the curiosity of one old squaw about something in the baggage of the trailer, enough to entice her out into the sun, and caught a snap or two on the sly before the Indian men lounging around caught on to my racket and warned her, then she darted off and squatted cross-legged again in the shadow of a cactus.

I offered my only lipstick to the prettiest belle for a pose, but with great strength of character she refused the temptation. The lipstick was about the only thing of value I had to offer. I had lost my face powder and rouge compact soon after we left "civilization," and I couldn't spare my tube of sunburn medicine—there are more deserts to cross.

Don't let anybody tell you that Indians have no sense of humor. Take Sophia Robinson, for instance. She was the one who was buying the blue "moskato" dress. Sophia giggled every time she looked at me and every time I spoke to her. I giggled too and I believe we could have become very good friends if there had been time. We could have planned, and probably have made, that new blue dress; she sews well, I learned, but designs terribly.

She was as much interested in my "now-cats" (shoes) as I was in her moccasins. She fingered the toes of my shoes, as I squatted with her in the shade of the trading-post wall, to see how tight they were on my feet, and she admired the corns on my toes (which she insisted on seeing) as much as I did the beading and stitching on her moccasins. She laughed because I thought beaded belts were beautiful.

Sophia had "gosmoskomonies" on her fingers, but don't worry, that is not contagious; neither will it wash off. It merely means "finger rings." How would you like to get married with a "gosmoskomonie" ceremony?

Somebody in our crowd made a "meh chulk"—but don't worry, candy fixed it up all right. You see a "meh" is a baby, and to "chulk" is to cry. We've been wrong all the time thinking Indian babies are papooses, they are not, they are "mehs," and they fear strangers and like candy just as do babies with fairer skin and less-brown eyes.

BABY CRIES

The baby who cried was named "Fern" and her little brother was "Canna," I learned from their mother. Other children's names were Amy, Canton, and Calvin. I did not ask the individual names of all the dogs about the village—too many—but I did learn that as a group they are called "katchunnies." A cat, if any, would be a "gotdorff"; but I saw no gotdorffs in the village—too many katchunnies, no doubt.

And oh yes, the little boy squatting by the door of the trading-post was 11 years old, in the fourth grade, likes to study geography, but was glad when school was out.

His name is Wasticakle, and the thing he was eating was a "popsickle," so you see, Apache Indians are really human beings after all. I was as favorably surprised with the Indians as I was the Yankees last summer and I really liked the Mexicans.

DOWN THE MOUNTAIN

Well, we are coming down the mountain ... and how. Such a climb as we have just had going up. We stopped at the summit for lunch and it surely was a welcome bite. The mountain air, the traveling, or something makes us ravenously hungry at every meal. Today we had just a good homey, family meal, canned corn, broiled bacon, tea, bread, and butter, sandwich spread, and marmalade. Most of the time we have a more elaborate meal, but we are hurrying on to Phoenix today, want to get out of the heat and on to the Grand Canyon as soon as possible.

Haven't had time to tell you how our expenses are running, and suppose this will be as good a time as any. Started to describe the mountain scenery, but couldn't anyway, so won't try. Enough to say, we have already worn out all the Oh's and Ah's in our vocabulary. The only thing I can say when I look at them is "great, wide, beautiful, wonderful world"—and I had already worn out that sentence in our own Tennessee hills.

Warning: Save your adjectives until you come out here.

I think I had better look at the typewriter keys and talk about camp expenses. When I glance over the edge of the road I get such an all gone feeling that—well, you know how you feel when you dream you are falling.

There went a bunch of real cowboys, driving a bunch of real cows and calves down a canyon.

I really wish we could stop and watch them but we can't stop to look at everything as long as we want to.

You should see what a happy system of braking we have. We have six wheel brakes and need 'em. One of the boys sits in the trailer and at a signal of two blows on the horn from the driver, he applies the trailer brakes; at one blow of the horn he releases them. But for all that, when we start down these mountains I press both feet as hard as I can on the floor, putting on my share of brakes and trying to help hold back.

I don't know whether it is elevation, or imagination, or lack of high-mindedness, but when I look down—down—down—those rocky steep slopes for what seems like six or ten city blocks for miles, I get so sick—so sicky-sick—that's the only word for it.

It affects each one differently. One sings, one is silent, one wants to preach, another to "cuss"! Another laughs hysterically, and another cries. It was the same way in the grandeur of Carlsbad Caverns. I wonder what it will do to us when we see Grand Canyon.

But I want to tell you about something considerably lower than the mountains—our traveling expenses. We counted up expenses at the end of the first week and this is the way our score read: At El Paso Sunday morning, we found from our speedometer that we had traveled 1,605 miles, bought 127 gallons of gas (getting something like twelve miles to the gallon) at a total cost of $23.91.

Our food for the week had cost $19.73; ice 55 cents; camping spaces $3; bridge tolls $3, and a $4 generator to replace the one we burnt out. I am not counting the cold bottled drinks that we buy along the road.

THE NASHVILLE BANNER
MONDAY, JULY 2, 1934

Maury Countians Stop Long Enough To See Wonders of Grand Canyon

BY LERA KNOX

Thursday afternoon—between Williams and Needles—

Can you imagine a gully as wide as from Columbia to Lewisburg, as long as from Nashville to Birmingham? Can you imagine this gully holding between its walls thousands and thousands of mountain peaks, all of different shapes and sizes ranging from baby hills and flat plateaus to tall, sharp peaks and bon-bon shapes a mile high? Then can you imagine those mountains and the walls that enclose them being splashed with bright yellow, red, brown, tan, orange, henna, flame, copper, rust, beige, brick, peach, rose, pink, orchid, lavender, green, blue, slate, dove, and taupe gray, dotted with dark green trees and shrubs?

Imagine all of that, then, if you can, draw over the farthest peaks a delicate soft blue hazy veil of atmosphere, you will have a small idea of what Grand Canyon is like. But not until you stand on Grand View Point will you realize completely that the word "grand" belongs entirely to this great natural wonder. You will realize that no other word in our very weak language fits it quite so well. After viewing Grand Canyon I think I can never use the word "grand" lightly again.

I was interested in seeing the canyon, of course, but I was interested also in seeing what effect the grandeur and magnificence, and vast wonderful beauty would have on the members of our party.

We have as many entirely different personalities in our group as can be crammed into fifteen people. And not the least of the pleasure of the trip to me has been the reactions of these varied personalities to the varied circumstances and environments we have experienced during the trip. And then, when the great moment came, when we looked into the abyss, I was so busy with my own reactions that I did not have time nor inclination to see and study the others.

I imagined that I would stand in silent, reverent awe before the great wonder, but I didn't, not just at first. The first thing I thought of was my children, it seemed that the canyon was drawing them, taking them away from me, and instead of silent awe, I had a horror, a terrible fear, a feeling of wanting to fight the canyon, and of an almost uncontrollable urge, to take the children just as close to me as I could and to run from the overwhelming fear of it. That was the afternoon of the first day. By the next morning, when I had seen the sun rise slowly over the cliffs and gently raise the soft blue mist from the rugged walls and peaks, I felt differently, an admiration and a reverence that hurt on the inside, and made shivers run down my spine, and tears came into my eyes, and all I could say was "Oh."

As for the effect the canyon had on the other members of the party, I can only repeat some of the expressions I heard: "Oo-oo-oo! Can't see any bottom at all." (The canyon was more than a mile deep there.) "Won't we have something to talk about when we get home?" "Oh! Let's go exploring it." "I feel like I want to jump off." "I want to throw rocks into it." "Ain't that sumpin'!" "Nobody could put a roof over that." "Wonder why they don't put a cable across it." "Wish I could go over it in an airplane." "I'd be willing to ride a mule to see the bottom of it." "I don't think much of the river, it looks like a spring branch."

"There's more to it than I thought there would be." "Well, I am disappointed. I thought the rocks would shine and glisten, but they don't, not much."

One of the party said of a group of people on the rim as we drove along looking, "Watch the folks stop looking at the canyon to see us."

Another one of the party, Stella, our "Campbell Kid," wrote two poems on the reverse side of business cards, while she stood on the edge of the canyon rim. This one which she allowed me to pass on to you expresses better the way we all really feel, than anything I could say:

> If my smile were as wide as the canyon;
>
> My faith as strong as its walls,
>
> My love as solid as the rock it's made of,
>
> Dear God, I'd be satisfied.

THE NASHVILLE BANNER
THURSDAY, JULY 5, 1934

Pacific Ocean Appears To Be Larger Than Duck River to Maury Countians

Group Treking to Chicago Fair by Way of California Find Mercury Doing Gymnastics in the Desert and Decide Catalina Island Outstrips the Cat's Whiskers

BY LERA KNOX

What a shocking lot of things can happen within a very few hours. When we left Barstow in the heart of the great Mojave Desert early Saturday morning, the air was hotter (as the sun came up) than it ever is at noon-time in Tennessee. As we traveled on toward the coast, and as the hands of our watches approached the noon hour the air grew cooler and damper just as we might expect it to do in late afternoon after a shower. By 3 o'clock, when we got to Riverside, a sweater felt very comfy, and when we reached Long Beach about 4, we stopped at a fruit stand to get fruit for supper; by that time we were complaining to the operator about it being so cold, and he apologized for the terrible heat wave that the coast country was suffering. That's climate.

After sleeping the night before with scorpions on desert sands, we were willing enough to roll up in blankets with crabs on the Pacific sands Saturday night. And we really did. We slept within 100 steps—(I counted them, and they were short steps, too, for one cannot step far in sand)—within 100 short steps of the Pacific Ocean at an auto campground called "Seaside." That was Saturday night. Some of the crowd ventured into the water, but I didn't. That looked like too much bath all at one time, even if it was Saturday night.

I am writing this Monday morning before breakfast. The rest of the "gang" are still asleep. I have to write when they are asleep or I get all their chatter into the story and that, along with my own, would be even worse than this.

Every day, the crowd says, is best of all. Yesterday, Sunday, was a real thriller. We went out on a big ship to Santa Catalina Islands. And of all the preparation we made for sea-sickness before we left, you never heard the like. And then, it was all useless. We were so thrilled at being on a real ship and on so much water all at one time that nobody had time to get seasick. We did get drunk however, but on seawater only. And we did quite a bit of staggering around until we got our "sea-legs" and learned to swagger and sway with the ship's movement like "Barnacle Bill The Sailor."

I can very well understand why seamen love their ships. Even a few hours aboard the S.S. *Catalina* won a warm spot in my heart for her. And the ocean does something to one on the inside—I mean something else besides turning over one's tummy. At first I felt a similar fear of it to the fear I felt at Grand Canyon, but like Grand Canyon, it awes but it also draws.

We made the glass-bottom boat trip at Santa Catalina, and just as we were all intent on seeing the fishes and sea-moss through the plate glass windows in the bottom of the boat, we heard somebody give a real "rebel yell" about a big fish that came too close, and Margaret said, "I'll bet he's from Tennessee."

"Well, it will do no harm to ask," I said. She did ask and found it to be Felix Fly of Nashville, who is "kin to the Flys in Columbia," and with him was John J. Brady of Hicks-Brady Company, also of Nashville. There is no telling how far these Tennesseans will and do go. Every place we go, we find them. But I forgot, Mr. Brady and Mr. Fly send regards to friends and to *Banner* readers back home—and Mr. Fly was not permanently injured by his fright at the big fish, but he promises, however, never to associate with anything more vicious than sardines and pickled herring from now on.

We made a trip out to the famous Bird Park on Santa Catalina, where birds from every continent and I think some from the moon are being kept and raised. It is an ideal place for a sanctuary back in the marvelous climate of the mountains of the island.

I can hardly describe the island better than to say that it has midsummer beauty in an early spring climate. The flowers on the island, which I greatly enjoyed, are the kinds that can be grown only in hot-houses back home, all tropical and subtropical plants, but the ocean spray or the Japanese stream, or something, seems not to let the weather come to the stage where one suffers from the heat.

That trip through the island was a joy, but the best was yet to come. After we got back on the boat, I got to thinking about something that might keep my mind off of prospective seasickness while going back over the channel, for I could see that the water was much rougher than it had been going over. I got to wondering what makes a ship go, anyway. I knew there must be something more to a ship than just decks, and saloons and cabins, and life-preservers. So I decided to ask the first man I met with a cap on a few questions. I soon saw one standing off by himself, went up to and introduced myself to him as a "hick from the hills of Tennessee spending my first day on the ocean, and, would there be a chance for me to learn something about the workings of the boat."

When he turned around I saw the word "captain" on his cap. Then I knew what a break I had made. For in all the books I have read about the etiquette of ships and sailors I knew that for a common, ordinary, country woman to walk up and speak to "The Captain"—well it just wasn't done. But he was lovely about it, "Sure," he said, he would "show me about." Then I told him about the rest of the gang, scattered over the ship, and he said he would show them about, too. I hustled to gather them up.

Well, he took us down in the very-next-to-the-bottom part of the ship—the bottom is a five-foot double floor space—and he showed us the machinery and wheels and shafts that operate the rudder. He let Jack turn the steering wheel (down in the bottom of the keel of the boat) which is used in emergencies. Just to think that with one finger on the spokes of that wheel one could turn a vessel as large as the *Catalina* was almost unbelievable. That experience certainly did increase my respect for little things.

Then to the engine room, and how beautiful and interesting that was. An indicator or speedometer, or something, was showing how fast the ship was going (seventeen miles an hour, the captain said, I couldn't read the nautical terms), and another instrument measured the distance we had traveled so we could tell when we got to where we were going.

From the engine room we went on through all parts and sections of the ship. Saw the provisions made to take care of "emergencies" (that word seems on every seaman's heart, and well it should be, I suppose; at any rate I was glad it was). At least when we reached "the bridge" where "no passengers were allowed" and saw the man steering the ship with a big wheel, not by looking out the wind shield where he was going, as I do when I drive Elizabeth T, but by looking at a compass balanced before him.

Then it was that the captain told us a big secret. He was born in Tennessee, on old Stone River, near Murfreesboro. We should have guessed it before, that one so kind and courteous, must have had a good place to start from, but few of us did. He told us too that the *Catalina* had made her first voyage just ten years ago on July 1, and that unconsciously we were celebrating the ship's birthday, with Capt. A. A. Morris, who sends back greetings to fellow Tennesseans, especially to his cousins, Walter and Jimmy Leathers on Overall Creek, in Rutherford County.

THE NASHVILLE BANNER
THURSDAY, JULY 5, 1934

Tennesseans Tour Way Into Sanctum of Movies

Hollywood, Ca.—(UP)—

Fifteen enterprising Tennessee tourists who spent only $9 apiece to travel here in a "bus" built from an old flivver, today received the rare privilege of parading through the heart of a large Hollywood studio.

The tourists, eleven women, two men, and two boys, arrived nosily at the studio gates and demanded entrance. Studio officials "fell" for the idea, invited the guests to drive in, and escorted them to the set where W. C. Fields was working. Fields, himself a tourist enthusiast, swapped stories with the visitors and showed them the ins-and-outs of movieland.

TENNESSEE SCHOOL TEACHERS IN HOLLYWOOD—Traveling from Nashville, Tenn. To Paramount's Hollywood studios at a cost of only $9 each, this group of teachers and their friends received their first peek inside a studio. Here the party is on the *Mrs. Wiggs of the Cabbage Patch* set with a trio of the children playing in the picture. Mrs. Lera Knox, leader of the motorized "covered wagon" expedition, is on the extreme left. The three little actresses in the center are Virginia Weidler, Carmencita Johnson, and Edyth Fellows.

THE NASHVILLE BANNER
FRIDAY, JULY 6, 1934

It Takes More than Policemen, Gates to Keep Tennesseans Out of Hollywood

Maury County Farm Caravan Rolls Up to Film Capital And Like It So Well They Just Pitch Their Tents and Are Given Royal Welcome—Studios Given Inspection

BY LERA KNOX

Hollywood, Calif. July 2—(By Mail)

So this is Hollywood! Really it is. We are camping tonight in the auto parking space of Hollywood Bowl, right under the sycamores at the Intersection of Highland and Cahuenga, if you know your Hollywood. We have special permission from the Police Department to camp here tonight, if anyone asks you. Reason: I asked a policeman who was looking over our outfit in front of Paramount Studios this afternoon, "You don't want this outfit to stay in Hollywood tonight, do you?"

"We don't want you to leave," he said. Then he told us we could spread our tent here, and it's a dandy place.

Well, we've had some experiences today. We left Long Beach this morning after visiting the *Long Beach Sun and Press Telegram* and giving them greetings from Tennessee and all along the road from there here. Then we drove on over to Los Angeles, stopped at the post office where we were overjoyed to get some "*Banners*" and other mail from home. We scattered about town then for a small while looking in shop windows and all about. I went to the *Los Angeles Times and Examiner* offices and told them about our gang being in town and that we were parked at the corner of Alameda and Macey. They sent reporters and photographers around to get stories about our crowd. After lunch we drove out to Pasadena and went into the Rose Bowl for a little visit and to sneak some pictures. Just as luck would have it a caretaker was going in as we came to the gate, and he showed us around. They are getting ready for a big circus and fireworks display there on the Fourth of July.

We were trying to get to Paramount Studios and at the corner of Melrose and Gower where Paramount was supposed to be, we thought we found a huge studio. I crawled out of the caravan with my letter from Mr. Sudekum in one hand and one from the *Banner* in the other and marched in just as though I wasn't a bit afraid and gave my letters to Mr. Information, near the door.

He said, "Did you want to see Paramount?" I told him I did. Then he said, "They are next door on Melrose. This is R.K.O."

I said, "Well, while I am here I don't mind seeing your studio if it is convenient." He sent me to the publicity department, and they were very courteous. Mr. Dick Pitinger told me the production department was just finishing *The Age of Innocence* and that if we would come back tomorrow we could see part of that being filmed. They had "knocked off" for the day, of course; it was 5:30 when we were there.

VISIT PARAMOUNT

Then we drove next door around the corner (which was really a long Hollywood "block") to visit Paramount Studios. I had learned by that time that my best luck was with the publicity department. That is where I headed for and where I found luck.

Mr. Delapp, who talked with me and came out to meet the gang, told us that they were making *Mrs. Wiggs of the Cabbage Patch* and that he "would be delighted to have us see it. The actors will be out on location all morning in a less interesting part of the picture, but will be back at the studios at 2 o'clock Tuesday." We are cordially invited to be back at Paramount at that time where, we will see not only Mrs. Wiggs, but other Interesting People and Things. He said if he could really count on our being there he would put on a few specials—I don't know what they will really be but we will surely try to be there.

While we were parked in front of the "No Parking" sign before Paramount Barber Shop, dozens of grinning faces gathered around the "Minnie-HaHa" and our jolly, wise-cracking Tennesseans. One who left the barber's chair and came out with the lather drying on his face, followed by the barber razor in hand was Harry Revel, author of "Did You Ever

See a Dream Walking?" "Underneath a Harlem Moon," "Love Thy Neighbor," "An Orchid To You," "You're Such a Comfort To Me," "I'm Dreaming With My Eyes Wide Open," and a number of other popular songs. He certainly did enjoy the appearance and good humor of our crowd, autographed many of the girls' notebooks with names of his songs, and decided, he said, to write a song about the crowd, to be called by one of the slogans painted on the trailer "We're Broke and Tired But Happy."

Other celebrities who came along and giggled at our gang, and left autographs in payment for the fun they had with us, were Bing Crosby, Henry Wilcoxson, Jill Gaffney and Bill Klein.

THE SAN JOSE MERCURY HERALD
SAN JOSE, CALIFORNIA
FRIDAY MORNING, JULY 6, 1934

Tennessee Party on Way to World's Fair Stops Here

15 Making Trip Via Pacific Coast Have $60 Budget For Six Weeks

San Jose was struck by T.N.T. yesterday.

But the T.N.T. in question was not the high explosive, but "Tennessee's Notorious Tourists," a band of fifteen Tennesseans who are enroute to the Chicago Exposition of Progress via the Pacific coast.

The expedition is unique in many ways. In the first place, the party has for its motto, "Six Weeks on Sixty Dollars," and the way they are holding to budget indicates that they will make it.

The party is composed of 11 women, two men, and two boys. One of the men is an expert mechanic, who drives and takes care of the car. Of the remaining members of the group five are school teachers, two are ex-school teachers, one a home demonstration agent, and the rest students. Lera Knox, member of the editorial staff of the *Nashville Banner*, is a member of the party, and is writing day-by-day accounts of the trip for her paper.

$25 AUTO

In planning the trip the first thing was to secure transportation. A '26 model automobile was purchased for $25, and was thoroughly reconditioned by the mechanic of the party. A trailer was built for $100 and $24.70 was spent for a tent. This brought the cost of transportation and housing up to $149.70 for the fifteen people for the trip. Five of the party ride in the automobile and the other ten ride in the trailer. To date—fifteen days after starting out—their expenditures have been: Gasoline, $55.44; oil, $6; bridge tolls, $3.40; repairs to burned out generator, $4; food, $49.90.

Meals are planned by two dietitians in the party, and that they are well balanced is demonstrated by the fact that the two overweight members of the party have reduced while the underweight member has gained four pounds. Members of the party are divided into three shifts of five each, each shift preparing one meal a day. Three people prepare the meal and the other two do the dish washing and cleaning up.

ONE DESIRE FADES

The party has had numerous interesting experiences since leaving Tennessee. Their ambition on starting was to slide down the slopes of the Grand Canyon, take a shower bath under the falls in Yosemite, and wade in the Pacific. They abandoned the sliding idea after getting a glimpse of the Grand Canyon, and have still to reach Yosemite. But they have gratified their desire to wade in the Pacific. The party slept one night on the sands of the Arizona desert, after traveling all day in a temperature of 110 degrees, and the next day slept on the sands of the Pacific shore at Long Beach. There they nearly froze, after their sudden change from desert heat although Long Beach residents apologized for the heat, assuring them that it was "very unusual weather."

The T.N.T. party stayed in San Jose last night and leaves this morning for San Francisco. They will go east by way of Salt Lake City to Chicago, where they will spend several days at the fair. Then they will make their way down the Mississippi valley back to Tennessee—and at a cost of $60 per person for the entire trip.

THE SAN JOSE MERCURY HERALD
SAN JOSE, CALIFORNIA
FRIDAY MORNING, JULY 6, 1934
[EDITORIAL PAGE]

Editorial Analysis

BY A. M. M.

"Neighbors" From South Visit City

We spoke yesterday of the trek of vacationists to California—a day too early to mention the T.N.T. party of fifteen who rolled into San Jose. It's merely another alphabetical contraction—that rather fearsome three-some of initials—expanded, to satisfy curiosity, into "Tennessee's Notorious Tourists." Their slogan is "Six Weeks on Sixty Dollars," and it looks as though they'll make it come true!

They're seeing the country, having a glorious time, and getting healthier every day. We're glad to welcome vacationists of this type and happy to show them the wonders of California. We hope they are the harbingers of many more parties like this.

In this great country of ours we don't have an opportunity to "get acquainted" and become neighborly. Distances are too great, though the automobile is doing its share to bring distant communities into friendly touch with each other.

THE NASHVILLE BANNER
SUNDAY, JULY 8, 1934

There's a Lot of New Ground Between The Corn Patch and Movie Studios

Maury Countians, Making a Roundabout Trip to Century of Progress Exposition, Pause Long Enough to See Hollywood, and Decide Plowing Easier Than Movie-ing

BY LERA KNOX

Hollywood, Calif., July 4 (By mail)—

We're in the movies now! We're not behind the plow! But from what we have seen of plowing and movie-ing, the plowing is by far the easier.

You think I'm joking, or exaggerating, or something, when I say we're in the movies, but really, I am not. Paramount photographers made a number of "shots" of us yesterday. They were filming *Mrs. Wiggs of the Cabbage Patch*, when we came to the studio by appointment at 2 o'clock, and Mr. Delopp had the cameramen ready to "shoot us" with members of the cast.

The actors on location yesterday were:

Mrs. Wiggs, Pauline Lord; Miss Hazy, Zasu Pitts; Mr. Stubbins, W. C. Fields; Bob Redding, Kent Taylor, Lucy Olcott, and Evelyn Venable. And the girls who were playing Mrs. Wiggs' children Asia, Europena, and Australia, were Edyth Tallowes, Virginia Weidler, and Carmencita Johnson.

The stocky good-natured, sun-burned, be-spectacled man, who was lounging in a Scattergood-Baines chair before the set, was Norman Taurog whom the actors pointed out with pride as "Our Director." "He's the man who put over *Skippy*, they said.

The hardest work I saw Mr. Taurog do that afternoon was carry on a rooster fight and phantom boxing match with the littlest Wiggs girl. Everybody on the job loves Mr. Taurog, I could see that. "He's so patient and so considerate," they said.

The man who was really doing the shouting and ordering about was Edward Anderson, assistant director. They were shooting the Opera House scene in a small town near "The Cabbage Patch," while we were in the studio. The setting and costumes bespoke of the "Gay Nineties."

You've probably heard that it is hard, very hard for an outsider to get into a studio. If you have, that's not half of it. One person, if he were the King of Siam, and if he had a truck load of credentials, might barely get a nose into one studio; and that would be an accident. But for fifteen people to get into four studios—well to put it in the pet phrase of the gang—"that's something!" It never could have been manipulated but for the very kind courtesy letters we had from Tony Sudekum, president of the Crescent Amusement Company and from the *Banner*. To them we owe all the marvelously good times we had in Hollywood, Burbank, and Universal City.

At Warner Brothers and First National studios they were making *Flirtation Walk*, a West Point picture, and at the time we were there they were rehearsing a Hawaiian dance number on one of the big sound stages. A very large Hawaiian orchestra led by Sol Hoo Pi, descendant of the royal family of Hawaii, was rehearsing numbers to be used in the picture, and apparently having great fun.

In another part of the set, on one of the great sound stages, Dick Powell and Josephine Hutchinson were being photographed in *Gentlemen are Born*. The scene we watched was taken of a gala on New Year's Eve in a Chinese restaurant. The rich girl had come to the restaurant for adventure, it seems, and there she met the impecunious hero.

Mr. Powell was wearing a navy business suit, blue shirt, and blue-gray carnival cap. Miss Hutchinson, who although she has made a great success on the stage, they said, is playing here in her first picture, was wearing a confetti-strewn brown polo coat and small hat. Two others in the "action" that we especially liked were the Chinese waiter in a black and silver coolie coat, and a very beautiful Chinese cigarette girl.

On another stage Frank Morgan and Barbara Stanwyck were playing the climax scene in *Lost Lady*. The acting was so good that our party wept at the death of the hero as much as did the heroine.

These plays will probably not be released until late in the fall but "our gang" will be eagerly watching for them to see if the camera-eye saw the action as we did from the sidelines.

Understand I have never been a movie fan, not by any manner of means; the legitimate stage has always been my favorite; but after seeing pictures made and knowing the characters in them I shall be intensely interested in some of the releases to be made in the fall. Don't wonder if I wear my old last winter's coat another year in order to see some screen shows that we have seen in the making.

Not the least of the interesting things in movie-land are the sets. Mr. McVeigh, who showed us about the place, took us first through the streets of Dublin, where signs on shop-windows told us that the O'Leary's, O'Connors, and Doyle Brothers were doing business there. Just around the corner or on the other side of the same scenery was a small Western town flaunting such signs as "Miner's Hotel" and "Last Chance Saloon." Nearby were a small artificial lake and the front end of a ship where Joe E. Brown played *Son of a Sailor*; next to that was a Russian street scene, where Leslie Howard and Kay Francis had just finished *British Agent*. Another "set" was covered with snow which had lain on the ground for two months under a blazing California sun—you're right, it was a special kind of snow. In fact, it is more often known as gypsum, and it does not make your fingers tingle like our Tennessee snow does. Other plays which have been finished so recently that the scenery was still standing were *Madame DuBarry* and *Dames*.

Another real treat of the day was a trip through Universal Studios. John LeRoy Johnston, director of publicity for Universal, was especially courteous to us, in part payment, he said, for the best food he had ever eaten, down in Tennessee in 1926-28 while making screen tests. We saw the sets used in *Hunchback of Notre Dame* and *All Quiet on the Western Front*. And we made some pictures of members of our party in the same old settings used for those productions.

In driving around the lot we found a group of actors, directors, and cameramen before a dummy theater making street scenes for *Gift of Gab*, in which the actors are Edmund Lowe, Gloria Stuart, Alice White, Ruth Etting, Phil Baler, Gene Austin, Victor Moore, Arline Judd, Sterling Holloway, Hugh O'Connell, Beale Street Boys, and Downey Sisters. The director was Karl Freund.

The players were just taking a recess between shots as we drove by in our hand-painted covered wagon, and they had as much fun over us and our "traveling accommodation" as we did over them in their khaki-colored face paint. You'd be surprised to see real movie actors in make-up. To look at even the close-ups you'd never guess that the hero's smooth square jaw is in reality a sickening yellow brown, and that the heroine's apparently kissable lips are a discouraging blackish purple.

Let those who will attach glamour to the making of moving pictures. Let them idealize and idolize and moon over actors and actresses. Let them stand in line for places as "extras," and envy the stars. I think I can never do any of those things. I do, however, admire the actors, not for their beauty—I saw little of that—but for their grit and patience, and hard-working stick-to-it-iveness. That's what it takes to make them what they are, and I envy none of them the tiring, monotonous, nerve-wearing grind that they endure every day.

THE NASHVILLE BANNER
FRIDAY, JULY 13, 1934

In California They Have Two Kinds of Weather, Good and Unusual, Claim Native Sons

Tennessee Farmers on Roundabout Trip to Century of Progress Exposition Pause at San Francisco, but Keep Ninety-Eight Blocks Between Them and Stevedores

BY LERA KNOX

Oakland, Calif., July 8,—(By Mail)—

Well. I surely am glad that ninety-eight city blocks and the bay separate us from the water front today. All is not so quiet over there as yesterday, I hear. I talked this morning with E. W. Macon, vice-president and general manager at the Western Pacific railroad, and nephew of our own Mr. "Fins-Furs-and-Feathers" Wilson. He said things are still very much unsettled, with several labor union meetings scheduled.

Our party has spent the day in and around Oakland, ninety-eight blocks from the bay. Some went to church, some went driving over the city to points of interest, some took airplane rides over the city and harbor, and some just lounged around camp and ate four meals between breakfast and supper (according to observations of a little boy in the auto camp where we are stopping).

Tomorrow we start eastward. May be in Reno Monday night—but without serious intentions. We go to Reno merely because the highway leads us there, not for a divorce as some other folks have.

We will stop, or expect to, at Salt Lake City, Yellowstone, and Omaha, en route to Chicago, to pick up mail, and will be glad to get any that may be there. Some of us have had no word from home, and none of us have had a *Banner*, except the edition of the day we left. Think of going three weeks without a *BANNER*!

I do not know whether any of the dope I have sent back has been fit to print or not. It has been dashed off in such a hurried, harem-scarem, way, either as we jolted over the road or as we stopped for supper or between getting-up-time and breakfast.

NOT HOMESICK

So, not knowing how much you have already had I hardly know how much more to tell. If I had a letter from home, I think it would get me out of some of this dumps I am in tonight. I'm not homesick—can't afford to be—just tired, and can't snap out of it, and have such a million things to tell you it makes me too sleepy to write. I'll feel better in the morning, I know. I ought to feel better after I get this story off my chest, if I ever do—but how to begin? The only way I know to tackle it is to begin where I am and back up over the past few days' experiences like a crawfish going upstream.

We've been in California a week today, and what a week! I don't know whether it is because of our experiences in crossing the desert or whether they are really that way, but the flowers in California seem brighter than any I have ever seen, except in a seed catalog, and maybe even a little brighter than those. The fruits here are as much better than others we have tasted as oranges are better than onions, and bananas are better than carrots—shriveled carrots and strong onions at that. And the folks here—well they do more playing, and more resting, and yet get more work done than any other folks outside of a fairy-tale book, I believe.

Just drive along the beaches and you will see thousands of men, women, and children lounging on the sand or on the grass plots, wearing belts and little more except their customary coats of tan. Drive through the parks, even the woodsiest ones way back in the mountains, and there they are, resting or playing around their impromptu camps—sometimes the tent for the whole family consists of a sheet spread over a limb for a dressing room in which to change from trunks to shorts, and back again.

As for California's climate—well, I haven't seen much that would do to brag about, the only thing I can say is what her native sons say—"It is very unusual." If you are sweltering and broiling in the sun about noon time, they say "This is very unusual weather." If you are freezing and shivering in late afternoon they console you by apologizing for the "unusual weather." I don't think Californian's have the best climate—they just think they have. And they believe that "there is nothing good or bad but thinking makes it so." But just the same, even the most loyal Californians would not "think" me out of a woolen sweater and into a bathing suit with that wind whipping in over the bay at a rate that makes one think Admiral Byrd left the door open in Little America.

PLENTY OF HILLS

Another thing that has been under-estimated in advertising is the number of hills on which San Francisco is built (I dare not say 'Frisco, although it is easier to spell. Folks here do not like the abbreviation, I understand.)

It has always been my impression that San Francisco, and Rome, and Pulaski, Tenn., were built on seven hills each—but from what I saw of San Francisco there must be at least seventy times seven. It is just one hill after another and new surprises and new beauties over each hill.

Through the courtesy of the Simmerville family of San Jose, we were able to see a great deal more of the famous Santa Clara "Valley of Heart's Delight," of San Francisco, Oakland, San Mateo, Burlingame, Palo Alto, Berkeley, and nearby cities and suburbs, than we ever could without the guidance of those who knew the country. And it was because of the Simmervilles that we made the side trip to the great California Redwood State Park.

As I stood beside those giant shaggy-barked monarchs of the forest (several of which were large enough to enclose my big eighteen-foot kitchen and the cold back-hall that joins it.) I was ready to believe every word of *Alice in Wonderland*. Do you remember about Alice eating the cake or drinking the liquid that made her very, very small? I felt as though I had eaten or drunk some of the same kind of stuff.

One gets an idea of how very insignificant one is out here where one cannot see the tops of the trees or the bottoms of the canyons.

We enjoyed watching the keeper call and feed the deer of the park. There are between four and five hundred, he said, but only a dozen or so came down from the hills at twilight to eat oats from the visitor's hands. We made some pictures of them.

An outstanding tree to us is the laurel or madrone that grows in the "Great Basin." It has a leaf something like the "green bay tree," but when Mother Nature says "shed," it sheds its bark instead of its leaves. The bark is a reddish brown and it looks very pretty under the dark green leaves. The drive through Redwood Park is so far the prettiest we have seen in California, unless one considers the drives lined with trees loaded down with plums, apricots, pears, English walnuts—and of course the grape vineyards hanging on the hillsides, and oranges and peaches in other parts of the State.

We saw world-famous Stanford University, and ex-President Hoover's home (but he probably never knew we had been so near). Then we saw Golden Gate Park and the "Gate" itself. Saw University of California and Mills College for girls. Visited Chinatown, of course, and liked the "Chinks" very much. One of them has adopted the name "Joe Knox" and has opened a coffee shop right near where we parked.

I'll just have to take off time later to tell you all about the rest of the trip we had. Too tired tonight.

THE NASHVILLE BANNER
SATURDAY, JULY 14, 1934

Anyway, Public Enemies of Desert Give Fair Warning Before Striking

But What's a Rattlesnake or So to a Crowd of Tennesseans, Especially Maury Countians, Who Like Their Hills And Pickles but Know How To Take Their Salt?

BY LERA KNOX

On the Nevada-Utah State Line at Wendover, July 11—(By Mail)—

Public Enemy No. 1 made his appearance in our camp this morning. He is a public enemy, and he is No. 1 in our experience. He is a 15-inch rattler with one rattle and a button. He didn't get into our tent—there was not room—but he gave plenty of excitement to the folks at a cabin about fifty feet from our tent.

We noticed a strange looking dog around our camp when we started cooking breakfast. He had the fattest face we ever saw, and we wondered what breed he was. In a little while, however we found that his fatness of face was due to what was in his blood and not in his breeding. His owner, the man at the cabin, took up the car seat from where it had lain beside the door all night, and in doing so he heard a buzzing inside it. "A large fly," he thought, and turned the cushion over to shake out the bug and there lay Public Enemy himself, No. 1; the first live rattler we had seen. He didn't stay alive long. We had no occasion to use our snake medicine except on the poor dog, who evidently got his "swelled head" trying to protect his master's doorway. When we broke camp at 6 o'clock Pacific Time (7, Mountain Time), the dog was pretty sick. They were going to bathe his head in gasoline or kerosene and make a mud poultice for the wound. But his owner had little hope of his recovery, for the poor old fellow was 17 years old.

Two hundred yards from where we camped we crossed the Utah line.

I don't know now exactly what time it is, but less than forty miles from Salt Lake City, and on our drive of 100 miles this morning we have seen some peculiar looking country. For miles and miles we drove through fields of solid salt as white as snow, and hard enough to hold up heavy traffic. It gives one a strange feeling to get snow-blindness in the midst of a hot dry desert. But that is what happened to us. Believe it or doubt.

Now we are pulling into Magna, near Salt Lake City. The houses are getting thicker. Manufacturing plants are on one side of the road and great, dirty looking, cracked salt beds are on the other side. The place makes you think "This must be where desolation is manufactured." You know how even a spot of good Tennessee earth looks the next day after someone has emptied an ice-cream freezer bucket of brine on it. This place looks the same way, only a million times more so. I confess I cannot appreciate the beauty of the salt mining section much more than I did the beauty (?) of the gold mines I saw. But when I think how potatoes taste without salt, I admit that the stuff is useful, if it is not ornamental in its crudest state.

Then I think if the Great Salt Desert, which we crossed this morning, could be boxed up into table salt and sold for 10 cents a box, it would really make enough to pay off the national debt.

If all the salt in Utah and all the dill in California could be made into a pickling brine, and if all the Rocky Mountains could be made into cucumber hills, what a pickle we'd have in America!

Seeing Salt Lake City today, just driving in, tell you about it in next story.

THE NASHVILLE BANNER
MONDAY, JULY 16, 1934

Maury Farm Group Pauses to Inspect Site of Brigham Young's Triumphs

Salt Lake City Found To Be Ideal Place for Gentlemen Who Prefer Blondes, and for Inquisitive Reporters Who Would Delve Into Mysteries of 'Private Lives'

Salt Lake City, Utah, July 11—

Well, I always reserve the right to change my mind and today I have had ample opportunity to give that right plenty of exercise. When we blew into Salt Lake City this morning, we had two or three things in mind—to hear the organ recital at the famous Mormon Tabernacle, to get some letters from home, and perhaps to get in touch with the Chamber of Commerce or a good newspaper and learn some interesting things about the city and state.

As soon as we found out that Salt Lake City was breaking out with a meat packer's strike (no we did not think it was put on as an exhibition for our benefit) we knew that the newspaper folks in town would be as busy as the *Banner's* city editor at 10 o'clock in the morning and that they would not have time to take any notice of even our T.N.T. party; so we decided to get our mail, hear the music, eat our lunch, and move on. Experiences on this trip have taught us to keep distance between ourselves and striking men and striking snakes.

We drove into the shade of a narrow street just off State Street to eat our sandwiches. A kind of friendly "neighbor" looked out her back door, saw us and came out with enough ice tea to really "set us up"—and we were hot and tired and thirsty.

As we "took tea" and munched sandwiches there on the backdoor steps with her, I began asking some questions about places of interest in the town. She told us of the huge copper mines nearby, where miners are slicing mountains and sifting copper out of them.

We regretted that we did not have time to drive out and see the mines, and then she tried to think of something else. "Well, Brigham Young's grave is just around the corner," she said.

That sounded interesting, so I asked some more questions which I thought were "leading." She couldn't answer all, but she said, "I can't tell you much, but Mrs. Dougall, Brigham Young's oldest daughter, lives just across the street from my front door—she will tell you."

"Whoopee! Wow!" I answered quietly. "Do you suppose I could meet her?"

"Why certainly," said my neighbor-for-a-day.

I left my tea and the last half of a peanut-butter-graham cracker sandwich somewhere—I don't remember where—got my notebook and pocketbook under one arm, my camera under the other, and with Margaret and Jack as attendants and

250-pound "Tiny" as a bodyguard, I set forth around the corner and across the street to meet the "Princess." And princess she is: a real jewel and a gentle lady.

She has given her life to young people. Old people bore her, she says, and the middle-aged are entirely too slow. Her greatest joy is in serving as councilor to the president of the Young Women's Mutual Improvement Association, an international organization of which she is the only honorary member. The organization has 100,000 members and I am sure few of them are more youthful in spirit than Maria Young Dougall, who will have her eighty-fifth birthday party on the tenth day of next December.

"Ri-ra," as her fifty-two brothers and sisters call her, has preserved her school-girl complexion to a remarkable degree. I failed to learn the secret, but I do know it is not by cosmetics, although it may be heredity or environment or both. We saw more fair-skinned, natural blonds in Salt Lake City than any place we have touched this side of the Mississippi.

I have seldom met a more delightful or entertaining person, and after I learned that we all might have the privilege of knowing her, I sent word back to the covered wagon, and the rest of the gang left their teacups to join in a delightful hour of talking and listening with the oldest living child of Brigham Young.

Mrs. Dougall took out three old albums which were highly prized by her father. One contained pictures of crowned heads of Europe and members of their families and prominent Americans; another had uncles, aunts, cousins and friends; the third had pictures of Brigham Young's nineteen wives and forty-two children—Mrs. Platt, Mrs. Dougall's very loveable daughter, gave me these family statistics—Mrs. Dougall said with a twinkle in her eye that "she could not remember."

"This was one of my father's wives," she said as she pointed to the picture of a woman who looked like a twin sister of Whistler's mother. "And she was one of the dearest, sweetest women who ever lived. We all loved her. I think no girl in America had a happier childhood than I had. You cannot imagine how wonderful it was to have so many brothers and sisters to play with. And we were always given the pleasantest surroundings."

Mrs. Dougall was born in a log cabin across the street from where she now lives in 1849—two years after the pioneers came in from the East and one year after 1848 when in answer to prayer, the seagulls came into the country and destroyed the devastating army of crickets that swooped down from the mountains to consume the pioneers' first crop and leave them to starve a thousand miles from food and civilization.

Now you know why one of the most prominent monuments in the town is erected to "the gulls."

Mrs. Dougall's earliest memories, she said, were of hard working people building houses and making roads. I did not ask of experiences with Indians, for I had heard already that

Brigham Young said it was "cheaper to feed Indians than kill them."

How we should have enjoyed a long stay with this charming new-found friend, but we had to be on our way. An hour had passed already. She insisted, however, that we do go down to the corner and go through the big "Lion House" where she and her many brothers and sisters spent their childhood and where "every wife had a room" but all came together at mealtimes in the big dining-room in the basement, and in the big "prayer-room" or parlor, in the evening. The entire house is not furnished in the period furniture, however. A large part of it is used as a community social center and school.

Next to the personality of "Princess Maria" I think I admire more than anything else about Utah, the indominitable spirit of the pioneers who settled there. On a monument to this "Handcart Veterans" who came over bringing all their possessions and the younger members of their families in handcarts, I found this inscription:

> Nor gold nor glory their exalted quest,
> Who won for East the wide unconquered West,
> They toiled o'er frozen crest, o'er parching plains.
> Eternal wealth in higher worlds to gain.
> Forever in remembrance let them be
> Who gave their all for Truth and Liberty.
>
> Orson F. Whitney

THE NASHVILLE BANNER
TUESDAY, JULY 17, 1934

No Matter Where You Go, You'll Find Tennesseans Right in the Limelight

Even Out in Utah, Where the Salt Is Thick and Forest Fires Rage, You're Likely to Run Across One of Your Old Neighbors, Maury County Trippers Have Discovered

Salt Lake City, Utah, July 17—

Well, another holdup! And if I give you a hundred and twenty million guesses you would probably not guess by whom. I couldn't have guessed it either, just off-hand, so you're forgiven.

We were a few hours out of Salt Lake City and had passed through Ogden where we saw a real wild, forest fire raging in the mountains above the town. (We thought a new volcano had broken loose or that the country was putting on a fireworks display for us.)

There has been a mystery to solve at Ogden. We saw an innocent-looking young man with a chin-enveloping six-week's growth of beard, and immediately decided, that, as it was not the time of year for college hazing, the mysterious man must be disguising himself with a beard. But to our great surprise, two more men came down the street behind beards of similar length, though different color. Others came out of shops and across the street—all with beards of different styles and shades and they looked hard at us and our "covered wagon."

"Gangsters!" we thought, "Maybe Dillinger himself hides behind one of those sandy or gray or bristly beards. And we were eleven women, two boys, one man (one stayed on the coast so we were only fourteen now). We had also one jack-rabbit-rifle but it was under all our grub boxes and luggage—besides we had no ammunition. Finally one brave curiosity-laden soul must know the worst. She asked one of the bearded giants a question, and learned—Ogden is having a big celebration near the last of this month in honor of the pioneers, and every man who attends without his beard must pay a fine. The barbers in Ogden, Utah, are really having a depression.

But that was not the hold-up I started to tell you about. We weredrivingalongasinnocentlyandpeaceablyandunsuspecting as could be expected, when a big car pulled along side honking as wildly as an ambulance in Main Street on Saturday afternoon. It slowed down in front of us and out popped twelve arms and six heads. We slowed to a stop and as we did, the car's doors opened and six bodies and twelve legs scrambled out.

Then a Comanche's Yell, which, when interpreted in Tennessee English asked "Is that Lera Knox and party?" I wondered what we had done.

"Don't you know us?" they yelled. "We are the Darwins from Cookeville!"

You bet a heap we felt good. They had been out on the road for only a week. They are still tender-skinned from their first coat of sunburn. We are as browned as veterans of the road. The first five coats are the peelingest, you know. They are going on to Yellowstone and we are too. Hope to see them there tomorrow, sometime. Just to think that they were in the tabernacle at the organ recital this morning at the same time we were. They were bathing in the lake while we were visiting with Brigham Young's daughter. Among us, we Tennesseans are really seeing a large slice of the West.

In the party were Mr. and Mrs. Dero Darwin and Margaret Darwin of Cookeville, Blanch Darwin of Gainesboro, and Christine and Walter Johnson of Eric, Okla. They had actually read some of our stories in the *Banner*, so I know now that my pay check must be "inching" along toward the first of the month or something not too far away—that encouraged me to write another story or so. Lookout!

Seeing them reminds me to tell you of a lot of other folks who have been attracted by our Tennessee license plates and all our signs to come up and reveal themselves. One of our first surprises was Dixon Sowell in Texarkana, a boy from my own neighborhood.

Then grinning, jolly, Joe Love, Jr., formerly of Culleoka, now of Prescott, Ariz. He wanted to know if we had any fried chickens in our grips or grub-boxes. And of all the folks! Howard Alexander, another boy whose home was hardly more than a mile from Knoxdale Farm—he was the motor cop who held up traffic in Pasadena to greet us. The word "greet" reminds me of the County Court Clerk at El Paso, his name is Greet, and in addition to being a good fellow and loyal Texan, he claims the honor of being cousin of Mrs. Mora Farris, Columbia. The deputy sheriff of El Paso, who told us about much of Old Mexico and Juarez, was a native of Coffee County, Tennessee. He thinks that Manchester is just about the best place on the globe except El Paso, of course. His name is Kirkpatrick, and he has been an officer in Texas since he was much younger than he is now, he said.

Alex Alexander, a prominent oil man of Texas and Arizona, saw us in Prescott, and asked to be remembered to M.E. Johnson, our big, boosting, booming, public-spirited president of Columbia's Chamber of Commerce. (Pardon me, Mr. Johnson, for neglecting to tell you sooner).

The portly gentleman who saw us "mirating" over the dimensions of the *Macon*, the big dirigible "Eye of the Navy" near San Jose (tell you about that too, soon as I get time), was the Reverend G.F. Higgenbottom, a Baptist minister who has held a number of revival meetings in our State. He sends greetings to relatives and friends in Tennessee. George Foster wants to be remembered to his cousin, Miss Elizabeth Turner, a teacher in Nashville. He is employed at the Naval Air Base where the *Macon* is "camping," or dwelling or stationed or located or hanging—I don't know the proper word.

J. E. Johnson of Long Beach wants to be remembered to his friends among the Shriners in Nashville.

Tom Mudd, formerly of Decatur, Ala., says "Hello" to friends and relatives in the southern part of Tennessee and Northern Alabama. We met him at a filling station in San Monica Calif.—Tennesseans as far as we went.

LOST IN LONG BEACH

One night while we were camped in Long Beach, the night we came back from Santa Catalina Island, we got on the wrong streetcar, and got off at the wrong stop. We told the conductor that we wanted to go to "Seaside Camp" and that it was located on the beach between the end of the boardwalk and the "bucking" bridge that raised up for ships to go under. It seems that any conductor who knew his city could have directed us, but little did he care if a gang of noisy, giggling Tennesseans got lost in the wilds of Southern California. He charged us 15 cents each fare over from Wilmington and put us off, we don't know where.

It was Sunday night. Everybody was gone to church or visiting. Nobody seemed ever to have heard of "Seaside Camp." Finally we saw a light in a sort of little office beside the street. We knocked, and asked the man who came to the door if he could please tell us the location of the "bucking" bridge and the boardwalk. He tried to tell us to go five blocks this way, eight blocks that way, then ten blocks the other then far as we could, and turn to the right. That was terrible news for tired feet. What we thought of the Long Beach street car system is unprintable—but the street cars were all too far away to hear our remarks, much less our thoughts.

We tried again to understand his directions, but our stupidity was pitiful. Finally he decided it would be easier to take us than to tell us. There were eight in the bunch, but he packed us all into his car and delivered us safely beside the sea between the "bucking" bridge and the boardwalk. That was the night we had the fish supper feast, and we were glad to invite our heroic rescuer in as honored guest. Just before he left, we learned that his name is Ted Tye, and he hails from Southern Kentucky.

Another "native son" whom we have met in the West is C.C. Lindsay, formerly of 2010 Broad Street, across the street from Samuel C. Davis' drug store. He is a relative of Miss Fannie Pilcher and Stuart Pilcher, he said, and he wants to know "what has become of Dave Wrenn who used to be with Wrenn Banking Company on Union Street."

A man, who passed us in highway traffic between Los Angeles and San Jose, yelled, "I'm from Waverly!" We found a Cookeville boy in Long Beach, but did not get his name. Maybe someone in Cookeville will know who is missing from there and will recognize him from this description.

Eris Johnson, formerly of Murfreesboro, now of Laguna Beach, and Miss Nina Manier of Lewisburg Huntington Beach, send love to folks back home. One of the best sports we have found is Jim Mullins, better known as "Moon," and he has a notorious brother called "Kayo." Moon hails from Kentucky and Tennessee. He is principal of the high school in Grant's Pass, Ore., and a leader of the "Cave Men" there. He was very eager for us to go through Grant's Pass so he could have us "captured" by the organization. Jim was visiting on a "business" trip in San Jose. The "reason" is sometimes known as "Beth," and we loved her too.

And did I tell you we saw W.H. Chamberlain, brother of J. N. Chamberlain of Nashville, in Kingman? He is a cousin of Edgar Foster of the *Banner*, and a friend of L.A. Bauman, and he "used to carry the *Banner* in North Nashville in '83."

T. Herbert Prichard of El Paso and Juarez wants to be remembered to friends in Tennessee and Kentucky; he wants "Katie" to write him. L.P. Henderson wants his regards sent to the Newton families in Nashville, and Roy Bosson, formerly of Sparta, now editor of the *Sentinel-Record* and *New Era*, has not forgotten his old hometown of Sparta. Mrs. Mary Hale Manier of Hot Springs introduced herself as the daughter of the late Dr. J.H.P. Hale of Nashville and a cousin of Joe Holman of Holman and Marr, Nashville Architecture.

KNOXVILLE NEWS-SENTINEL
WEDNESDAY, JULY 18, 1934

Tennesseans Go to Fair in Covered Wagon

Traveling by way of San Francisco's Golden Gate, this group of Tennesseans arrived at the World's Fair for a two-day visit after traveling 6800 miles in a motorized covered wagon for $40 apiece. They are, left to right (front), Margaret Knox and Mrs. Lera Knox, Columbia; Edna Johnson, Dickson; Mrs. Goodrum, Columbia Gladys Wall, Columbia; (second row) Jack Knox, Columbia; (back row) Camilla Manier, Holland; Bess Anderson, Franklin; Mrs. Henrietta Kearney, Columbia; Stella Campbell, Columbia; Florence Burkett, Columbia; and Frances Mathews, Columbia.

THE NASHVILLE BANNER
THURSDAY, JULY 19, 1934

Rambling Tennesseans Remember Yellowstone for Thrills and Chills

Prepared for 100-Plus Temperatures, Party Encounters January Climate in July—Find Most Beautiful Drive through Shoshone Canyon, 'Most Scenic 70 Miles'

BY LERA KNOX

Just Out of Cody, Wyo., July 15—(By Mail)—

We shall always remember Yellowstone Park as the place that gives thrills by day and chills by night.

The first morning we waked to find a half-inch of ice on our water-bucket. The second morning the hydrants were frozen. And that was July 13 and 14—believe it or doubt! We had equipped ourselves, you know, for desert travel, in a temperature of 110 to 120 degrees, and we were not long off the burning desert when we waked in the morning to find our dish towels frozen as stiff as marble biscuit-boards. The few clothes we had removed and washed the night before were stiffened in the trees on which they hung.

If you could have seen how red were our noses and how stiff our little pink toeses, if you could have heard our teeth chattering, and felt the chill-bumps on the complexion of our extremities, as we shivered in our blankets around a smoky camp-fire, you would have said, "January climate in July ain't so hot!"

But it was fun—not at 5 o'clock, in the morning, I'll admit—but as the sun, and campfire, and sooty-black coffee warmed our congealing blood, we began to recount our experiences trying to keep warm during the night.

All these statements and insinuations are indeed incredible when one considers that fifteen minutes' drive brought us to steaming geyser basins where mud and "paint" and crystal-clear water were boiling and bubbling, and shooting jets of steam 250 feet into the air.

"Old Faithful" herself, in vapor, and in her usual steaming manner, gave two magnificent performances while we were in the geyser basin.

As we came in sight around the bend of the road, she rose in a majestic column of white mist and daintily spreading her skirts made such a curtsey as you would expect from a maiden of 1847.

And yet as lovely as is Old Faithful, as marvelous as is Grand Canyon of the Colorado, as romantic as is Santa Catalina, as vast as is the Pacific, as inspiring as is "Rock of Ages" in the bottom of the earth in Carlsbad Cavern, none of these things in my opinion have quite the breath-taking beauty that we saw in the Grand Canyon of the Yellowstone while viewing the lower falls from Artist's Point.

MOST BEAUTIFUL DRIVE

The most beautiful drive we have found in the 5,320 miles we have traveled to date is through the Shoshone (three syllables, please) Canyon between Yellowstone Park and Cody. It is advertised by the Cody Lions Club as "The Most Scenic Seventy Miles in the World"—and we believe the Lions.

Cody is a very "dudish" little town, proud of the fact that it has a claim on "Buffalo Bill," Will Hayes, and W. R. Love, New York capitalist.

To tell the truth, it looked for a short while as though Cody was just a bit too high-toned for common country folks from the "Volunteer State." It was near night, we were terribly tired, we went to the three tourist camps of the town and found either no room "in the inn" or outside, or "no accommodations for so large a party."

Finally we decided to beard the Lions in their places of business.

I found one in a furniture store and accosted him thus: "You didn't say in your advertising along the highways that there was not room in Cody to pitch a tent! If we don't find a camping space somewhere, we will be forced to shake your dust from our tires and inflict our presence on the next town fifty miles away."

Then the Lion sprang to his telephone and finally found a place for us behind the cow-lot down the Ingraham's dairy farm. Don't think, however, that we were uncomfortably or unpleasantly situated. You see, this place behind the cow-lot is a lovely apple orchard which the Ingraham family have converted into a campground for such wanderers as we.

In the shade of the next apple tree to ours were camping thirty-four Boy Scouts and four scout leaders from Humphrey, Nebr. They made jolly good neighbors, very gentlemanly, remarkably well-disciplined, but having a whale of a good time. I think it speaks well for the boys that in the final count-up, not a green apple was missing from the tree under which they camped. I don't know whether that could be said of our tree or not—I have had to pass around the medicine kit several times this morning.

This group of sightseers is making a two-thousand-mile journey through Nebraska and Wyoming on a loaf of bread, two cans of pork and beans and $5 each.

They hired a truck and trailer for $120, half down and half on safe-return, and the remainder will take care of other expenses. They buy eggs by the case for breakfast, have baked ham for lunch, and mulligan stew, pork and beans, or soup for supper.

Such a trip as they are making is worth more than can be estimated to each boy, and it is possible only because the boys are well trained and completely disciplined. When a boy becomes unruly he is allowed to walk a mile. If that does not tame him, another mile or more is added, we learned.

They had just been over the same road we are to follow and we had just traveled the road they were taking, so we were able to exchange road information and experiences with them. The boys were on tip-toe to see the Yellowstone bears and to know something of them.

The best we could tell them was that the rangers know what they are talking about when they say (and post on signs) "It Is Dangerous to Feed Bears."

Another thing hard to believe is that black and brown and cinnamon bears walked around our tent and trailer just like dogs around a farm-house door. One sneaked into our grub box, which was sitting on the ground at the end of the trailer, while we were eating supper with our table propped against the side of the trailer. A scolding and a stone sent him scooting, whereas if we had started feeding him he would have fought us for more.

J. A. stayed in camp one day while we took a drive through the park. He had spread his crackers and left a jar of peanut butter on a cot beside the tent, and had turned to fry some flap-jacks on our little camp stove. When he turned around a two-year-old brown cub was sitting in the middle of the cot enjoying his lunch.

THE NASHVILLE BANNER
SUNDAY, JULY 22, 1934

Despite Climbing Mercury, Wandering Tennesseans Make Good Time in West

BY LERA KNOX

Near North Platte, Neb. July 17 (By Mail)—

After four weeks on the road we feel that we are really just learning to travel. This morning we rousted out at 4:45, and after baths and semi-baths (we have learned to take baths or let them alone) and after breakfast (we are never willing to let that alone) and after dressing (such as it. was) and packing (that must be done expertly or all cannot be put in), we got away at 5:45 Mountain Time—and there are only sixty minutes in an hour of M.T. (whether you believe it or doubt).

In spite of rough, dusty, hot highways and narrow, bumpy detours we are making very good time. We came from beyond Casper, Wyo., to Oshkosh, Neb., yesterday. But we were really in a hurry yesterday. Shall I tell you why? Please don't let this story ever get back to Wyoming.

We were driving along on a monotonous road when something that looked like a bunch of wild "dominicker-brown-leghorn" chickens crossed our dusty path. Just to see if we could pick up a chicken-dinner we took out the 22-rifle. Then came a car along. "Hey! Dead sage-hens cost $50 each in this State," the driver called to us.

Well, we immediately lost our appetite for chickens—especially chickens that might taste like they had been raised in the United States Treasury. All the rest of that day we would even take a detour in preference to driving by a sign that advertised "Chicken Dinner."

Please forgive me if I talk about the weather. There is more of that in this country than anything else. This is the "drought-stricken area." Cattle are being shipped out by trainload and truck-load. They are driven along the highways; and in some places are turned into the cornfields.

The corn is from two to three feet high and is brown and twisted. From what we can learn, the people west of North Platte may get something out of their corn if it rains within the next ten days. But those east of North Platte have no hopes—I heard this in a barber shop where I took Jack for a haircut, so you may attach whatever credit you choose to it. You may take my word for it, though, that it really is dry out here, and the hottest summer ever known, they say.

It was 117 degrees along this road yesterday, but when we came along telling about the pipes being frozen in Yellowstone

Saturday morning, folks got ashamed and turned their thermometers back to 113 degrees. It is hot enough though, at that. You know how hot taffy-candy is just before it is cool enough to pull—that's how hot the metal parts of my typewriter are as I try to write this at 4 o'clock in the afternoon.

It was so hot that we ate scarcely any lunch today. We are going to have sandwiches for early supper and drive late tonight—hoping for cooler air after dark. We may make it into Omaha tonight or early in the morning. We are traveling this afternoon like an old plowhorse when he turns at the far end of the corn-row and starts back in the direction of the barn. You know how, if you have ever been with him; if you haven't, I can't tell you.

We are not homesick of course, but, well, East is east, isn't it?

We have lots of fun all along. There are four or five rhymesters in the gang, who, when they lack anything else to do, make poems about one another or circumstances, or incidents. No reputable publisher has bid for the poems yet—but we have hopes.

It is hardly fair to you and to me that some of the funniest things that have happened are unprintable. But you need not think because I cannot tell you, that "O. G, There ain't no jesters" in the gang.

We have for instance, a crew of "sign pullers." They collect, beg, buy, borrow, or swipe every movable sign that interests them, and then fasten it up either inside or outside the trailer. The last sign is very simple. It merely says "Ladies." But they got quite a "kick" out of stealing it and tacking it up under the window where they stick their heads out.

I do suppose the bunch does need to be labeled. With all the sunburn and dust that is on us after four weeks' traveling, I doubt if our closest relatives would recognize us at tent-time on days we make 400 miles. I frequently hear the expression, "I'm glad my mother can't see me tonight."

But we have learned many things on this trip, besides history and geography. We have developed a new sense of values. We feel that the things that are going into our heads are more worthwhile than the dust that is settling on our scalps. One girl says she is going to spend her first week at home half time in the bathtub and the other half on a double-springs mattress under a Tennessee shade tree—mosquitoes prohibited.

I imagine you have wondered whether fifteen people can get along together for six weeks with no disagreements, no fusses, and no losses of temper, no tears, or hard feeling. Maybe they can. I refuse to commit myself. I do know, however, that our gang has done remarkably well. When you consider that we range in age from 13 to 55, in weight from 93 to 250.

I will confess, however, that we have "inside information" on one strike that has not as yet been in the papers. The grievance was "pork-and-beans and cold-slaw" for two or three days, in succession. The gang complained and mumbled and almost mutinied—I guess that is a good word—isn't that what Columbus' crew did? The "dieticians" for the week said nothing. But late that night when we drove into camp at a small town where they "roll up the sidewalks at 6 o'clock," we unloaded, tired and hungry, wanting to know how soon supper would be ready. Then the pantry chief announced, "As we couldn't please you with our buying, we quit. We didn't buy anything for supper."

And there we were 2,000 miles from home, tired, starved, and supperless. We foraged around the slumbering little city and finally aroused a kind cafe-keeper who let us have a little strong-flavored but weak vitamined milk and a few ancient eggs. Next morning we paid 10 cents a cup for coffee and 25 cents a flap for hot cakes, and by noon we were ready to eat pork and bean sandwiches frosted with cold slaw and grin about it.

Understand, we are not trying to tell anybody how to settle a strike, but we know what cured ours. Sometimes the way to one's head is through one's stomach.

We just stopped at Grand Island, Neb., 6:20 (E.S.T.—changed our time at North Platte) and a tousled-headed, ruddy-faced young man came up to the car and wanted to know if we knew anyone at Petersburg, Tenn. He went to school over there just after the war, he said, and wants to be remembered to Prof. R. K. Morgan, and many others, especially Dr. and Mrs. Charles Marsh. Mrs. Marsh, he says, he can never forget the good things you gave him to eat. It makes him hungry even yet to think about Petersburg. His name is Bruce Barham, and he played on the football team for Petersburg against C.M.A. (Columbia Military Academy.)

THE NASHVILLE BANNER
SUNDAY, AUGUST 5, 1934

Still Dazed by Sights On Great Western Trek

Maury Farm Woman Finds Time to Figure up Expenses of 7,346 Mile, Five-Weeks' Jaunt to 'Frisco and Back, at $45.32 Per Person

BY LERA KNOX

Home again, and still unconscious, or dazed or stunned or just "knocked cuckoo" by the sights I've seen and the experiences I have experienced. I can hardly believe it yet, that a green country woman and a group of friends could have made the 7,346-mile Southern-Western-Northern trip we did at an average actual cost of $45.32 each and return to tell the story.

I must apologize to those of you who read the fifteen stories the *Banner* has published about the trip, not because the things I wrote were inaccurate or exaggerated, but because I could not make them big enough to describe the situation as they appeared to my wondering eyes, and because I could not make them long enough nor numerous enough to cover all or even the best of our experiences. But time for writing was so scanty, and my body and mind were so tired, and the editor was so crowded for space-that—well, we just couldn't give it all to you.

But I promise this. As I get my bearings; regain consciousness, etc.; get caught up with the five weeks' work I left undone at home; and get rested a bit, I will begin putting squibs from the trip into the regular Sunday "Scrap Bag" and you may still "tour the West" with me in retrospect.

I promised to give you an account of the trip's expenses. Each time I have figured it up I get a different set of figures, but that's due to my arithmetic, algebra, and geometry.

Following I am giving the expenses as they showed up from the figures of three of the expedition's "bookkeepers," and I give the mileage from the speedometer.

Left Columbia June 18, returned July 23. Traveled through Tennessee, Arkansas, Texas, New Mexico, Arizona, California, Nevada, Utah, Idaho, Montana, Wyoming, Nebraska, Iowa, Illinois, Indiana, Kentucky, sixteen states, Mexico and Islands of the Pacific.

In five weeks we traveled 7,346 miles on 584 gallons of gasoline.

ITEMIZED EXPENSE ACCOUNT

Rent on 1926 model car for six weeks	$25.00
Cost of building camping-trailer	98.00
Cost of 14x16 tent	24.70
Cost of 584 gallons of gasoline	114.47
Cost of oil and lubrication grease	9.89

Cost of two new tires, one tube, three rims, and tube repairs.	20.18
Cost of second-hand generator to replace one burnt out.	4.00
Bridge tolls and National Park entrance fees	9.45
Driver-mechanic wages for five weeks	200.00
Food and ice and fuel for cook stove.	128.52
(Note: There were fifteen in party for two weeks.)	
Camping spaces for thirty-five nights	19.90
	$654.11

Average actual cost per person for trip...$45.32

Average total expenditures of each member of party including cost of trip, souvenirs, films, cold drinks, laundry, messages home, new clothes, etc....$67.50

On the first half of the trip to San Francisco the actual cost per person was $19.59.

The last half of the trip from San Francisco to Chicago and home cost...$25.73.

THE NASHVILLE BANNER
SUNDAY, AUGUST 12, 1934

The Scrap Bag

Maury County Farm Woman Finds the Sunsets Framed By Her Kitchen Window Are Better Than Any out West—Crafts Turning Toward The Past

BY LERA KNOX

Well, it has been several weeks since you had a Scrap Bag to reach into and maybe you won't find much in it this time, but even the homeliest things look better to us after being absent for a while.

You may have much to endure during the next few weeks. I am so chuck full of things we saw on that Western trip that I'll be likely to talk too much about my "travels"—never been used to seeing much before, you know, so the sights I did see went pretty hard with me.

Be thankful for one thing, however: I never had an operation. If you will let me inflict my travel yarns on you, I'll let you tell me all about your operations and the symptoms thereof.

There is a river in Arizona—I cannot spell the name of it, but it is the river that Prescott is near (Hassayampa?)—they say if you drink the water of that river with your head downstream, you will never leave Arizona; if you drink with your head upstream, you will never tell the truth again. I drank some water of that river, and I didn't stay in Arizona. But I drank it from a public fountain, and I did not have a map to find what direction the river came from, so there is no telling but what I had been exposed to prevarication.

I had this coming to me, I suppose; anyway, I took it chin-up and grinned about it. In fact, I can still grin about it and hope you can do the same. A typical, dude-ranch, movie-hero-type cowboy with fifteen-gallon hat, loud-plaid shirt, fancy belt, and fuzzy chaps came up to the car in Prescott to know how we liked Arizona.

Well, that was before we drank the water from that river, so I honestly told him I didn't like Arizona at all.

"I don't blame you," he said. "I never did like it myself until I saw what could come from Tennessee."

I can see more pretty sunsets in three days from my kitchen window than I saw in five weeks in the West. That's the truth. The sun doesn't really set—not prettily, I mean, in the Western States. It just drops over the edge of the plain or below the tip of a mountain without leaving a single bright colored streak or gold-tipped cloud behind it. The reason, I suppose, is there are no clouds. We scarcely saw a cloud as big as a man's hand while we were gone, and did not have a drop of rain on us. But I was going to tell you about sunsets. We did see two that were very pretty on the two afternoons we were in Wyoming. We might have seen a pretty one at Salt Lake City, but after we found out that another strike was breaking there, we didn't wait for sunset.

Anyhow, I have learned one thing or two—one is that it takes clouds to make beauty supreme, and the other is that I have a picture every day before my humble kitchen window that all the wealth of the West cannot produce.

Another thing we all learned is that this United States of ours is not a mere patchwork of pink, blue, green, yellow, lavender, states all pieced together and stitched across with black threads called rivers. It is a living, breathing, working, (striking) country made up of vast stretches of land, huge mountains, and people—other people just like us, and a great many of them.

Something that made a great impression on us was the unusual percentage of blonds (natural, I mean) in Salt Lake City. Of course, we saw plenty of synthetic blonds in Hollywood, but the blonds in Utah are real and permanently blond, not just prematurely.

Perhaps we noticed their fair complexion more because we had just come from the coast where complexions are darkened by both sunshine and Spanish blood, but the fair skins, and the red or golden scalp-locks in Utah were extremely noticeable to us. They were more prevalent even than they were here in Tennessee where we boast of our pure Anglo-Saxon inheritance. There must be a reason for the blonds in Utah. I did not find it in the atmosphere, and I am sure it is not in the drug store.

But I must not talk entirely about the West. Let's turn east a bit. Last week I was in East Tennessee at the Farm Women's Convention at Knoxville and a treat of the week was a trip into the Smoky Mountains. One stop was at Gatlinburg where we were to visit the shops at which the handicraft articles of the mountain people are displayed. One woman in the group seemed not to understand what it was all about—not even the name of the town. She asked me as we came down the Main Street in Gatlinburg, "Is this where the Battle of Gettysburg was fought?" (I can't blame her for mixing her history and geography though, for I got so mixed up in spelling the word I had to look in the dictionary to see whether it had an "e" or "y" in the middle of it.)

I noticed the tendency throughout the week at this gathering of farm women was back to the old, and the native; to the good old days and the things that went with them. The songs used were the old hymns and the mountain ballads. "Sourwood Mountain" was a favorite, and "Little Sir Echo." "The Keeper," "Old Water Mill," "The Lark in the Moon," "The Belles of St. Mary's," "Down in the Valley," "Whip-poor-Will," "Home on the Range," and "Morning Come Early" were equally popular.

"She'll Be Comin' 'round the Mountain" was as popular and was used as the foundation for as many parodies as "It Ain't Gonna Rain No More" a few years ago. And "The Old Spinning Wheel" was sung and hummed as much as "Casey Jones," "Rainbow," and "Red Wing," all put together in their day.

Watch the music of the nation and the fingers of the women if you would know the trend of the times. I lived with 200 women for five days and did not see or smell a cigarette nor hear a jazz tune—now believe that or doubt—the world's not all bad yet.

The trend in handicraft is certainly toward the crafts of our grandmother's day. Knitting, crocheting, weaving, quilting, basketry—even spinning, carding, and home dying have come back—and you need not think that this was just a bunch of the hickest "hicks" that were at the University—they are the cream of the crop of farm homemakers, the leaders in their communities back home. History is certainly repeating itself among rural people and city people, too; if the taste of the women is a gauge we may wear hoop-skirts before spring.

And perhaps you have been wondering how the farm, the farmer, and the pup, also the cows, chickens, and garden got along while the wife and children were gadding about. You might have expected me to come home and find five weeks supply of soiled dishes piled up in the kitchen sink—but you guessed wrong. The dishes were washed, the table set, a ham was boiled, a cake was baked, the washing and ironing were done and put away, the beds all made up and swept under, and the kitchen floor and front porch scoured. I'll confess it was more than I expected. But Daddy and Uncle Fayette and Aunt Dora and Uncle Jimmie had really been on the job for three days getting ready for the return of the prodigals. A farmer's wife is not such an absolute necessity after all, I learned, but just a very desirable asset. So ladies, don't feel too important about your job. Somebody else really could handle it as well as you do. Just maybe not in your special style.

THE NASHVILLE BANNER
SATURDAY, SEPTEMBER 1, 1934

The Scrap Bag

A Former Tennessean Sets the Maury Farm Woman Right On a Few Things She Wrote About Arizona. Says the Two States Are Not Made for Comparison.

BY LERA KNOX

Ho! Ho! Here comes a delightful letter from Arizona "to try to set me right" about a few things in "The Scrap Bag" of August 12. It is from "a loyal Tennessean who has not yet drunken from those Hassayampian (glad to get that word spelled) waters either up hill or down hill," and he has been in Arizona nearly six years—long enough to get acclimated, I judge. He "takes up" for his adopted State in such a charming manner and maintains such an admirable loyalty for Tennessee that I beg to quote some expressions from his letter. In my opinion they "doeth the heart good like medicine." He says in part:

"It was my privilege to leave Peoria (Ariz.) June 17 on a journey that took me as far east as Alexandria, Tenn., and return via Chicago, Milwaukee, Omaha, and Trinidad, Colo., thus we must have passed twice within a few miles of each other. I was in Chicago July 18-19 and on the road in Iowa July 21. While you were detouring north to Carlsbad Caverns I was detouring south in the Davis Mountains of Texas. I read your account of the trip as published in the *Banner* while I was in Tennessee, and with all you said about the roads (the detour to the Caverns) and the heat in Arizona, I thoroughly agreed. Then I followed in my mind your trip to California, on the ocean-side camps, in the Redwoods, to San Francisco and across to Salt Lake City. After getting back to Arizona I finished up your trip in the six weeks' stack of *Banners* awaiting me. Also I was able to go with you into the Smokies, for I had been through them seven years ago and you very accurately described the difference between the Western and Eastern mountains in calling them 'clothed and unclothed.' My wife and I have often mentioned that very fact.

"I hope your writings will help to make the people of Tennessee 'park conscious' until they will at least visit the one right at their doors. It is my honest judgment that 75 per cent of the people of Tennessee and adjoining states could in the next ten years make one visit to that great park, if they will learn how to travel (as your crowd did and as we do, for we too had our tent and camp stove). So keep your pen working until you see a steady stream of 'Minnies and automobiles' going to the Great Smokies. Then, when many of them have made that trip they will see how possible it is for many to go to our National Capital and others to come to the great West. Now this is my first reason for writing.

"In my second reason I rather beg to disagree with the substance of some of your comments. As a writer I think you erred in making comparisons and using such words as "better—best, more beautiful—most beautiful," etc. Were we as Americans compelled to select one and only one mountain, I would readily agree to making that the Great Smoky, but we are not forced to be satisfied with one. Each of our great mountain ranges stands out sublime in its own peculiar grandeur: the Smoky with its clouds and fogs and foliage and all that makes its beauty; the western mountains with their minerals to blend to gorgeous coloring, and their dizzy heights, their ruggedness, their awesomeness—well, all that makes a western mountain. They are not made for comparison and contrast but are the great counterparts of our great America.

"But having made one "first trip" across Arkansas, Texas, New Mexico, and Arizona to land in the town of Miami, I will excuse you for being "homesick for those Columbia foothills with their blue grass and Jersey cows." I believe if you made many trips over the Miami-Superior Highway through the Claypool Tunnel and down Devil's Canyon or over Yarnell Hill and the Prescott Road, you would say that they have their peculiar beauty.

"I think the Prescott cowboy gave you about the best answer possible, for one must stand up for his state. But I am sure he did not know what is around Columbia, Tenn., or he would have understood your reply, While I admit the good and beautiful of

Arizona, I will frankly say that any one who leaves Tennessee to seek a better home in any other state simply does not know what he is doing. Now don't you ever dare to tell that on me, but it is the truth." (Pardon me for quoting this, Mr. Hickman, but I am not telling who said it. I haven't mentioned your name, you know.) "The fact is many inhabitants of Arizona have come from the States of the North Middlewest where the summers are as hot as Arizona and the winters are too cold to mention. Therefore they are justified in acting like they had been drinking "upstream and downstream"—but that does not apply to Tennesseans.

"Now about the sunsets. No, it does not "take clouds to make beauty supreme." I was in Tennessee the same weeks you were in the West and I did not see a beautiful sunset while there, but I know it does have them. You were in Arizona at "the most wrongest time" to see any of its special and peculiar beauties. The winter and early springtime is when the gorgeous beauties of Arizona are seen, even our Grand Canyon hides its beauties, its supreme beauty, in the summer. It is our custom to often drive out on the desert to watch the sunset and for two hours watch the changing colors in a cloudless sky. But you made the mistake that many do, that is to assume that the country is always like the few particular days on which they see it. Many visitors come here in winter and praise our climate and the beauties of the mountains and the citrus groves and the lure of the deserts. But, say, they are not here in June as you were or

July and August as many of us. So we adopted (not yet adapted) Arizonians just smile and think of the reason why they talk as they do.

"Just to make my point clear about 'comparing' I recite an incident that happened just a few days before we passed through the Columbia country. A friend of mine in West Tennessee had made a hurried trip the nearest way (via Camden-Waverly) to Nashville and returned the same way (shame on him) and this was his report: 'I don't see what keeps those people in Middle Tennessee from starving to death.'

"Imagine how we laughed when in July we turned off the main highway purposely to go through the hills of Lexington, Parsons, Linden, Hohenwald, Columbia, and into Nashville. Every time we go to Nashville we travel this road for we love those Linden-Hohenwald-Columbia hills, and to tell the truth, the best crops we saw on our entire 5,500-miles were in those three counties from Columbia to Nashville, and then to think 'what keeps those people from starving.' But it just shows on what meager facts many people form an opinion. So while some people 'do not like Arizona at all,' the federal cotton reports put Arizona second to top in normal crop production and that's that." (They must grow that cotton on cactus plants, Mr. Hickman, I can imagine a record breaking production if every cactus would produce just one boll—but who would want to pick it?)

"So while we talk and write of each other's states, let us be just and leave out 'comparatives and contrastives' and all be Americans. As a business proposition on the side you tell any of your friends dissatisfied with Tennessee for them to stay where they are and to make Tennessee the greatest State in the Union, for it is geographically and climatically favored above any other state in the Union. But tell the farmers to clean up the fence corners so tourists can see what they grow, build a little larger and better tourist cottages and to advertise their State more, above all to 'know their own State better,' and to make one great State of Tennessee instead of those three measly little states that most of them know now, East, Middle, and West Tennessee, such that they think of going to a foreign country if they dare to cross the Tennessee River. I think you have started a big thing and I want to see you finish it. I will agree with the biggest and best things you can write for Tennessee even though I defend Arizona. If I drink of Hassayampa my head will be upstream. ...

"I failed to mention how thankful you should have been not to have an Arizona cloud or rain while touring our State. We do have them and woe to the tourists who happen to be caught in one. The day of our return, July 28, a rain from Lordsburg, N.M., to Safford, Ariz., filled all those 'dips' in the road to overflowing and we splashed through, water up to our running board. (This is not a 'believe it or not' but actual facts.) Then we do have even 'gentle clouds' that fringe with gold and every other color. June, the last of the month, is our usual beginning of rainy season, and the dry season for the coast country. So having made a hurried trip you were fortunate in selecting the weeks you did."

Thank you, Mr. Hickman, for this letter. My family and I thoroughly appreciated it and I believe *Banner* readers will. I stand corrected on all points regarding Arizona climate and crops. All I know is what I saw in passing, and I admit I wore sun glasses, and drank from the Hassayampa. I may get up enough courage to come back to Arizona some fall or winter to see if Grand Canyon can be any more beautiful then when we saw it, and to see if Yarnell Hall's fresh gravel has been smoothed down enough that one can keep his eyes on the scenery and not on the road. I know there must be a fascination for folks somewhere behind those rugged hills and sticky cacti or beneath the flood waters in the "dips," but just now there is still enough homesickness for Tennessee in my soul for me to say of Arizona "distance lends enchantment."

A NOTE FROM THE TRAVELS EDITOR

To prove that acorns don't fall far from the tree, following is the first article published by Margaret Knox, shortly following the T.N.T. trip.

Margaret Knox Morgan

THE NASHVILLE BANNER
FEBRUARY 15, 1935

Visit to Home Of Ill-Fated Ship Recalled

Margaret Knox Was Member of Party of Tennessees Who Inspected Dirigible

Editor's Note: The writer of this description of the ill-fated naval dirigible *Macon* is the daughter of Mrs. Lera Knox of Columbia, feature writer for the *Banner*. She was a member of a party of Tennessee women who made a bus tour of the West last summer before visiting the Century of Progress exposition at Chicago, and whose experiences were described by Mrs. Knox in a series of articles written for the *Banner*.

BY MARGARET KNOX

The recent disaster of the *Macon* off the coast of California revived memories of my trip to see that giant dirigible last summer. Since her maiden cruise several months ago, the *Macon* had been housed at the United States Navy Dirigible Base at

Sunnyvale, a few miles south of San Francisco. On the 1,000 acres of land surrounding the hangar of the lighter-than-air craft are various buildings which the United States Government erected. The naval headquarters and quarters for the guards are on part of the track while nearer the hangar are workshops, water tanks, a 2,000,000-cubic-foot helium storage tank, and the helium distributing, storage, and compression works.

The $5,000,000 hangar is the second largest of its kind in the world, having an over-all length of 1,118 feet, width of 308 feet, and vertical clearance of 180 feet. The main doors, two at each end, weighing 500 tons each and are operated by electric motors. The 100-ton movable mooring mast would extend out of the hangar for several hundred feet before it released the airship. In addition to the *Macon* several smaller dirigibles and airplanes have been kept in the hangar.

The building itself is so large that eleven football games could be played simultaneously without interference from the other games on eleven regulation size fields.

The dirigible herself did not entirely fill the space in the hangar, but she was extremely large. She was 785 feet long by 145 feet high and her nominal gas volume was 6,500,000 cubic feet. Her eight engines had a maximum speed of 84 miles per hour. She carried a normal flying crew of fifty men, although there were eighty-three men on board when one or two of her twelve helium cells burst as she neared Sunnyvale the evening of her disaster. Five airplanes could enter or leave this queen of the skies while she was in the air. When she went on one of her four or five cruises each year, usually experimental trips, she carried these planes, a radio, seven gun emplacements, electric lights, and telephones.

PART III

Country Woman Goes to Europe

PART III

Country Woman Goes to Europe

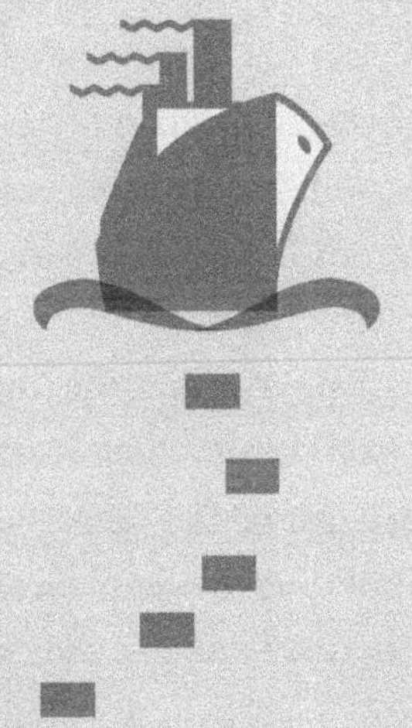

A NOTE FROM THE TRAVELS EDITOR

Parts of Middle Tennessee, particularly that area around Columbia, were on the edge of the plantation country of antebellum days. In 1918, when Mother and Daddy were married, he bought a portion of one of those former plantations—70 acres that included the former manor house.

The house was two-story, with large columns on the front. The windows, first and second floor, were large, and under each first floor window was a set of wooden doors. Neighborhood myth had it that when the Confederate troops had been in the area, soldier husbands and sons of the family that lived there then would slip home and tap on those doors at night to be let in.

The interior of the house was also large in scale. All rooms were 18 feet square, with 12-foot ceilings, and each room had a large fireplace. Written on a basement wall was the date, 1835. The large front hall had a wide, graceful stairway. Mother always said she looked forward to seeing me descend that stairway when I would be married in front of an open fire in the living room. That happened in December, 1941; when I was married to Stanton Morgan, originally from Dover, Tennessee, and a classmate from the University of Tennessee.

Lera and Alex sold the farm to a phosphate company shortly after that. Jack had joined the Air Force on the day after Pearl Harbor, received a medical discharge, then moved to Evansville, Indiana, where he became involved in building fighter planes.

The old house had no electricity, and as an elderly woman said of the Tennessee Mountains, "They're purty to look at, but they're hell to live in!" Not long after Mother and Daddy moved to another farm and started a new restaurant, a tornado went through the country and took the old house down-our version of "Gone with the Wind!"

I soon became a camp follower as Stan was transferred around the United States, and then to Europe. With the 94th Division he went through France, the Battle of the Bulge, and across Germany to Czechoslovakia. He signed up for the Army of Occupation, came home to the States to get me, and we wound up in Germany.

The next summer Mother decided to make the trip to Europe, also, and the following summer, too. Just as the trip to the West Coast was covered in the *Nashville Banner*, the segments that follow were first published in the *Daily Herald* of Columbia, Tennessee.

Margaret Knox Morgan

THE DAILY HERALD
COLUMBIA, TENNESSEE
WEDNESDAY, MAY 21, 1952

Country Woman Goes A-Flying

Editor's Note: Mrs. Lera Knox, experienced writer for newspapers as well as accomplished farm and business woman, left this morning for a European tour to visit her daughter in Germany. Below is the first of a series of articles she will write for the *Daily Herald* and the *Maury Democrat.*

BY LERA KNOX

Well, here goes!

Believe it or doubt, in this good month of May, 1952, anything can probably happen—once.

Four days ago I had no idea that this old country gal would ever fly through the air on anything else but a broomstick.

Now I hear tell that I am to leave Nashville at 11:25 this morning and arrive in New York City at something after 4 p.m. the selfsame day. How's that for surprise?

They say something about the best laid plans of mice and men, but they seem not to have considered the (perhaps) better laid plans of women. Well, those can "gang aft aglee," or aglay, or away, or wherever the plans of mice and men go.

My flying to New York, strange to say, can partly be blamed on, or credited to, the new highway. When the *Herald* and

Democrat reported that U.S. 31 would be closed, the man who had leased our little open air farm market and grocery on the Pulaski road got discouraged and decided he wanted to cancel his agreement—and that, when I was to leave by bus for New York en route to Germany.

That meant we had to hustle around and get someone to help Alex operate the grocery, in addition to keeping up the farming and other activities. We found Mrs. Kincaid, and her son, L.C., and I think they'll do a bang-up job.

We had to take inventory and figure up all that, measure gas in the tanks, and do all the odds and ends of things that have to be done when a business makes a change—then we had to scratch up some change to pay for that inventory; and now after scratching around for about three-and-a-half 28-hour days I feel changed myself.

But today I'm heading for Nashville and the big DC6 (or 7 or 8 or something-or-other). My aeronautical arithmetic is about as bumfuzzled as my aeronautical knowledge.

In New York—

(Wow! What a time this country bumpkin will have in that town!) I am to be at the Paramount Hotel—thanks to a good travel agent—for three nights. Then at high noon on Saturday, May 24, when the big superliner *Liberté* watches New York wharf move off and leave her, I'll be right there—Cabin 755D—with my brand new far-seeing glasses; my new poodle hair-do, under last year's tam; my 8-quart size over-the-shoulder bag; my three-and-a half grips; umbrella and dual-purpose raincoat, for England; second-hand typewriter, which spells like a post office pen; my Kodak, Jr., which I'll try to keep hidden, so I won't look so much like a tourist; and a various assortment of other et cetera.

The folks who own the *Liberté* declare they will take all that, and me too, to Le Havre, in six days for $175 plus $5 head tax—I don't like taxes but I feel obliged to take my head along.

Margaret and Stan, our daughter and son-in-law, plan to meet the boat if Stan's leave is granted; if not, I go to the Hotel Franklin Roosevelt (they speak English) in Paris; then perhaps on to Frankfurt, or wherever they meet me along the way.

We plan first to visit the Benelux Nations; and perhaps to England. I look forward to saying, "So this is London." I'd like to watch them change the guard; and to peek over the back fence at Elizabeth's Garden, if the busy Queen has had a chance to make one this spring.

Of course, Switzerland will be a must. Meg and Stan seem to think that is the most ideal country in Europe; they like the Swiss people very much. Wouldn't it be fun if I could run across the woman I met in Washington in 1936 at the Triennial Meeting of Country Women of the World? I'll never forget how she astounded the other 7,500 of us country women with the bragging statement that even then every home in Switzerland had electricity! It struck me forcibly because over in the enlightened area of Neeley Hollow, Maury County, Tennessee, U.S.A., I was filling lamps and ironing by fireplace heat.

Back to the Big Journey: I plan to see everything that is see-able so I am taking along two pairs of bifocals, and when one pair gets tired of looking I can change to the other.

I must chat with Tilman Knox in Munich, and two or three others of the Knox nephews in the same vicinity. And by the way, I'd just love to have dinner, supper, or a snack with your son George, Bill, Hal, or Tom or Jerry—I may need a gigolo, and I'm too Scotch to hire an escort when Meg and Stan can't go. Alex says he won't care, that is if I can save a few Knox nickels. He's Scotch, too.

And I'd love to visit your daughter Sue, your cousin Betty, or your Aunt Mary—I'll need to borrow a lot of kinfolks in Europe if I stay till my ticket runs out in September.

Any card or letter addressed to Stan will reach me. He is

Capt. Stanton A. Morgan
2nd Bn. 8th Regt. 4th Inf. Div.
A.P.O. 39% P.M.N.Y.N.Y.

I may not have time to write you back how your kin folks are behaving over there, except through the *Herald* and *Democrat*, because I'll be so busy changing bifocals, but I'll tell you plenty when I get home, I bet.

But after all the turmoil I've had getting off, I wonder if I'll ever get there all in one piece.

Yours on the way to be a-flying, a-floating, and a-seeing.

THE DAILY HERALD
COLUMBIA, TENNESSEE
THURSDAY, MAY 22, 1952

SOCIETY CLUB NEWS

Country Woman Goes Fast

BY LERA KNOX

Editors Note: The following story was received by wire special to the *Daily Herald* from Mrs. Alex Knox in New York, who left Wednesday for a four months stay in Germany during which she will tour Europe.

Bulletin—

I left the *Herald* Office at 9:30 a.m. Wednesday and by devious detours because of road blocks arrived in Nashville at 11:30—that was the only leisure lap of my journey. At 2:30 I was in the nation's capital and at 3:50 the plane settled down to a stop at La Guardia Field—but I didn't stop!

At 5:30 I was backstage at the Kate Smith evening hour, ready to help her if she needed me. To my surprise and chagrin she didn't. Fascinated, I saw the show through, thus missed an intended date to be one of Arthur Godfrey's friends. The crowd was lined up for blocks to see him stalk around the stage.

Tennessee hillbillies really stole the show! The crowd was wild about June Carter, Anita, Cousin Joedy, Cedar Hill square dancers. And when Kate wound up the show by singing "Tennessee Waltz," she paved New York for me.

Every time I say "Howdy Doo" to anybody, the answer is "Oh! You're from way down South!" Us Rebels might win that war after all!

At 7:30 (OGT—ours and God's Time), 9:30 (EDT) over a 30-cent Automat dinner, I was chatting with a Mrs. (Obviously Rich) Williams about what to do with caterpillars on Park Avenue, and how to make rose geraniums bloom in a north window. I told her she would have to ask Mama, Mrs. D.A. Vaughan, back in Columbia about geraniums.

At 9:05 (OGT) but bedtime (New York Time), I was backstage at *Guys and Dolls*, (STO—Standing Room Only). A gorgeous blond was showing me how to push instead of pull to get the door open. She was lovely and she knew I was from Tennessee.

The story of my flight up here will follow by mail. It was really out of this earthy world—and may take a whole edition.

P.S. New Yorkers are grieving tonight over the death of John Garfield, but rejoicing over the Dodgers making a world record of 15 runs in one inning.

THE DAILY HERALD
COLUMBIA, TENNESSEE
MAY 24, 1952

Country Woman Flies High

BULLETIN

New York, Saturday a.m.—Was escorted to pier by a parade of Boy Scouts. Almost missed boat. She (the boat) waited. Now Country Woman is "all aboard."—Lera Knox

BY LERA KNOX

New York—

Aboard the A.A. Flagship *Arizona*, belted to a window seat, insured for $5,000—cost only a quarter—I seemed the only nervous person about.

I twist and crane my neck trying to see what's over, under, and beyond both big wings, wonder if any celebrities are aboard. But everyone on there looks like just ordinary folks—except of course the crew—and everybody is reading, or chatting, or just sitting as though they were on an ordinary bus or train. But not me! There was nothing ordinary about this experience for me. And those others couldn't fool me—I knew good and well that every other person on that plane had made at least one first flight.

The thing that struck me first as Tennessee farms slipped out from under that right-hand wing flap and got smaller and smaller was the way the little creeks seemed to nuzzle up against the river like pigs around an old sow, and the cute little brown ponds looked like baby chicks squatting in the green grass; very short grass, it must have been.

At first, I could see cows and recognize them for what they were, but I couldn't see them switching their tails, and even with two pairs of bifocals, I couldn't see any flies on those cows.

In a moment or two, I noticed white smoke coming from under the flaps, and I thought sure Alex would collect that $5,000—but, no, we were up in the clouds.

As I looked at my native state from there, I could appreciate more and more the slogan, "Keep Tennessee Green."

Thirty-seven minutes to Knoxville, and lunch enroute, the stewardess said. Now the houses that looked like pinheads are getting larger, and roads that looked like thread are as big as pencil marks. Are we coming down? Must be—engines are un-revving. Can see propellers go slower and slower. Wow! Concrete's not as soft as the clouds.

While we stopped at Knoxville, Bearden School children filed through to see the plane. Curious, I followed. The Captain or somebody in uniform took me to be a teacher or student and graciously started to usher me off with the school gang. I said, "Say, I paid $59.23 to go to New York and I want my money's worth." Was his face red! He exclaimed to a buddy, "Bill, she's a passenger."

Up again, I believe I am looking down on the Blue Ridge Mountains of Virginia. Below—a muddy little river has a yellow streak along one side. Must have rained up country. There are so many big lakes, somebody must have made a dam. From the map, it must be Douglas Dam.

You've heard of being big by a dam site. This lake must be by a dam site bigger. (Even a preacher might read that, if a copyman doesn't change my spelling.)

It's a bee-a-u-ti-ful day for flying! So clear, I could almost reach out and pat the Smokies on their heads, except that my window is closed. We're definitely above the clouds and we seem also to be above the sun for he just shines in my south window when we go down below the clouds again. Barns and houses look one-sixteenth inch square, set in a bright and cloudy field-scape down there.

God must love shifting sunshine and shadows over His earth below!

Wish I had a thermometer out on my wing so I could tell how cold or hot it is out there.

Looking down on the clouds is like looking down on a cotton field, white for picking, except that the foliage is hazy blue, and field-dotted with miniature towns when we can glimpse through the "Cotton."If a giant Paul Bunyan could stride through with an oversize cotton-picking bag, I'd bet he'd harvest many a cloud-ton of the acre.

Wish they had markers on the towns down there so I could see where I am, geographically speaking.

I used to love to look up at the shapes of clouds and imagine one was a house, another a horse, or an elephant, or a Santa Claus, or an old woman smoking her pipe. Now, I'm looking down at the shapes of the clouds' shadows on the ground. I see a Christmas tree, dark green; a sausage patty—it's green, too, and right beside it is a huge green doughnut. Could it be that my eyes are influenced by the two years I served sausage and doughnuts at our little Knoxdale Café before I leased it to make this trip?

Clouds are thinner, fields are clearer. Maybe we are easing up on Richmond? I see a wide, straight, green strip that may be a fire break or a power line clearing.

We are going 260 miles an hour, they say, but really the propellers are the only things about the plane that seem to be moving, and they seem only a blur of air, such as you see rising from a stove on a cold day. It's the beautiful earth that is the magic carpet slipping out from under the wing like a rug from under a chair.

No clouds below at all, now. Wide double highway down there. We must be coming to a town. We are. Big city sprawled out like the letter "Y." Airport like an "A," with an oversized crossbar. Apple orchards galore. They look like green-sprigged calico.

I see a long slope. Could that be Shenandoah Valley? I've once seen that from below, but it didn't look that way.

Faithful old propellers. I can turn away and look at the landscape, and when I look back at them, they're still going. Bless them! I'm praying for them, for I'd feel awful bad to have Alex collect that $5,000 insurance that I paid a quarter for at the airport. I'd rather lose that quarter, and a lot more, than lose altitude suddenly by prop failure.

Another lovely river and wide bands of green and brown running around the hills. Wherever there are dams there are those beautiful striped green fields. I'm getting my T.V.A. taxes' worth in the beauty of those fields, contour-striped in bands of two-tone green and brown.

Another town, the landscape looks like a crazy quilt with patches of green and brown, each patch is bordered in fancy stitching, gray highways, yellow roads, black railroads, deep green rivers, and brown little creeks.

It's a far piece across this land of America and there are lots of little farmhouses like ours. "Knoxdale Farms" might not look so important to an air passenger 7000 feet high, as it does to me there at home in the garden.

Big forest. We must be topping a mountain. I'm yawning more and the clouds are getting thicker.

Now, the country below is beautiful and I want to tell James A. Lavender (our beauty loving neighbor) that I really have seen something else as beautiful as Maury County hills. I know now what it is. We're coming into Washington, D.C. There are sand barges on the river below. Here is the airport.

As quick as that, we're down, and beside us a big plane labeled "Canadian Royal Air Force." The control tower above looks like a big turquoise jewel in a high platinum mounting setting.

Washington—three hours after leaving Nashville!

I'm enjoying this trip so much that I think as soon as I get back I'll dust off my old Spanish dictionary and start out for Mexico, American Airlines.

While the engine warms up to go again, the *Arizona* has the motion of curbed power. It reminds me of holding a spirited horse in check—albeit a powerful big mustang, with plenty of spirit!

I didn't realize how many people might be working in that air business until I watched various matters handled with so much efficiency and dispatch in Washington, D.C. It was amusing to see them pull long squirmy black gas lines out of pits under the plane and drag them up on to the wings to refuel my friend *Arizona*. They looked like Paul Bunyan fishing worms.

I should like to have stayed at Washington airport thirty days rather than fifteen minutes.

Off again at 2:45. Gee, but those props are revving. I'm getting airport talk now, you see.

I wish the nice people in Washington would put their names and house numbers on their roofs. However, it was nice of them to paint those roofs all shades of red, blue, and green.

There goes Lincoln Memorial, Washington Monument, but I don't see the Capitol dome.

Those airline stewardesses have had nurses' training, so I've heard. Well, they have certainly transferred their bedside manners to wonderful seat-side manners.

For a few minutes, things almost got bumpy. It reminded me of riding over Bigbyville Road in a Model-T on frozen ruts. But the stewardess began passing mints and chatting in such a friendly manner I even forgot to nibble the nuts.

Now, the cotton clouds below have slipped off and left a hazy blue-green floor. Could that be water? It must be. Here's land again.

Land, water, clouds—all moving along westward—and we're just sitting up here watching them. We must be just east of Baltimore or is it Philadelphia?

Now, we're all in snow. The clouds are completely white, except for occasional blue shadows to make them interesting. Those clouds give one a comfortable feeling. They look so soft to fall into, but I still don't want Alex to collect that insurance.

It's getting a little rougher at 3:30, and white all over, but my nerves are much more calm now than they were a few hours ago when Alex was whipping our old Plymouth along over the Bear Creek Road detour through the metropolises of Pottsville, Leftwich, Rally Hill, and Match, Tennessee. I feel more safe here than I did on those curves.

This must be Philadelphia. It looks as clean as a picture postcard and there's a big cemetery then more water. No, I'm wrong. It's New York—La Guardia Field.

When I started to leave my seat, I seemed more attached to that flagship than I realized. I made several efforts to rise, but each time I sat back down. I unloaded the bundles from my lap and tried again. Again—down. Then I noticed that my seat belt really did hold. I hadn't trusted it too much at first. I unstrapped and walked out into a stiff breeze and a lot of jabbering lingo. Was I at Le Havre? No, just New York—and a lot of "dose guys" must have hailed from down on Toity-Toid Street.

THE DAILY HERALD
COLUMBIA, TENNESSEE
MONDAY, MAY 26, 1952

Country Woman Goes A-Rambling

New York—

National Broadcasting Studios seem to have been searching the city for me Thursday afternoon from four to six, and where was I? Rambling around The Cloisters, like a good girl should!

It seems that they did not take into consideration the fact that, coming from The Bible Belt, Land of the Coonskin Cap, I might gravitate toward anything that looked like a cathedral or a woodsy spot—that's The Cloisters. Will tell you more about it or them when I have time to look at my guide book, but for now, can only say it seems to be a sort of religious museum perched high above the Hudson in a natural-looking, master-size, rock-garden—and you know how I am about rocks and gardens.

You see, I simply can't stay off those blessed 5th Avenue busses. I can get more for my money there than anywhere else, even the Automat. I'm not exactly certain about this, for I was too busy seeing to count, but you can ride 200 blocks on one of those busses for 12 cents. Maybe it's only 198, but to be sure I got my money's worth. I got off the bus at the end of the line and walked two blocks. 200 blocks for a dime and 2 pennies. That's a bargain even to a Scot!

But back to NBC and why they were hunting me instead of me hunting them, when broadcasting studios seem easier to find in New York than Country Women.

The penciled scribblings I made on the Flagship *Arizona* were so shaken up by the time I got to the Hotel Paramount, I couldn't make them all out, so I took them downstairs to the public stenographer, for they say she can read anything—maybe even people.

The man at the next desk to hers heard us trying to read and dictate the stuff, and he must have been a tattletale, or at least to have the party line tendencies that makes one tell someone that tells someone.

Then, to be sure I had my air facts correct I called American Airlines to see if they would clear such an epistle as I was writing. Mr. Johnny Coneybear (no, the word Island doesn't go in the middle of the surname) a Public Relations Representative, met me in the Paramount Coffee Shop at lunch, and when we started to read that lady's typing, we found that although she can read anything, she can't exactly interpret Tennessee diction, having been in New York all her life. But Jack C. has been in Tennessee long enough to speak our language—he established the radio station at Oak Ridge, and operated a chain of newspapers once or twice—so he helped me interpret her typing, and respell and interline her copy.

The finished product wasn't very pretty and he hated for me to send the *Herald* and *Democrat* such a mottled copy, so he very graciously offered to have his secretary re-copy same and rush it by fastest A.A. plane to Columbia.

He asked if I would share a few carbons to show some of his friends. I said, "Sure, throw 'em away, if you wants." (See, I'm talking East Side already.)

He asked, too, if I would care if he tried to sell any of the stuff for me. Remembering the $3 I'd paid that stenographer; and the tips; and the telegrams I'd sent back home, I gave him the green light but quickly.

When I returned at 6 p.m. to dress for a 40-cent dinner at the Automat, I found a message to call J.C. at Murray Hill 3-9000. Every phone number in New York must have 5 numbers, so the operator told me, "so we just add another zero and then see who we get."

Jack had already commuted to his home at Amityville, but his secretary was waiting up for me. He called Jack back at 8:00, Long Distance, and exclaimed, "Hasn't NBC found you yet? Where on earth have you been?

"Bussing, as usual," was the answer.

"Well, NBC wanted you backstage for two shows this afternoon, but those shows are over now, better let them find you Friday."

I shall.

Friday: Bob Simmons has summoned me to his office (and he's not the City Judge, but Somebody at NBC) for orders or tickets or something to *Kate Smith Hour* and *We The People TV*. Also German Consulate General must visa my passport, so must hurry.

P.S. Special—

I find the New York Telephone Directory very handy in many ways, not necessarily in the way we country people are said to use a Sears Roebuck Catalog. But like the catalog, it's thick, and I find that with a little help from a waste paper basket planted underneath, I can use it for a typewriter desk. And this little second-hand portable, which spells like a post office pen, needs all the support that New York Public Utilities can give it.

The Telephone Directory probably has many other uses, too, if one is well versed in ABC's; but being from the allegedly barefoot South, I do a lot of my talking on the Information Line.

The Information Lady seems to know a lot of things, maybe even Chinese; but she must be sort of hard of hearing, or she doesn't understand TENNESSEE-ESE: I have to repeat everything I say, talk very slowly, and sometimes spell a word for her, Western Union style!

With her help, however, I find that, for all its bigness, New York has fewer wrong numbers than Columbia, sometimes.

THE DAILY HERALD
COLUMBIA, TENNESSEE
JUNE 12, 1952

Country Woman in New York

Mrs. Lera Knox Reports On Big Town

Editor's Note: This belated report on the activities of Mrs. Lera Knox, our globe-trotting correspondent, was mailed from Europe, where she is now visiting her daughter and family. Other dispatches will appear from day to day.

BY LERA KNOX

You love New York in June? How about May?

Well, May is OK, too.

Folks up here say they have been having a heck of a lot of rain, but the day I arrived the sun came out.

The big town, to me, is full of love, joy, and pity; and pardon my saying so, but among the objects I pity most, are the dogs. Poor beasts! Every dog I saw was dragging a mere man or woman around on a leash, and I regretfully noticed that some of the dogs seemed somewhat embarrassed at what was on the other end of the leash. But dogs have endurance; I know that from our own dogs' experiences at Knoxdale.

And New York is broadminded, I'm sure of that, but it does seem a shame that so large a part of the population can't let a poor canine live a dog's life.

Passing Central Park I noticed something that looked like a locust tree in bloom. That seemed strange, for I thought all black locusts had bloomed white and shedded weeks ago. In the Cloister gardens however, I saw the plain old purple iris, the first to bloom, the one we call flags, blooming among the rocks. That all goes to prove how far New York is behind Tennessee, botanically speaking.

But back to the sad and happy in New York: though dogs are to be pitied, cats seem to fare better. I saw a fat cat, marked like a Holstein cow, and apparently as contented, sleeping peacefully in a crowded delicatessen window on Sixth Avenue, "Avenue of the Americas," they call that now. I didn't stop there for lunch.

Most of my lunching and dining were done at the Automat. That is the place where you drop your nickels and dimes in a slot as you would in a juke box, but you get food, rather than music. Since the high cost of living has developed, they have added several slots for quarters. And it takes two nickels now to please the coffee slot enough to make it measure you out exactly one cup of coffee.

Rice and carrots are still classed as 5-cent foods, but everything else has gone up. I lived mostly on rice and carrots while in New York so I could save up for a cup of coffee at

Maxim's in Paris. But really all the food I tried tasted good. Some of the current theories on diet were exploded right before my eyes at the Automat.

A small, thin man came over to my table and set down three enormous servings of three different desserts. He quickly gobbled those up, then went back and got two more. Even then he walked out of that place a small, thin man.

By getting up early and taking a tramp down Broadway I had a chance to say "Good Morning" to the people who gather the garbage, clean the windows, and mop the sidewalks. They are New York, too, you know, as much so, perhaps more than the people who make the garbage and clutter the sidewalks the night before.

Upon being questioned, they thought it was a nice morning, that it was not likely to rain that day, and all that sort of stuff; but I continued to clutch my umbrella, for they say that anything can happen in a big city.

I find that people in New York are just as friendly as you want to make them. And also, they are glad if you want to make them friendly.

It seems hard to get an early breakfast on Broadway, and I didn't see a Truck Stop anywhere.

Childs' Restaurant in the corner of Duffy Square had a sign that said, "Open All Night." Perhaps so, I thought, but they seem to close in the morning. But walking on around the corner however, I saw six sleepy looking waiters, two waitresses, and a cashier dozing. At least they were up, so I went in and asked if I could get a cup of coffee. All went into action. Even the cashier roused, and rubbed his eyes.

I looked at the clock, it was 5:00 a.m. I imagined the counter at Knoxdale Café would be about full at that time of morning. But I was alone with several service people, not including the cooks and manager at Childs. Rambling around the room, my eyes leveled off on a large sign which proclaimed: "Occupation of this room by more than 200 persons is both illegal and dangerous."

When I saw that sign and looked back at my lone self, I spluttered and burbled so into my coffee, I had to have my coat cleaned when I got back to my hotel. But 5:00 a.m. is 5:00 a.m., and Childs' had probably needed that sign two hours earlier.

I saw several radio and television shows in the process of production or rehearsal. And I judged by the bits of conversation which I caught on streets, buses, and in lobbies, that the great summer onslaught of tourists is on.

Polls taken at audience participation programs proved the audience to be predominately out-of-towners.

At one time I could have tapped H.V. Kaltenborn on the shoulder, except for two reasons: (1) I didn't want to seem forward. (2) There was a double thickness of glass between us.

Lagging behind on a guided tour of NBC Studios as we passed the newscasting rooms, I noticed a large pink-faced, white-haired man with a sheaf of copy in one hand and a cup of tea, with lemon, in the other, ease himself into the small room and take the place at the mike-desk. I stared curiously, and was just about to recognize him from his telecasts, when he turned around, smiled, and gave me a friendly salute. A glance at the clock told me it was five minutes until time for Kaltenborn. So I was practically certain of his identification, but I am not sure he recognized me.

I enjoyed the two Kate Smith programs very much. Kate is so much herself—and that is much indeed. I had an opportunity to see the *Old Gold Show* telecast, but feeling that I needed a treat instead of a treatment, I went instead to see *Guys and Dolls*. With standing room only, and that at $2.40 per pair of feet, and seats at $9.10, and not available, I decided that show must have something. It has. It is a ridiculous exaggeration on Broadway. And Broadway evidently loves to see herself ridiculed, especially with clever songs, gay costumes, and catchy dialogue.

I believe I mentioned getting lost backstage during the finale on Thursday night, and the lovely, friendly blonde who showed me how to open the stage door. Well, imagine my surprise on Friday night to see that very self-same blonde playing the "Doll," Miss Adelaide, herself.

I knew it couldn't have been the same person, for the Star would have been obliged to be on stage for the finale, and yet, I knew almost definitely that the girl who opened the door for me and said, "You have to push hard against it, Honey," on Thursday night was positively "Miss Adelaide" on Friday night.

I pondered and puzzled until I opened my "Standing Room Only" program. A slip of paper fell out; it said:

"At this performance the role of MISS ADELAIDE will be played by BEVERLY LAWRENCE."

Evidently my escort of the evening before had been not the star herself—who was evidently on stage for the finale—but the star's understudy who was giving Miss Vivian Blaine a Friday night off for a long weekend. But Vivian or Beverly, the show is great!

Even though I am as green as any tree that grows in Brooklyn, I get around in New York. I'd like to tramp from the Cloisters to Coney Island, from the Battery to Baker Field and talk and laugh with New York about herself. From *Guys and Dolls* I see she likes to laugh at herself. And I'd like to talk to New York about Columbia and vice-versa.

You two towns ought to get together sometime. The sum total of what you could each learn and enjoy about the other would indeed be a revealing tale of two cities.

But there isn't time now. I must be off on my European Campaign. So New York will have to get along without me until September 29. That, however, should give her ample time to prepare my ticker-tape parade.

The *Liberté* sails at noon Saturday, and I shall probably be sitting on suitcases and trying to fasten them for the next six hours.

THE DAILY HERALD
COLUMBIA, TENNESSEE
FRIDAY, JUNE 13, 1952

Country Woman All At Sea

BY LERA KNOX

S.S. *Liberté* flagship of the French Line (Compagnie Générale Transatlantique)

Two natural tendencies that I follow with all ease are getting lost and being late.

Two of New York's noticeable tendencies are tightening belts and suitcases, and being in a hurry. We got along very well, however, until the time came for me to leave.

I didn't feel I could possibly get lost between the Paramount Hotel, on 46th Street, and Pier 88 at the end of 49th Street, especially if I took a taxi. As for being late—well I simply wouldn't. So I got up at 5:00 a.m. on D-Day (D as in Departure). But by the time I had done a little packing, a little writing, a little primping, and a lot of loitering over breakfast, (the people who come into an Automat for breakfast in New York are a great part of the greatest show on earth), and by the time I was really ready to start my session of sitting on suitcases, it was getting about that time. Instructions for the *Liberté* said all passengers must be on board by 11:00 a.m. At 11:05 I was still sitting on suitcases.

The bell boy, elevator man, and taxi driver all helped with the rushing however; and at last we were taxiing down 49th Street, and just across the street from the pier when the Boy Scout Parade came marching right down the street we were ready to cross. It was a national or international or maybe just a local parade of boys coming down to see the ships. Sure I had a seat of honor; but it was getting to be a very uneasy seat. It was much after 11:00, people were scurrying, whistles were blowing, and I had visions of the *Liberté* pulling right out leaving me in what had been its shadow.

You can always count on a group of Scouts to stop to the rescue of a lady in distress, though. Of their own volition they stopped the parade and let the taxi pass. Porters of the French Line rushed out at double-New-York pace, gathered me, bags, and baggage into an elevator and rushed us up: then down a line of blue-coated inspectors who called for passport, tickets, baggage checks, blue slips, pink slips, what not, numerous other addenda which were stuffed away down in the depths of what was by that time my 10-quart over-shoulder bag.

When I finally set foot, on what I thought was the ship, I feared that there was surely a mistake and that I had been ushered not on board a liner, but right into the midst of a mid-summer Bargain Sale, in Macy's Basement!

Really, if a ship was there, I couldn't see the ship for the people. It was men this time, not Boy Scouts, who slightly eased my hypertension. It couldn't be either Macy's, nor even Gimbel's, I thought, for that many men could never have been dragged to a bargain sale, either on land or sea! Then a whistle blew, and I was relieved again, for I didn't believe Macy's had a whistle like that—even though New York business does do a lot of "blowing."

But the crowd continued to distress me. If this were really *Le Liberté*, how on earth could Mrs. *Liberté*, or Madame, ever bed and board such a huge hunk of humanity for six days?

But the problem soon began to work itself out, a large part of the hunk began to scoot and be scooted down the gangplank to wave and weep from the pier and a large part of the remainder of the hunk crowded to the rail to do a bit of waving and not a little weeping from there.

Not me, however. I wanted to see if I really had a berth on that boat, so I started rambling. Six decks down, and one deck up; two halls over, three halls back, I found my 3 1/2 bags and typewriter.

How could Madam *Liberté* bed so many people? I soon found out. She stacks 'em up.

The "D" following the 755 on my east-bound ticket meant approximately 12 square feet of mattress space plus one plump pillow, located a little higher than my nose. Talk about Grandma's four-posters! My bunk had no posts, and no automatic elevator; only a nervous looking little ladder up which I was to hoist my 140-odd pounds.

Why, I hadn't skinned up a ladder like that since I used to climb up in the barn loft to look for eggs!

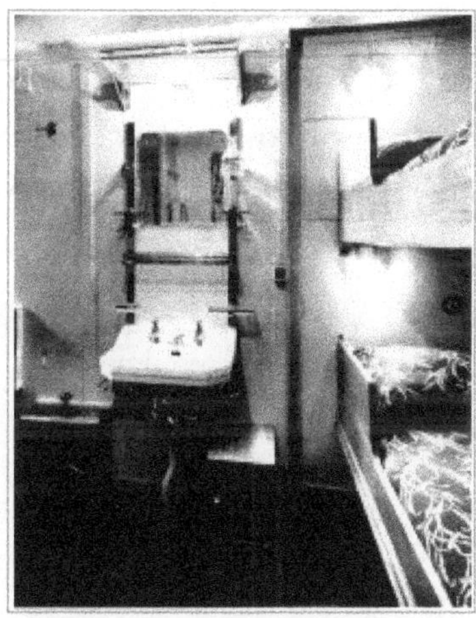

Besides, there were to be three other unknown persons in that 6'x10' room, plus baggage. One other would be on a par with me, nose high; the other two would be beneath us. I had heard that only the younger persons were given upper berths, and looking at myself in the mirror I wondered what kind of "old bags" would be below.

I couldn't do a thing but laugh and like it. My ticket was stamped. My grips were aboard. The gangplanks were gone. And the *Liberté* was by now high and dry—except the evidently very large part of her which must be below the water.

Speaking of high, I decided to go up those umppty-odd stairways again and see what was going on upstairs.

In my going up flight after flight, ambitious to rise to the top, like good country cream, I passed a room that looked very interesting. A sign beside the door said "Salle a Manager, Dining Room." I glanced inside, and said to a jolly looking girl nearby.

"I think I'll like the dining room. I see that Sally is the manager."

She spluttered and explained: "'Salle a Manager' is French for Room to Eat." I spluttered too, and we both rose toward the upper deck, or Pont. I was learning by then that all signs on the ship were written first in French then in English.

Why, oh why, hadn't I paid more attention at CHS when Prof. W. P. Morton was conjugating French irregular verbs, instead of spending so much time passing notes for Eldridge Denham, Eva Gilbert, and Elizabeth Voss; or writing notes to Erwin Hardison, Rufus Baker, and Bob Hunter? I can realize by now that those notes never got me anywhere, and a knowledge of French would really help me go places on a French Liner!

I didn't need French, however, to climb stairs, though I thought a liniment, French, Scotch, or British, might be needed by the time I got back down those stairs and up my ladder to bed that night.

But I kept climbing, and going in and out doors, stepping high over thresholds—when I didn't stumble over them.

At last I saw daylight, I went through that door, and there was the ocean again. She was still there. And the dock was right where I left it and the people were still waving and weeping and laughing.

When I began to take my bearings and inquire, I found that I must be slightly lost again.

Where I seemed to be was top deck First Class; where I was supposed to be was several decks lower, Tourist Class. (I later learned that "Pont" is "Bridge"—which may explain my lofty position.)

That country-cream policy of rising to the top seemed to have gotten me lost again. I didn't worry too much, however, for after all I didn't really know that I was in the wrong place until somebody told me, and nobody had told me yet. And by that time I had brushed enough of the 40 years of dust off Prof. Morton's French to remember "Je ne comprehends pass le Français," or something like that, and I could still shake my head even though my knees were weak.

So I simply sprawled myself out in the most comfortable First Class deck chair that was empty, and it was from there, waving at people I never saw before, and rolling a couple of tears into the Atlantic, that I watched America leave me for the first time.

THE DAILY HERALD
COLUMBIA, TENNESSEE
TUESDAY, JUNE 17, 1952

Country Woman Breaks Ice

Or At Least Mrs. Knox Chips It

BY LERA KNOX

Atlantic Ocean, et al.—

Refreshed from a nice nap on deck, and not wanting to stare at the Atlantic and thus probably incur seasickness, I decided to look around at the people on board and see what they were like.

The conclusion on the whole matter was that everybody else was just like me; they wanted to be friendly but didn't know just how to go about it. I decided that somebody ought to break the ice, and it has frequently been my job to do the things that nobody else wanted to do, so I plunged in.

I grinned at the young man in the deck chair next to mine and said:

"Bon jour. It's a nice day, isn't it?"

He sat straight up, took off his sunglasses, looked at me, and said:

"Oh, you speak English! How nice! Now I'll have somebody to practice my conversation with."

He turned out to be an excellent young person, originally from Switzerland, but also somewhat world-traveled. He had been in the States for several months and was on his way back home, after a visit in Paris. He told me more about Switzerland than I could ever have learned from guide books. And he also enjoyed practicing his "conversation" on me. I gave him all the latest I knew in American slang; which was something he said he could not get from guide books, so we both made what was to us a very profitable international exchange.

Our conversation waked the girl on my left, and we soon had drawn her into the chatter. She was Amy Florio, of the Bronx, so that brought us in another dialect, and a lot of fun. She's a "peach," that Amy, and a "peck of fun." She works at the Federal Reserve Bank of New York, which she announced is "the largest and biggest and richest bank in the world, has five floors down under the street, and has stored gold bullion from all over the world though of course gold varies in its worth due to its alloy content," all that, and a little more on one breath.

My Swiss conversationalist and I felt so much more financially secure after meeting Amy, I ventured to stagger, (a la sea legs) into the bar and spent 15 cents for a package of chewing gum to help us keep our stomachs steady until lunch, second sitting.

Amy didn't exactly offer to lend us any money, but we knew that she knew where to get it, so we felt that just knowing her had helped to steady our financial standing, if not our deck walking. We were going over "the banks" (Newfoundland, I think), and the waves were a bit whiter at that time.

Amy very generously offered to help me out with my typewriter, which by then was getting very sea-sick indeed. But after attempting one line she cussed it out in Bronx, which amused Switzerland very much, and gave it back to me. "Too slow," she said. "Throw it over board." That's all I can quote for publication.

Having two extra sticks of chewing gum, we coaxed into the conversation Amy's friend, who used to work for The Bank, but now is with The Government. The recipient of the fifth stick of gum was Carolyn Cantelli, a joy if ever there was one. She had just finished Parson's School of Design, and was traveling with 20 or more of her classmates on a European study tour. She introduced several of her friends, and I felt that my 15 cents for gum had been well spent.

Sharing cabin 755 with me and two elderly German-born American women is Miss Brigitta Stanfelt, of Sweden, who has been in America for 18 months, studying physical therophy,[1]

---

[1] Therophy, n. —revolutionary blend of therapy and philosophy, designed to cure a patient's illness through greater understanding of the human condition.

weaving, and several other matters. She's a delight to know. She asked if she might give me a word of advice. "Certainly," I said.

"Well, while you are in Europe, don't act American," was the advice.

"Do you mean, 'Don't brag?'" She nodded, and a gesture said a lot of other things. Which I didn't quite understand but will try to follow, because I considered that advice quite a compliment, and very confidential. I always think of Brigitta as "The big Swede" but I don't call her that. She permits me, however, to call her "Leif," for short, as in Leif Eriksson. We had several discussions as to why Leif Eriksson didn't stay in the States once he arrived there, and how different the world might, or might not, have been if he had.

Leif continually shocked our other two cabin-mates, Madam Anna Hanke, and the other German woman, both of whose bodies have been in America for 35 and 43 years, but whose souls are still in Germany. Madam Hanke said she never had felt that America belonged to her. And the other woman said she had not bought a new dress for five years, had been saving everything to go to Germany in 1953, and now was afraid she would have to pay duty on her new wardrobe. She was very uneasy about customs.

About all the Big Swede and I ever saw of our two roommates were the tops of their very white "poodle haircuts" as they got up and dressed early in the mornings. I whispered to Leif that we might as well stay in bed because there wasn't room for our feet on the floor until we had "expelled the Germans."

Leif's practice of going around completely in the nude shocked our neighbors greatly, but my opinion was that she had a figure she didn't need to cover up. I explained to Madame Hanke & Co. that really they could see there was not enough room in that cabin for four women and all their clothes, so as Brigitta was the last one in every night she had to leave her clothes outside to get into the cabin and up to her bunk

During the first couple of days out the Dining Steward was too busy to assign us to our proper tables, so it was catch-as-catch-can when it came to getting chairs. For the second dinner I caught a chair beside the big round table next to the kitchen door. The atmosphere was distinctly appetizing. Shortly after I sat down our table annexed Texas, Spain, and Paris.

Texas was there with triple strength in the forms of Steve, Tom, and Helen. Spain was represented by Luis Romano, accordion player from Madrid; and Paris by a plump little brunette exchange student to "Bryn Mawr" whose name I never did quite catch, and by Mr. E.C. Solari, or "Cam" for short, he said. There was also a young doctor of laws, who with Texas made a large part of the life of the party.

Steve, whose last name is Ely, is tall, straight, and blond, very tall. Tom, (whose last name is Connelly, and he's not the Senator, he says), is tall, dark; muscular and very handsome as is Steve. Helen is a sparkling middle aged attorney, also from

Dallas; she might have been the mother of either, and such a good sport that Tom and Steve had as much fun with her as with any traveling companion they could possibly have selected for an automobile tour of Europe. Their car was up in the garage on Boat Deck, and they had no particular plans. Steve said when they got the car on the ground again they were just "going to point her nose in any direction and follow through." The trio were as jolly as any passengers on board, and aided and abetted by Cam, Luis, and the young DLL (is that doctor of laws?), and the French student, our table made so much noise we couldn't hear the ship's chugging, nor the clatter of pans in the kitchen.

Shortly after dinner, Texas annexed Sweden. Brigitta had so much fun dancing the Swedish schottische with those tall, lanky Texans everybody in the lounge stopped to watch them throughout the evening. Never before, I think, had she so much deserved the term "Big Swede." She would swing Tom around and up and down the floor until he was exhausted enough to flop into a chair, then she'd take on Steve and give him the same treatment. They had their lessons in Swedish Physical Therophy that evening.

The palship between our neighbor Texas and our neighbor Sweden became so hearty, wholesome, and genuine I felt that the Atlantic would be re-salted by international tears when we docked.

Right here I'd like to advise the United Nations and whoever it might concern, that as a result of my un-congressional investigation during two days at sea, my one woman's opinion is that if we'd travel more, we'd fight less.

During a brief lull of the evening's fun, I said "Hello" to a boy in knee-pants, next chair to mine. He politely introduced himself as Guy Van Meenen, of Paris and U.S.A. He has been in the States eight months with his brother going to school. He is a very genteel young Parisian, son of a French editor, 13 years old, and an ardent admirer of the "Dodgers." He is carrying a baseball and bat back to Paris with him, and his ambition is to "teach my friends the great American game of baseball." From then on I called him "Le Ambassadeur du Baseball." And he always grinned when I said it, perhaps at my accent. I found in him the excellent interpreter, which I needed with the stewards.

The slender, blonde, very dignified young woman in the corner aroused my curiosity. She was alone, and not too unapproachable, I decided. In fact she seemed very glad to be approached. She was a bit homesick she admitted; had been in Johns Hopkins and other American hospitals.

I said, "Oh, you are ill?"

"Oh, no, I am a doctor. I study dermatology."

Later when I went down for the ship's doctor to inspect my smallpox vaccination, I mentioned meeting Dr. Weisenbach, from Paris, and described her. He said she is the youngest M.D. ever to get a degree in France. She finished her medical studies when only 23 years old. Her father is one of the world's most famous dermatologists.

Later I mentioned having heard of her father. She was surprised.

"How did you know?" she asked.

"Oh, I get around," was my answer. And that is what I am trying to do.

Right here I want to nominate as the most peace-pactful words ever spoken or gestured on land or sea.

I was standing in the narrow hall near the dining room door waiting for second sitting, when I noticed a plump, smiling, very white-haired little lady at my elbow. I smiled and said, "Good Morning."

She smiled and shook her head, saying "No speaka."

Then I said, "Bon jour." She smiled even more, and said "No speaka."

So we both just grinned and shook hands.

Then it happened: She put her arm around my waist, held my hand, looked up at me, and said:

"I no speaka, you no speaka, but we all LOVE."

I sniffled and agreed, "Yes, *Liberté* and Liberty makes us all love everybody always."

I don't know who she was, I don't know where she came from, but the strange little woman, with the heart of a girl, had struck the keynote of the journey for me.

Seven languages could not have said as much as her smile and her warm, impulsive caress.

THE DAILY HERALD
COLUMBIA, TENNESSEE
THURSDAY, JUNE 19, 1952

Country Woman "Lion" Hunting

BY LERA KNOX

Ship's rumors, like country gossip, spreads like blue mold on a tobacco bed. Belinda Timmons Priest, the Maury County product, whom I met the first day on board, told me that her husband had told her that he had read in the papers that "Sugar Ray" Robinson was to sail on the *Liberté*, May 24.

A former French war bride, now mother of four lively little Americans, who slept next cabin to ours, joined in the conversation with a frantic hand-clasp and the exclamation that sounded something like "'Oh, Shugarre Ray Ro-ban-sogn!" And she made as though to do a Frank Sinatra faint.

"Well, if he's here I'll give him a knockout of an interview, and maybe I'll get an autographed boxing glove for you," I told the ex-bride. She beamed.

Using my "Laissez passes" I passed through four doors and up three flights to the Information Desk 1st Class. Mr. Information was busy, but while I was waiting for him a very nice looking young Negro woman came up near the desk, and was waiting, too. A large, also very nicely dressed and well groomed Negro man followed her, and then another. I thought I would probably get more information from them than from the desk. I did.

I asked the woman if she knew whether Robinson was on board. She asked the man next to her, and he explained that Fighter Ray had not kept his date with the *Liberté*, because he had made another date to fight somewhere. We all introduced ourselves, then. The man asked if I was not from the South. How did he guess! I had only said to him "Thank you."

I told him I was from Columbia, Tennessee, very proudly. Then he asked if I knew of Meharry Medical College in Nashville. "Certainly," was my answer.

He turned out to be Dr. Edgar Keemer, graduate of Meharry, 1936, and his friends were Dr. and Mrs. Melvin Fowler, all of Detroit and all on their way to Scandinavia for the Summer Olympics. They are personally acquainted with Robinson, they said, and they told me more about him than he probably would have himself. But I didn't get the glove.

On my next venture into the realm of celebrities, alias "Lions," I took with me as escort Guy Van Meenen, who is planning to introduce baseball to the French youth.

We first met Milton Katims, famous young conductor of NBC Symphony. I introduced Guy to Mr. Katims as "America's Ambassador of Baseball to France." The "Lion" beamed, and said. "Sure enough, fellow, what a team."

Then the two of them launched into such a chatter about Dodgers and Giants I was hardly able to get Mr. Katims' attention long enough for him to agree that the Atlantic is a Great Symphony.

I really knew very little more to say to him, however, for my musical education got only as far as "The Happy Farmer." And I married him.

Mr. Katims did however reach into his pocket for a piece of paper and wrote out his summer schedule for me. He would be in Paris until June 7, (my birthday, but he was not letting that influence his plans, I was sure.) Then to Prades, France, for the Chamber Music Festival with Pablo Casals until June 30. Make some recordings for Columbia (not Tenn., but records). Then a visit with Toscanini in Italy. Next he would fly from Rome to Israel to guest conduct the Israel Philharmonic Orchestra for four weeks. Then fly back to NBC. He wrote that much for me, then he and the "ambassador" went to bat for the Dodgers again.

The thing that surprised me most about Milton Katims was his extreme youthfulness. I had always thought of orchestra conductors as having long white hair. But not this one. He appears to be several years younger than thirty.

The thing that I liked best about him was the sacred way he mentioned "The Maestro" Toscanini. His enthusiasm over that visit in Italy was the only part of the conversation that exceeded his interest in the Dodgers.

While the menfolks were in their 4th and 5th "inning" of the interview, a young Negro woman, tall and very slender, passed by, turned, came back and asked Milton what she should play for the Ship's Party. He answered "Oh, something light," and was back with the Dodgers again. He did, however, introduce her as Lois Towles, Hollywood's great concert pianist, and Lois and I went into conversation. She used to teach at Fisk University.

If you can imagine a huge ocean liner, nearly 1,000 feet long, or about as long as a city block, I would reckon, stack it up 8 or 10 stories, or decks, high. Fill it with small rooms, large rooms, lounges, offices, porches, cubby holes and corridors; sprinkle it with 468 First Class passengers, 499 Cabin Class passengers, 466 Tourist Class Passengers, 1,080 crew members; all speaking with different languages and accents; paint it white with red chimneys, set it afloat with a rhythmic, rocking motion in a giant tub of glistening blue, sudsy water—you will have a slight idea of what the *Liberté* is like. You will have an idea why, while on board, I would rather ramble than write. So I rambled.

In my ramblings around I met an average-size man, in average size horn-rimmed glasses and a slightly above average sports suit; with an average-size fringe of slightly-graying hair around an average-size balding pate—in other words all about average for a man of about 47 years, more or less, maybe.

His name turned out to be "Jean Desses," and the ship's daily newspaper reports him to be a famous French Fashion Designer. When his name is mentioned among fashion-conscious women and girls there are always gasps and symptoms of swooning.

"Ah, Zhawn Day-zay" the French girls say, evidently pronouncing the name. An American girl told me M. Desses is one of the foremost up-and-coming designers of the world right now. Later, glancing through *Vogue*, I suspected they were right. But on the streets of Columbia he would pass for Dave Gordon if Dave had less hair, more years and pounds, and if he would wear average size horn-rims, and over-size sports clothes.

But as you folks in Columbia might guess from what I wear, all I know about Fashion is that it is not spinach, as a not-too-recent book declared it is. We spoke of the work he is doing on board ("because it is so quiet"); of the work he must do in Paris; of going to Deauville for a show on Sunday after arrival, the show he must put on the following week every afternoon at 3 p.m.; and of the big fashion show in Paris August 1-10.

Altogether I gained a very definite impression that this particularly world-famous French Fashion Designer is very much a working man.

I suppose I should have felt a little more self-conscious in my $11.98 blue-green, mail-order, nylon crepe, size 38, but glancing at his working clothes, and noticing that they fitted him about like my size 38 fitted me, I didn't feel too badly.

However, I did determine to be in Paris, August 1-10, for the Shows, if possible, especially for "Desses Day," August 4, and if it is at all possible, and if francs and marks are not revalued by then, I might come home in a Desses model, even if I have to live on hard French bread and non-potable European water until then. Meeting an artist like M. Desses does something to even a country woman's sense of Fashion.

As I said "Goodby and thank you very much," to M. Desses, a woman nearby touched my elbow and said unmistakably in English-a-la-Dixie,

"Say, where are you from? I haven't heard so much Southern talk since I left Bristol." And she didn't mean Bristol, England, either. I knew she must have meant the Tennessee side of the Bristol, Tenn.-Va. line.

She is Mrs. Allen Rucher, formerly of Bristol, and now of Lexington, Mass. Her husband is an economist and they are obliged to travel all the time, she said with a world-weary sigh. We had a grand little down-to-earth chat, and agreed that a coonskin cap would look very well hanging on the White House hat rack.

Searching for a map of Paris, in a map rack near the Information Desk, I was aided by John W. Burn, who is taking his young little 81-year-old mother to South France for the next two years, He knows Europe like Dale Younger knows

South Columbia. And he gathered up a book of maps for me and marked enough "must see's" to keep me in Europe during a 5-year plan. I don't know what kind of a "lion" he is nor what his work is, but he'd make a wonderful travel agent and publicity representative for the Continent.

THE DAILY HERALD
COLUMBIA, TENNESSEE
SATURDAY, JUNE 21, 1952

Country Woman Cracks NATO

Oh this French Bath Business! Grandma's was never like this!

Whereas, when on Saturday night Grandma thought it necessary for me to take a bath, she dragged the Monday washtub into the kitchen; wedged it behind the stove; filled it with slightly wiggle-tailed rainwater dipped from the barrel under the eaves, and slightly warmed in two tin dishpans on the kitchen stove; gave me half a leg of somebody's last winter's underwear for a washcloth; half a mealsack for a towel, a chunk of potent, brown lye soap; pulled down the shades; turned down the lamp; bade me to remember my neck; and walked out leaving me to lock the door and perform the remainder of the procedure. These French bath stewards do somewhat differently.

The French Bath Business is also very different from what the modern American traveler demands at every motel and hotel—a private bathroom for every person, or at least every couple.

So as far as I could discover, there are only two or three bathrooms or at most four, for the more than 400 people in our section of the ship.

To get a bath here one must make a date with a Continental. In my case he wears a white coat, and answers to the name August—rhymes with disgust—but he is very, very nice indeed. He keeps books on baths; and by making certain gestures and by pointing out the time on my wrist watch, he told me I was to bathe at 7 o'clock Sunday morning, Ship's Time, or about 3 o'clock God's and our time.

So promptly at 7 o'clock Sunday morning, a White Coat filled with a pleasurably plump and very polite Frenchman, tapped on our open door, bowed, pointed to me, and announced, "Your bath, Madame."

I scuttled down my nervous little ladder from Bunk D, and sleepily followed him down the 2-foot wide hall to a small room almost completely filled by a huge tub, a huge towel, a small mat and a small cake of soap, merely those and nothing more. He made an all-inclusive gesture, bowed again, walked out, and locked the door from the outside.

I glanced at the tub. It seemed enormous. I tested the water; it seemed just right. So I de-pajamaed myself and stepped in.

If that tub seemed large from the outside, it was a lake when I sat down, or tried to. Before I realized what was happening I was floating around, feet up and head down, and I'd never had more than three distressful swimming lessons in my life!

The tub must have been 7 feet long and I am 5 feet 5 1/4 inches in my bare feet.

My first thought was of the Life Belt back in 755-D above my bunk! The door was locked and August was evidently far-gone. I clutched, grasped, scratched, and struggled, but there was not so much as a straw to catch at! Even the soap dish was high above.

As I proceeded in my near-drowning process and gobbled down a mouthful of violently salty water, I realized that my Personal and Private Atlantic Pact, to let the Atlantic alone, was being broken. I was absorbing the ocean.

At long last my foot found that the tub had an end in it. I turned around, reached for a faucet, but it turned on the shower. Then the Atlantic not only was coming up on me, it was also coming down on me, and with what force! Suddenly I remembered it was Sunday morning and time, a very good time, for prayer. My first and very fervent prayer that morning was: "Please, God, turn that water off!"

I didn't say "Amen," however, till finally, with main strength and much awkwardness I had wrestled that faucet and the Atlantic back into place and got my feet firmly planted on that small mat! I never did get as far as the soap, so that was saved.

By the time I had blotted a considerable amount of the remaining Atlantic off my person and had climbed into my pajamas, I felt more composed, especially when I found I could open the door from the inside. So I walked out into the 2-foot wide hall, bowed to my White Coat, and said in my hybrid French, "Merci, Monsieur, bath tres bon."

I then realized if I had called "Mercy" from the bathroom he would have thought I was saying "Thank You."

In the tub I had very definite visions of *Herald* and *Democrat* headlines proclaiming, "Country Woman Drowns in French Bath Tub."

I was so glad not to make those headlines, I bowed again to August and said, "Merci, beaucoup."

He scraped and bowed and tried to tell me something about the bath being "la mer," and I remember that "mer" meant sea. I said in French, or English. "Sufficient," and I meant just that.

Wandering on down the hallway, trying to find 755-D again, I met our French maid. (Oh yes, we have one of those, too.) Trying to explain to her why I was out alone at that hour of the morning, I told her that I'd had a bath. And then I added what I thought was "la Mer," but she understood me to say "Ma Mere."

She exclaimed, "Bath, with your mother?"

I exploded: "Oh my goodness, gracious, Miss Agnes, no (though I don't think Agnes was her name). Bath with Mama! Absolutely not, and Heavenly days! Mama never gave me a bath like that!"

I found some consolation from the Big Swede, the girl who has a bunk on par with mine, 755-C. She explained, "We are not so dirty in Europe as in America. We take not much baths."

I concluded that if all baths in Europe were like the one I had that morning, I'd go European too!

I learned this, also, on the *Liberté*: When we hunt what we Americans call "the bath room," we don't find them so labeled on a French ship. They are evidently called by various names. But they are not too hard to find, for all doors are always open.

I stepped into one that I thought might be a proper place, but upon looking around at the furnishings I concluded that the sign above the door, which I had not noticed, was not "Dames." So I sneaked quickly out and down the hall to another open door. The word on the door of that one was definitely "Dames."

It seemingly made no difference, however, for the doors remained open, and the white coated stewards roamed in and out with their care-taking and cleaning, just as freely as the dames did.

Whatever there may be about the French that is false, it is not their modesty.

I realized I was starved. Not so much for food as for a glass of good, cold water. And it kept coming into my mind that European water is not fit to drink. As I pondered this more and more, I grew thirstier and thirstier. That mouthful of the Atlantic I had gulped in my bath didn't help much.

The waiter asked if I wanted "juice." I said, "Certainly, and water." He brought juice, and juice alone. He asked if I wanted coffee. I said, "Certainly, and WATER." He brought coffee, also alone.

One taste of that thick, black gooey broth convinced me that French coffee might be guaranteed to contain not more than 1/2 of one percent water.

I glanced out the portholes at the waves and grew thirstier. I tried in vain to brush enough dust off my memory of Prof. Morton's alleged French to remember the word that meant "to drink." It wasn't in there.

I glanced out the portholes again and remembered "The Ancient Mariner."

"Grandma" Mitchell had made us memorize certain portions from that, including, "Water, water, everywhere, but not a drop to drink."

Certainly, the venerable Ancient Mariner must have been aboard a French boat, and at that on "the morning after."

Finally, Britain came to my rescue in the form of a couple from London, Mr. and Mrs. Leonard Briggs, who are at my table. He is at the Foreign Desk of the *London Daily Herald*, he said, and he also said that Britain had been blamed many times for aiding the South, in a certain not very recent war, which we called Civil.

He told me the French word for water is "eau." I was ready and very willing to say "Oh," all right. So I said to the waiter very distressfully, "Oh." He replied, "Wee, Madame," and went on his way.

Then Canada helped out. Mrs. Pearson, on my right, from Vancouver, B.C., said, "You must say L'eau."

The next time he passed, I said, "L'eau," and pointed to the waves outside the porthole. He nodded and said, "Oui, oui, Madame." He seemed pleased that I realized that the sea is l'eau.

At last in desperation, I resorted to gestures, and to make them unmistakable, I snatched my empty juice glass, pointed threateningly to the Atlantic at the same time. He said, "Oui, oui," again and disappeared to the rear of the ship.

At last he re-appeared with a bottle about the size of a 4-ounce bud vase, filled with a reasonably clear liquid, and set it before me in disgust. It was my time to exclaim "Oui, oui, oui, and merci, merci."

After breakfast, which the French call "petit dejeuner," or "small lunch," I put on my coat, and sunglasses, tied up my poodle (hairdo that is) and found my way out on the deck to confer again with the Atlantic. Having participated of her in The Bath, I felt we were better acquainted.

Up to that time I had met very few of the people on board, and that morning I saw very few of those that I knew. I had understood that besides the crew of 1,080, there were 1,432 passengers aboard. In my arithmetic that meant 2,513 people; and I was sure there must be 2,512 accents, for everybody there seemed to have an accent except for me. Or perhaps the number should by then be 2, 512 $^{1}/2$. By Sunday morning I feared that I, too, was coming down with a change of language. So I scarcely dared to speak for fear I would betray it.

I settled down in a deck chair, pulled up my blanket, and all was GLORIOUS! Somebody said that the groves were God's first chapels. I tried to recall my history, and especially the first part of the book of Genesis, but was too languid to separate the land from the water in my remembrance of Creation. However, I believe from the evidence then available that the waves had a slight priority over the groves, adequate though groves are, as chapels.

It was too late by then to go up on the Boat Deck at the very top of the ship to the man-made chapel, and I was too tired for more stairs, so I just sat there wrapped up and blanketed in that deck chair and had a very, very Close Communion.

THE DAILY HERALD
COLUMBIA, TENNESSEE
MONDAY, JUNE 23, 1952

Country Woman Goes Gala but Not Entirely So

BY LERA KNOX

(Still on Atlantic)—

No story of a ship's voyage would be complete, I suppose, without a mention of the Ship's Party, or as we say on the *Liberté*, the "Gala."

It happened on the fourth evening out, and does this ship get around to the Gala in a hurry! We've made such fast time, and the sun has been moving so rapidly, we've had to get up every night at midnight and run our watches up an hour.

Incidentally, I figured that I have been losing an extra hour of sleep every night, which I must be reminded to catch up with on the journey back home.

By the fourth day out everybody already knew everybody else worthwhile, and everybody was in a mood to have a lot of fun.

The gala began with a bigger-than-usual dinner. Only by copying a chef's dictionary could I tell you all the things we had to eat that night. I tried eating some of all of it, for after all my $11.98 blue-green nylon dress doesn't fit very well anyway. And by that time I had gained enough confidence in French cuisine to know that whatever it might be called on the menu it would taste good.

Our menus that evening had ribbons on them, red, blue, white, yellow, all inscribed in gold with the word *Liberté*—as though we could ever forget. Following the example of the little grey-haired lady who LOVES everybody, (and kept the people at her table laughing throughout the week), I tied my blue ribbon around my Columbia "poodle hairdo," and set out to have as good a time as anybody that night.

I couldn't join in the dancing because, after all, Grandpa was a preacher, and it was against family laws for me ever to do anything worse than the Virginia Reel, and that on the sly. I didn't taste the champagne, because the ship would soon be docking and I wouldn't have the sea to use as an excuse for my staggering. But I could listen to the corks pop, and I could enjoy watching the different international games and dances and hold my sides laughing at my fellow passengers who entered the contests.

First came the Snowball Dance. I thought at first when that was announced that it might be somewhat chilly. But no, it was designed to melt whatever "ice" there might still be on board, except of course that downstairs in the refrigerators.

A volunteer couple went out on the floor, and started dancing. When the music stopped they separated and each chose a new partner, thus two made four. The music stopped again suddenly, and 4 made 8. The process was repeated until the floor was full and everybody was stepping on everybody else's corns and laughing about it.

A lull, then the Rubber Ball Dance. Every couple was given a small rubber ball to place between their foreheads; then they put their hands behind their backs and the game was to keep that ball in place, to dance to any kind of music, keep hands behind them, and never to drop the ball. Well, those balls had a way of getting around, as you can imagine. Sometimes one would find itself between the lady's eye and the gentleman's ear; sometimes it was nose to nose, cheek to cheek, or chin to chin, but it was all ridiculously funny. Each couple who lost out left the floor. And to show you what smooth dancers they were, two couples tied for the prize, though many of those dancers are probably still rubbing their eyes, ears, or noses.

Next game was the Statue Dance. The floor was filled with couples, and the contest was to remain in whatever position one found oneself when the music stopped, and to remain absolutely motionless, as still as Miss Liberty, without even a bat of the eye nor a giggle, until the music began again. Sometimes I was sure those poor ludicrous statues must have thought that the orchestra had gone to sleep.

I heard one man say that as long as he could be caught looking at the floor or the ceiling he got along very well, but when his eyes fell on a fellow fool he went down and back to the chairs.

It was in the Statue Dance that my cabin-mate Brigitta, the Big Swede, stole the show, alternately swinging the big Texans, Tom and Steve. But it was in a one-foot dance when she was left on one toe with one finger pointing skyward, Tom looked at her, giggled, and had to sit down, leaving her unsupported on one toe, that "Sweden" also fell. I tried to console her by saying that I didn't believe even Miss Liberty could have stood during all these years on one toe.

By that time my watch said midnight. And I realized it was time to run it up another hour. When I looked at it again it was already after one. Realizing that a respectable country woman ought not to be up and at a dance after 1:00 a.m., remembering the five hours sleep that "Longitude and Latitude" had already deprived me of, I gave my seat of vantage to the Little Lady who Loves Everybody, and went downstairs to Bunk 755-D.

By doing so, I learned next morning that I had missed the Purser's last party, as I had previously missed his first. After I was gone they brought out bells, whistles, caps, ribbons, all sorts of crazy, kid-like playthings, had more marches, games, contests—good clean fun and hilarious laughter—but I slept right along through all of it. Guess I'm slipping. It must be that birthday coming up.

I believe I felt better next morning than the 70-odd-year-old Little Lady who Loves Everybody. She stayed up with the other young people all night, but she brought her usual smile to breakfast, as did they.

THE DAILY HERALD
COLUMBIA, TENNESSEE
TUESDAY, JUNE 24, 1952

Country Woman Tends Tender

BY LERA KNOX

About To Leave the Atlantic—

On what was to be our last night at sea, having caught up with longitude and latitude, we didn't have to run our watches back an hour at midnight, so I expected to have a good might's sleep. Perhaps I did. But sometime, it seemed very shortly after I had gone to bed, I waked with a start; didn't know where I was; all was quiet; ship wasn't rocking, engines weren't chugging. I lost no time in scuttling down my nervous little ladder and tip-toeing into the hall. Imagine my surprise to see green!

Actually it was a sort of a flat green hill with some Japanesey looking little green trees along the top. I still felt "all at sea," and finding that little green hill in what I thought should still be the middle of the ocean gave me a start. Then I realized what had happened. We had docked in the harbor of Plymouth to "expel the British," at least those on board the ship.

I realized from what I had read about sailors that I should have shouted: "Ah, Land, at last!" But I had been having such a wonderful time on the ocean, I really didn't want to see land yet. If liners get to be much faster than the *Liberté* I think we should annex the Pacific to the Atlantic and cross both of them to get to Europe—the Atlantic will probably be wide enough, though, when I return to the States in September. And Miss Liberty may look as good to me as the *Liberté* did the day I left.

But remembering my duties toward expelling the British, I reached for a coat and sweater, put them on over housecoat and pajamas, and started for the dining room. All the people from my table were getting off at Plymouth, and Texas was seceding, too.

Most of the "expellees" were already at the tables with their hats on, pocketbooks well in hand and cameras swung over their shoulders. They were surprised to see me in coat and pajamas, and scarf around my bobby pins.

"Did you decide to see London this morning?" They asked.

"No, but did you all h'expect me to jolly well let youse bloody h'Englishmen get off this yere boat, taking my 'eart and all my 'aitches, and not let me know anything about it, did ye?"

So we broke our French rolls together, spread them with Normandy butter and Italian marmalade (by then I was able to call it "Marm-a-lardy"). And that morning I got a bottle of water without begging. That was the morning for the weekly tips.

Emily and Leonard Briggs had their last two eggs for breakfast. They said that after that morning they would have no butter and only one egg per week per person. It was worth the trip to see how they enjoyed butter and eggs. Leonard popped some more of his h'English jokes on us—I had always heard that the British have no sense of humor! His yarns beat anything we hear at home on television or radio.

Joy Pearson, from Canada, who had not seen her brother in England for 42 years, was thinning her French coffee with tears of happiness. She was taking her brother a ham that she had bought in New York. And she said:

"When he asks me what he can do for me, I shall say, 'Please, a pot of tea!' "

As a farewell gift Emily gave me her recipe for genuine Yorkshire Cheese Cake and Leonard told me his best joke on Churchill (I can't tell you that 'til I get back home, not that it is unprintable, but because it must be accompanied by an accent that can't be spelled.)

After breakfast we all went upstairs to First Class Lounge where they had to show passports and go through the red tape of dis-embarking. I watched them carefully so I would know how to behave when we arrived at Le Havre late that same afternoon.

Going out on deck I caught my first sight of the Union Jack in his (or her) own environment. It was flying from the top of "Sir Walter Raleigh," the little boat, or tender as they called it, which had come out to take passengers and baggage off the *Liberté*. The big ship could not get close to land in the Plymouth Harbor.

Then it all came over me. This was really PLYMOUTH, the very same harbor from which the MAYFLOWER sailed!

I THINK I HAVE NEVER LOVED AMERICA SO MUCH AS WHEN WE SAT AT ANCHOR IN THAT LITTLE HARBOR OF PLYMOUTH!

Looking back over our long, but seemingly short, journey across the Atlantic, and realizing the bravery of that little band of Pilgrims, I wanted to get down on my knees on any rock that might be on that rugged little shore, and say the biggest prayer of my whole life.

I didn't feel like this even when I stood in the top of the Empire State Building and looked into the diamond that is New York. In an instant I re-traveled my entire trip, back in the plane over New York and Washington, the hills of Virginia, the haze of the Smokies, the dams and lakes and roads and farms and homes of Tennessee, and back in our old Plymouth car around the detour road to Match, and Rally Hill, and to Knoxdale—it was a long way from our rattley old 1939 Plymouth car to this green bordered Plymouth Harbor. And the *Mayflower* was not like the *Liberté*. If it had not been for the extreme bravery of that venturing little group of Pilgrims, America might never have been ours. I celebrated my most

Memorable Thanksgiving Day on Memorial Day, May 30, 1952 at 4:00 a.m., ship's time.

Downstairs again, I took out my bobby pins and put on my hat. Maybe the Atlantic was wide enough after all. And I decided that I would not ask Congress to move the Pacific over to our East Coast so as to make ocean trips to Europe last longer.

We didn't get off the *Liberté*, until 6:00 p.m. that afternoon, but I kept my hat on all day.

THE DAILY HERALD
COLUMBIA, TENNESSEE
TUESDAY, JULY 1, 1952

Country Woman at the Rail

It takes a long time to get off a boat even after ocean crossed

BY LERA KNOX

Somewhere in Europe—

I had a long, long look at France before I ever set foot on her soil, or rather platform. That morning when the *Liberté* stopped at Plymouth to disembark the British, Canadian, and London-bound passengers, I got out of my bunk, hurriedly and partially dressed, even to putting on my hat rather than comb my hair, and went down to have breakfast with some very excellent journalistic souls from London whom I had met on board.

By the time I had reached the table my "habile" was about to become "dishabille"—in other words I was about to lose part of my hurriedly-put-on clothes. I tried to negotiate a loan from the British, but they had nothing to lend, not even a safety pin, but Canada came to the rescue of my decency and produced an almost blanket-pin from the depths of her handy bag.

After the green shores of Plymouth left us we chugged on toward Le Havre, and were due to land there sometime the same day, or so I could understand from the all-French-speaking crew and mostly-French passengers. But I got a shock while gouging my small silver spoon into my thick black after-luncheon coffee; I began to see derricks and wharves or platforms and a general conglomeration of nailed-up boards fly past our portholes.

"What is that?" I gestured to the waiter.

"Le Havre" was the answer.

I couldn't believe it. I jumped up, clamped my beret down closer on my still unbrushed "poodle," grabbed up my 10-quart shoulder bag, and rushed down to 755-D to gather up my other 3 1/2 bags. Ro-bear (Robert), my guiding and guardian angel of a cabin steward, tried to stop my on-rush, but to no avail. I thought he had enjoyed my company and generous (?) tips so much he wanted me to stay on and return to the States with the ship next trip, but I was not to be deterred. I had sighted land. Or at least lumber.

He finally prevailed on me to leave my heavy luggage saying the French porter would take those up for me, or something like that, but I snatched up my typewriter and handbag and proceeded to climb stairs. That baggage and my late luncheon were almost too much for four or five flights of steps, but I knew that land must be somewhere in the offing, or to starboard or port.

I didn't dare leave that typewriter to the integrity of whatever French dock porter might appear, although I knew by experience it could hardly write English, much less French. And I took consolation in the thought that whatever Mademoiselle might wear my probably pilfered homemade nylon frock to a French Fashion Show would not likely be a sensation, or would she?

I got on deck by the time the tugs were nuzzling the *Liberté* up to the boards. A big derrick picked up a gangplank, all banistered and covered, and long as a Pullman car, and aimed it right at my face. I found I was leaning against the part of the railing that was to come down to make an opening for said gangplank. I moved.

Then instead of people getting off the boat, people began to get on. First policemen, or at least uniforms, of all sorts and varieties. Then the crew—or what I judged to be the crew: men who looked as though they had hurriedly thrown off white coats and half-way jumped into grays and browns—began making 2 to 4 steps at a time down the plank toward the girls they must have in every port. But we poor passengers, who had come all the way across the ocean to get off at Le Havre, were held back by important looking uniforms.

You couldn't tell those uniforms a thing, however, unless you could speak French, and you couldn't ask them anything, for the same reason. You could only look and wait, and drool, and you can do that as well in English as you could in French, I found out.

I did a lot of looking, and not a little drooling; perhaps, after all, the United States Army decided to answer my prayer, that Stan might be allowed leave to meet the boat; or else that Meg might have obtained reservations and come on down to Havre to escort me onto the Continent. As bad as I wanted to get off that ship, which I loved so much, I hated to attack Europe alone with only a grin for defense, a few travelers' checks for food and transportation, and my only "arms" full of luggage.

I scanned the docks, piers, platforms intently for the sight of a neat, well-dressed young woman or an American Army captain's two shoulder bars. The only women I saw were old or fat or frowsy, and most of the army uniforms were French or at least frowsy. Then I remembered that Meg was at least older than when I saw her, and she had admitted that she was getting fat—but frowsy! Never! Wherever that girl might be I knew she'd be looking good, very good!, and Stan also.

That was about 2 o'clock Friday afternoon. At 6:30 that evening I was still at that railing, leaning on or off, looking and watching. I'd change bifocals every once in a while, but I couldn't see any more familiar faces with one pair than I could with the other. The same factory must have made both pairs of my glasses.

In my "off" sessions from the railing I'd trot downstairs to see if my suitcases had been picked up by the French porters. They were still resting placidly in their same piled-up positions.

"Ro-bear" tried each time to calm my nerves and lower my blood pressure, with the most pacifying of gestures, but I answered with gestures that meant "dead or alive I am determined to get off this boat."

Meanwhile the public address system was talking, but in French. People were milling around, and there was nothing for me to do but mill around too. Now and then a name would be called on the P.A. But not mine. Or was it? How would the French say "Lera Knox?"

Up to that time I had never heard a Frenchman call me anything but "Ma-dam" (accent on last syllable.) They didn't say "My-dame."

At last I detected in the P.A. intonations the word that sounded like "theater"—I realized that I might be making a show of myself, but so was every other impatient aboard. Then a word that sounded like "sin-e-emoah." Putting it all together I recalled that the words "cinema" and "theater" were on the door of a big room upstairs, and I observed that the French-understanding "impatients" were rushing upstairs. I did also. We took seats in the large room. But we were not in the mood for a movie—moving was what we were interested in. At least I could speak for myself.

One by one we were called out of our seats to line up and pass along an extended line of uniforms who wanted to see our passports, know how many cigarettes we had, how much money, and a lot of personal questions that were not listed in passports or who's who. We were checked to see whether we had tickets for the boat train, reservations on said train, red landing cards without which no one could leave the ship. Then I had to spend $30 good American dollars for a handful of stuff that looked like Grandpa's Confederate money, only bigger, and perhaps more valueless. Because, we were told, we were facing a 3-day bank holiday, and those francs would be handy in Paris. All of which was right, I guess. That many Frenchmen in uniform couldn't be all wrong.

Back to cabin again we were told to go, and to tell cabin stewards to release our baggage to French dock porters.

"Ro-bear" gave me an I-told-you-so grin. I admitted he was right. I might just as well have spent those four or more hours getting my money's worth out of a nap in berth 755-D.

But I was at least ready when the time came to get off, and I changed his grin to one of the "merci" kind with another American dollar for a tip for his trip which I didn't take. Shook hands with him and said "revoir" for the sixth time and climbed the stairs again behind a rough, but capable looking, perspiring and heavily laden French Dock porter.

THE DAILY HERALD
COLUMBIA, TENNESSEE
THURSDAY, JULY 3, 1952

"Country Woman" Writes Of Danes—And Of Maurians

Editor's Note: Today's communication from Mrs. Lera Knox, the *Daily Herald*'s "Country Woman" correspondent who is now touring Europe, is what was written as simply a friendly personal letter to the editor. But it contained so much news in it that (with some deletions) we are publishing it as part of the series.

Tom Brown, Lera Knox, and Bill Stanfill near entrance to Hamlet's Castle, at Elsinore, Denmark.

Back in Büdingen,
Oberhasse, Germany
11 a.m. Monday
June 23, 1952

Dear John:

As you can see above, we are back "home" again—but what you can't see is that we have had a most wonderful-trip-wish-you-were-here visit to Denmark.

Gosh! I LOVE THAT DENMARK! If Switzerland is more perfect, as I've been told, I doubt if I can take it—for a while at least. And it will be a little while, perhaps July 1 or perhaps a little later.

Even though it is somewhat chilly here—I'm never out of my sweater except to get into "longies"—and a coat feels good anytime, I don't care to rush into the "warmth" that is Berlin unless urged by someone other than myself. I'd rather send home for my winter coat—which I need more right now than the moths do.

If you don't believe that Tennesseans can make themselves known in far places, you should have had the experience that I had while standing in the Knight's Hall of Frederiksborg Castle, near Hillerod, Denmark, gazing innocently up at a magnificent tapestry.

Stan and Meg and I had ventured to take what is known as the North SeaLand Tour of a group of personally conducted tours over the island on which Copenhagen is located.

In order to get a seat on the bus I showed the guide a letter from the *Herald and Democrat*, which confessed that I am an accredited representative. After noticing the *Herald*'s letterhead, he politely exclaimed, "Oh, I know that paper: I've been in New York!"

I tried to explain that it was not the *Herald-Tribune*, but the *Herald and Democrat* of Columbia, Tennessee. But when he got on the bus he announced, "We have with us today a representative of one of the two largest newspapers in the United States!"

I looked around to see who that press-personality was, and found him smiling down on me. I could only shrink down in my coat collar. No time for explaining; the bus had started.

A while later we were standing, as I said, under a very important tapestry with the busload of other sightseers when Stan leaned over to me and said in a stage whisper, "That's a long way from Columbia, Tennessee, isn't it?"

I looked up and retaliated, "Yes, and from Dover, Tennessee, too, suh!" We have our little battles about our hometowns.

Just then I notice I was about to be surrounded by olive drab. In addition to Stan's uniform in front of me, I was being flanked by two uniforms of the same color. A soft voice on my right said, "Pardon me, but what newspaper are you writing for?"

"Why, the *Herald and Democrat* from Columbia, Tennessee —I kept trying to tell the guide—"

Then the voice said, "Well, I'm from Columbia, too."

And the Left Flank exclaimed, "And I'm from Columbia, too, and Hohenwald!"

It was Billy Stanfill from Thomas Avenue, South Columbia, grandson of the late Squire Drake Stanfill, and Tom Brown, reared in Hohenwald, but who worked for the telephone company in Columbia.

They said they thought they recognized me when I got on the bus in Copenhagen, from the clipping Billy's mother had sent him, but when the guide introduced me as a representative of one of the two largest newspapers in the United States, they didn't recognize the *Herald and Democrat*.

It was when they heard Stan joshing me about the tapestries and castles, about those not being in Columbia, Tennessee, that they began to be suspicious. And when I opened my mouth to speak, they knew I couldn't be from anywhere else than Dixie! We almost had a camp meeting right there in that sacred and historic hall.

So when we made an onslaught on Kronborg Castle, the Elsinore Castle of Shakespeare's Hamlet, a few miles farther along on the tour, I had an army escort that any woman would be proud of, and when we all tackled a marvelous Danish dinner at a little special and unspoiled restaurant in Copenhagen that the guide told us about, I had really good company. And when we three, aided and abetted by Meg and Stan, took in the whole Tivoli Amusement Park that night, you never saw five happier travelers.

And we all agreed not to tell on one another, but we couldn't resist sending a round-robin card from Hamlet's Castle to a teacher who had been Margaret's, Jack's, and Billy's English teacher. Guess she was a bit puzzled, and a bit surprised, but certainly no more so than we were—the funny thing of it all is that they are buddies of Tilman Knox. Tilman is my husband Alex's nephew, who had intended to be with them on the trip, but had his leave cancelled at the last minute.

And we talked about just about everybody else in Columbia and Hohenwald, in the army and out. We discussed Billy Corrigan and the name he made for himself introducing hillbilly music to Europe (may he be forgiven) through his famous Uncle Willie Gasthaus' radio programs, and just about as many other home folks as the hours and the dinner would permit.

I don't think, now that it is over, that they would object to my telling you the things on our menu that night, so you'll know why we had to take a long, long walk in Tivoli afterwards.

The dinner started with half a fresh boiled lobster each, with other appetizers of smoked herring, pickled herring, smoked eel, pickled eel, and fried eel, shrimp, salmon, plaice, cod, and other fish delicacies, delicious bacon, ham, pork, eggs, all served on those wonderful and famous Danish open-faced sandwiches called "smorgasbord" (pronounced something like smeared bread—but wonderfully smeared that bread was.) Then we had several delicious salads—those were only the introductions to the meal.

Following were hot roast beef, potatoes, cauliflower, and other vegetables, more delicious delicacies. Cheeses of various kinds, fruits, and a dessert of pancakes, ice-cream, and other sweets, and the total cost of our dinners was $1.45 each. I haven't seen or tasted such a meal since I used to go with Grandpa Ussery to preaching out in the country and went home with a church member for dinner.

We "skålled" or toasted in proper Danish fashion, and had one grand and glorious time. But we all walked straight through Tivoli Gardens until it was time for us to remember that tomorrow would be another day, and that the boys had to leave for camp early on that other day, tomorrow.

The morning *Stars and Stripes* carried a story about Tilman that explained the cancellation of his leave. He seems to be doing right by golf over here, and these people do love their golf. I'm mighty proud to be his kinfolks, from what I hear.

FROM *STARS AND STRIPES*:

"Garmisch, June 21 (Special)—Medalist Tilman Knox, ex-Tennessee pro from the 43rd Div., came from behind in the driving rain yesterday to capture five of the last six holes and defeat Murray Jacobs, VII Corps 2-up for the 7th Army golf championship.

Knox, five down with six to go played in the 36-hole final match, turned on a blazing finish to take five of the last six holes. Jacobs had held a 3-up at the mid-way point and 3-up again after 27 holes.

After halving the 28th, 29th, and 30th holes, Knox turned on the steam across the waterlogged greens for top honors."

THE DAILY HERALD
COLUMBIA, TENNESSEE
MONDAY, JULY 7, 1952

Country Woman Visits Denmark

BY LERA KNOX

No, I didn't shake hands with King Frederik nor Queen Ingrid, but I did have a chat with two of their Royal Life Guards, they of the Sam Brown belts and Bear Skin Hats. Though the fact that the Guards spoke Danish and I spoke English made our conversation more of a chatter than a chat.

I didn't parade Tivoli with their Majesties the three little princesses, but I did live almost next door to the private school which they attend.

I didn't have tea at the American Embassy, though I met some American soldiers who did.

Indeed, I doubt if Royalty, Parliament, or the Embassy even knew I was in town. The dressed-up policemen probably kept an eye on me, but they have very nice eyes, so I wasn't too nervous about them.

I don't know just when we decided it, but somehow after a day and a half in Denmark, Meg, Stan, and I just didn't mention going on to Norway and Sweden at all. We seemed to reach a sort of silent and unanimous opinion that Denmark was just as close to paradise as we could hope to get in ten days, and that ten days was all too short a time to spend there.

On the first day, Stan and I trailed Meg down a main street to what she designated as "three little rooms of my own private heaven, namely, Georg Jensen Silver Shops, Bing and Grondahl's National China Factory, and The Royal Copenhagen Porcelain Manufactory." Stan and I enjoyed these, but we didn't "Oh and Ah" and sigh so deeply and all but fall down and worship there in just the way Meg did.

And Meg and I dutifully (?) followed Stan to the best eating places in town, and to the snazziest night clubs and all those places where a man is advised by guide books either to take, or not to take, his wife—and mother-in-law.

They patiently toured bookshops, parks, museums, gardens, and such with me at times. But for the most part we agreed that to see the city most satisfactorily, "he travels fastest who travels alone."

Thus it was that instead of having a late hotel breakfast with them, I usually got up early, went down the street, and slipped into the little Kaffee Salon, almost next door to the city's large fruit, flower, and vegetable market, where farmers and hucksters ate.

There I mostly looked and listened and tried to be as much of a Dane as possible. In ordering breakfast, I didn't even open my mouth, for fear an accent might slip out. I just pointed, or nodded, as nonchalantly and inconspicuously as possible toward the cups and coffee urn, and held a finger over the particular pastry that looked the best. I then counted out my ores and took my food to one of the small inconspicuous tables.

To be sure the paintings on the wall of this little place, those of plows, the sunrise, the green houses, the flowers, fruits, and vegetables, were somewhat faded and stained. The air was thick from pipes, cigars, and cigarets, and humanity; the conversation was completely Danish; but the atmosphere was cordial and the coffee and cakes were good.

In order to stay a little longer, I usually went back for a second cup of coffee, which I really didn't need or want. But it was a good excuse. I even picked up a Danish newspaper and tried to read it—so I wouldn't appear too foreign.

I was very much pleased to be merging into Denmark's rural populace the way I was, when a very well-dressed young man stopped at my table and said as correctly as a Vanderbilt professor might:

"Pardon me, but the lady at the counter tells me you are an American. Can I be of any help to you while you are in our city?"

"Indeed you can," I exclaimed. "This headline says something about Truman. What has he done now?"

"Oh, that's the Steel Strike," was the answer.

One just cannot escape news.

THE DAILY HERALD
COLUMBIA, TENNESSEE
WEDNESDAY, JULY 9, 1952

Country Woman Finds Nothing Rotten In Denmark

BY LERA KNOX

Why, oh why hasn't somebody told us more about these interesting people and their beautiful country—the Danes and Denmark?

To be sure we have heard about "the melancholy Dane," Hamlet; and we learned in geography that Demark is a small peninsula with perhaps a few islands thrown in for good measure; and we found that Copenhagen is a hard word to say and a harder one to remember—but in my opinion, all that stuff should be put into a museum and labeled, "World's Prize Understatement!"

As for being melancholy, there seems to be little of such nonsense as melancholia in this country. On the contrary, I believe the Danes could out-wit the Irish, and a few other funny countries thrown in, with both hands tied behind them, and tongue in cheek. If the Irish, as the Irish say, are 98% wit, then the Danish temperament seems 99 and 44/100%

pure, clean humor and fun. I'd like to see the Irish and the Danes meet in a verbal battle. That would be an "Olympics" for the gods!

My first contact with a Danish person was meeting a sturdy little Dane on the train. He broke into our conversation with a clever quip expressed in excellent English, and assured our wondering minds that, "if a Dane gets angry with you, he won't fight today; he'll wait 'til tomorrow." I felt reassured, for I thought that by tomorrow we could either be in Sweden or in Norway.

Incidentally, this man is a professional wrestler. A picture from his billfold showed us that he has won enough medals to cover his very broad chest. So I judged that if this particular Dane didn't fight you today it wouldn't be because he was afraid or didn't know how. He just figured that if he'd wait 'til tomorrow maybe he wouldn't have to fight. Which seems a very sensible peace-plan for men and nations.

As for there being "something rotten in Denmark"—that is pure bosh! That first word in that phrase should be "nothing," and I do mean NOTHING!

The country is as clean as a well-scoured bowl of its own porcelain dinnerware. And that word CLEAN refers to the houses, the barns, the streets, the stores, even the fish market where the old women sit near the sides of the canal and peddle their fish. It refers also, I believe, to the minds of the people. I doubt if there is even one dirty joke or dirty fly on the peninsula or on any of the islands. I didn't see even one little nasty gnat flying around the lights above the neat sidewalk cafes.

There's nothing "buggy" about Denmark either.

I asked someone if the country has no insects at all. I thought maybe it is just naturally that lucky. The answer was, "That DDT is effective."

Evidentially it is applied, too.

Standing on the street corner, my first morning in Copenhagen, waiting for an endless stream of bicycles to pass, I thought I had never seen such a friendly mass of people in all my life—not even in Sulfur Springs, Texas; and not even in Columbia, Tennessee, on Mule Day. Every cyclist that passed me waved his hand.

By the time I could get my left hand out of my coat pocket and my right hand unloaded enough to wave back, I realized that actually they were signaling for a right turn.

Turning right around the corner, I found myself walking into a beauty-lovers' Special Annex to Heaven.

It was, I judged, Copenhagen's market for her country neighbors. And Rural Denmark had turned out heavily laden, and in an extremely good humor.

If you could imagine the two blocks in your downtown all leveled off, enlarged, and neatly paved with cobblestones, then jam-packed with folks, flowers and fruits, and vegetables of seed-catalog quality leaving just room between each row of carts, trucks and wagons for a pedestrian or bicyclist to pass. Then let it overflow, this beauty and abundance that I am talking about, you can get some idea of the size of one of Copenhagen's farmers' markets.

To be perfectly accurate, and to put on the record a small part of what I walked through, I took out my little black book and jotted down notes as follows:

A lady crossing the street to board a tram with a large basket of flowers and a loaf of bread. A small pushcart attached to the rear of a bicycle piled high with cauliflower, onions, beets, carrots, and trillium—just like the trillium that grows wild in our woods back home. Next cart packed with daisies done up in florist paper, and bunches of oak leaves and elm branches. A woman with vines growing in little pots, also pots of begonias, geraniums, and fuchsias; and bunches of radishes, herbs, salsify, pink daisies, fern leaves, and sweet Williams just at the opening bud stage. A large truck piled high with rhubarb, stacked like stovewood, and half a dozen boxes of new potatoes on the rear, and a great lot of long green things that must be zucchini or cucumbers.

Parked wisely in the shade of the big truck was a sort of wheelbarrow affair, also powered by a bicycle, loaded to the brim with attractive packages of peony buds, Queen Ann's lace, orange-colored lily buds and blooms; nasturtium; lupines in a half-a-dozen colors; ragged robins, also in bunches; pink carnations, rosebuds in lilac paper; strawberries half as big as hens' eggs; gooseberries as big as green gage plums; rosebushes with roots wrapped; rubber plants in pots; pink geraniums; and cineraria, wrapped and in pots.

The lady in charge of those had confidently hung her pocket book on the rear of the truck and was rapidly transferring the contents of the wheelbarrow-arrangement to her pocket book in the form of *kroner* and *ores*. A kroner, by the way, is the Danish dollar, except that at the present rate of currency exchange, a kroner is worth about 14 1/2 cents of our money, and an ore is 1/100 part of a kroner.

In a little Kaffee Salon, handy for the hucksters, one could buy a cup of very good coffee for 30 ore, and a hunk of delicious bread or pastry for 35 ore. I was tempted to have lunch there.

But curiosity kept me moving on to assemblies of more pink rosebuds in purple paper; water-lily buds in bunches; limbs of trees and climbing rosebushes in bloom, all parked in buckets of water, to keep them fresh. Another seller had mixed bouquets from gardens and woods; celery and tomato plants; mustard for boiling; mushrooms in baskets, herbs in pots; fennel, leeks, chives and cherries, columbines; asparagus; peas; small potatoes; rhubarb; and spinach. Cabbage heads and lettuce were in abundance, and cauliflower heads, which themselves looked like bouquets of white hydrangeas, were packed in bushel baskets.

And purchasers were there in great numbers. I soon noticed that the wholesale buyers were usually dressed in long white coats or aprons, and most of the sellers wore long tan coats like dusters, or raincoats, or trench coats. Everybody seemed to trust everybody else for pocket books were left lying around as carelessly as were the potatoes.

As to the vehicles on which the produce was loaded, there were, as I mentioned, bicycles with baskets either fore or aft; carts attached by bicycles either fore or aft; old Reo trucks, ancient Packard cars; A-model Fords; new Chevrolets; home-made wagons with horses eating out of nosebags; shiny new English limousines; and believe it or not, even a few ox carts drawn by milch cows. Denmark certainly has a variety of transportation as well as produce.

And the Danes are wise to believe, it seems, that "when the farmer has money, everybody has money." And the farmers were really taking in money that morning.

I learned that every Sunday, the market is just as full as on that first morning I saw it. And also in other parts of the city the same performance, or a similar one, is repeated. Down in the older part of town by the canal, not far from the King's residence, is another market where the boats from the neighboring islands come up the middle of the shopping street loaded with vegetables, flowers, fruit, cheese, fish, and all sorts of country produce. This also is a busy section.

And down next to the Parliament building is another canal that is essentially the town's fish market. There, in the shadow of a monument of an old fisherwoman, surmounted by gulls, is a long line of bonneted old ladies peddling their fish alive from their perforated bottom boats. They'll skin or dress their produce while you wait: eels, shrimp, fish, lobsters just any live thing that comes out of the water. You pay your ores and take your choice.

I know you think this is all a sort of fantastic fairy-tale dream. But not so. It all happens everyday but Sunday. And on Monday and Friday and Saturday, the markets are twice as busy.

But by 10:00 a.m. every morning the flower and vegetable markets are as clean as your kitchen table, or as clean as it ought to be. And at 2:00 p.m. the whole fish market space, even the old statue, is all washed up by the city fire hose and the gulls go elsewhere.

Certainly, there's not so much as a rotten temper in Denmark, and I can tell you there are no flies on this countryside, with or without DDT.

THE DAILY HERALD
COLUMBIA, TENNESSEE
THURSDAY
JULY 10, 1952

Country Woman Abroad—Meets a Great Dane

BY LERA KNOX

I may as well admit that I am incurably a book-drunkard, and can no more pass a bookstore than an alcoholic can pass a bar—unless on a non-stop express. And there are few non-stop expresses in Copenhagen. Besides, I had read in my "how not to get fat" book that one must walk half a mile for each half a pat of butter. And that Danish butter is very good indeed, so I was doing a lot of walking, and consequently a lot of stopping at bookstores. The fact that most of the books in most of the stores were in Danish made little difference. I could at least look at the pictures. Cartoons are the same in any language, if there are no words connected with them.

Wandering around trying to find the Town Hall Square, I discovered a little shop that had in the window several books with English titles. I went in, picked up the nearest, and looked it over. The title was *Meet the Danes*, and the price was K4:85. Gosh, what an awful nice little book. Then I realized that K meant kroner, which was about 14 1/2 cents in our money, and the 85 would be ore, so the total price would be bout 69 cents (not plus tax) which would be about what a big lunch with dessert and drink might cost. I wasn't hungry, and did want to "Meet the Danes," so I counted out kroner and ores, took the little book, walked out and sat down on a handy park bench.

That's one thing I like about Copenhagen. Park benches are always handy. I decided to read my lunch hour out. But I had no sooner scanned the first couple of pages until I found myself rushing back to Mr. Kai Worm the "Boghandel" as the sign above the door said, and asking the young man,

"Do you speak English?" "Certainly," was the surprising answer.

"Then tell me how I can find the publisher of this book. He seems to be here in Copenhagen. Please."

Smiling, he picked up the telephone, spoke a word, dialed a number, jabbered a few words, smiled again, wrote something on a slip of paper, and said: "The editor will be glad to see you, at this address." I looked up the street on my map, and decided to walk it—I might find another bookshop on the way. I forgot entirely about lunch. But every now and then I'd sit on a park bench and read a little more from the little book. The man who wrote that book was saying just exactly what I wanted to say about Danes, but I couldn't find such words as he put together, in the way he put them together, in any other book, magazine, or newspaper I had ever seen.

Following Bregade, which is Danish for Broad Street, I came directly to Amalienborg, the Palace of King Frederick!

Certainly the King didn't have anything to do with that book! Was I lost again? I looked at the slip of paper, and at my map. The slip read "21 Ameliegade." I was just a little mixed in my spelling. The correct address must be nearby, for the street sign said "Ameliegade." I dodged around the castle, and found No. 22.

On the opposite side of the street where No. 21 should be was only a tall and completely blank wall. I reasoned that it must be the side wall or back of the castle.

Now Danish policemen are so dressed up in blue uniforms and brass buttons, they look like they might be Admirals of the King's Navy. But they really aren't. One gets the impression that the city government had found on sale somewhere some handsomely tailored uniforms, and had had some men tailor-made to fit the uniforms. But the reverse is probably true. I could not help thinking that in Denmark policemen could be only ornamental, and were not intended to be useful. Once I asked a policeman about a location of somewhere, and he had to ask a taxi driver.

But up against this blank wall I had to ask somebody. I saw a policeman, and looked about for a taxi driver. There was not a taxi in sight, so I ventured to show my slip of paper to the officer. He smiled, and pointed at the blank wall where I thought No. 21 should be. I must have looked as blank as the wall.

He smiled, and pointed to a small door in another wall down the street a little way. Danes must have their little jokes, even in numbering houses, I thought.

I walked across the street and down to the door in the next blank wall. I knocked, properly I thought. But no answer. There must be someone at home, for "the Editor" was expecting me, Mr. Worm had said. I ventured to open the door, heavy though it was, wondering if the policeman was watching me.

No wonder no one answered. The door led to a sort of wide long hall like a porte-cochere, and beyond this was a sort of court yard, paved with cobbles that were very well worn. Kilroy or perhaps a lot of Kilroys, must have been there before. A sign on the wall said 1751.

I looked around, and closely. The one sign on the one door that I could find suggested that I was in the Italian Embassy; I turned hurriedly and scooted out to the sidewalk again, and closed the door softly.

I looked about again for the policeman, but cop, cycle, and all were gone. I scratched my tam, and made bold again. Well, nobody had told me to get out, and I could speak Italian as well as I could Danish. On the next "tour" I passed the Embassy door, and found another courtyard, then another open hallway, and another door. This one luckily had several names on it, and at the bottom was one that looked like the name in the front of the little book, "Hans Reitzels, Forlag," and "Forlag," according to my little pocket dictionary, means "publisher."

I pushed the door open ever so gently, found another hallway, some stairs. I tripped up those very easily, not knowing but that the next door might be the Russian Embassy—and I don't speak Russian so well, either. On the second flight, however, I found the same title, "Hans Reitzels, Forlag."

I tapped lightly, but before the door could be opened, I bravely pushed it open and said to the girl at the desk, "Do you speak English?"

To my surprise she exclaimed, "I certainly do, and it's so good to hear a Southern accent! You must be Mrs. Knox." She's from Florida.

It is really good to be recognized by a Southerner in a Danish publisher's office, upstairs next door to the Italian Embassy, and second door from the King's castle. I keep on liking Denmark.

I explained to her that I had found the little book, liked it very much, and would like to quote some of the things "Bo Bojesen," the author, had said about the Danes.

She introduced a portly gentleman from the next room and he very graciously told me it is proper anywhere in the world to quote, if you use quotation marks. Well I certainly would use those, and gladly.

Then, as dubiously as I would test a tub of water, putting my foot in and not knowing whether it would be hot or cold, I said: "This author, who and what is he? Where is he? Living or dead? And would he just maybe, barely be possibly available for perhaps a handshake or maybe even an autograph!" I don't think I have ever been childish enough before to ask about an autograph. But I ventured.

"Why, certainly." (Certainly is a word the Danes use lavishly, and I like very much the way they say it, and like them when they say it.)

Then he gave me the author's real name and told me he lived out of town, but sometimes comes in. He picked up the telephone, jabbered a bit, then turned and said, "He will meet you at Frascati (a popular and friendly sidewalk cafe) at 4:00 this afternoon." He showed me a caricature on the back of the little book, and said, "He looks like this, only is thinner."

I was at Frascati at 3:30, even though I had to miss part of a city tour to be there. I was watching for a very tall, very thin, very dark man with big glasses, small mustache, and big cigar. At 4:15 I was still watching. A man behind me might have been "the Dane," but he was too fat, and not as dark as the cartoon, and he was nervously smoking cigarettes. But he did have the mustache. I had turned again to look him over, when someone caught my shoulder, and said apologetically, "I am so sorry to keep you waiting. My bus was late."

Never trust a pen-and-ink drawing! He was not dark at all, but very blond, slightly graying, and the little mustache was blond also. But how could an artist draw a blond mustache with black ink? Bo Bojesen did have a cigar, however not a very large one, nor was he so very tall, nor so very thin. I'll never quite know how he recognized me among all those other Danes and foreigners, for he didn't have a cartoon of me.

We chatted very pleasantly for too short a time. His wife is from Manchester, England, and he is making it his job and business to translate American poetry from the first in the 1600s to the last in the 1900s into Danish. So we had few language difficulties. I wished sincerely that I had known more about American poetry so I could speak understandingly of the things he was interested in.

We did find some subjects of common interest, however, for instance the Danish policemen. I told him I think they are very decorative. He replied, "They think so, too."

I won't give you his real name, for fear the policemen might feel too ornamental and get useful in his neighborhood.

Once upon a time, he told me, not bragging at all, that he wrote some poetry that another nation didn't like, and as a result he spent a few winters in Danish summer houses, and once left town hurriedly in a clanging ambulance, right through the Nazi lines. There was more, but it's not for publication, not about his poetry, I mean, but some escapages during the occupation of Denmark.

Wondering at the energy of a person who would try to translate into another language all the American poetry that I had not even ventured to read in English, I asked the old question that has probably been asked of every author.

"When do you work?"

"When you want to? when you feel inspired? or when you have to? regularly or at certain hours?"

The answer was: "I write when I want to, when I don't want to, and when I have to.

"My secretary comes at half past nine in the mornings, and by that time I am supposed to have had my breakfast, taken a walk, and read all the papers.

"We work until about 3:30 or 4:30, then I have dinner, take a walk, read the papers; and work until about 2:00 the next morning."

"But what do you do in your spare time?" was my next sensible question. I've heard that in an interview you should always ask a "personage" about his hobbies.

So I made the question more to the point. "What is your hobby?"

"Why, hopscotch, of course. My wife and I have no children. We are not talented in that direction. But I have a number of friends ranging from five to seven years of age; and we have some wonderful hopscotch tournaments during the time that I should be reading the papers."

"What, no garden?" I asked. I had observed that every good Dane has a garden.

"Oh, again, I have a neighbor. And that is better than digging one's own garden." I was realizing all the time what a smart man he is.

Meg and Stan came along at about that time, by previous appointment. I told them I would be at Frascati until I met The Dane, or thereafter. We all went around the corner to Coc d'or for a delicious dinner. It was so nice to have our food ordered in Danish and explained in English. "Bo" and Stan discussed wars and peace; the Swedish-Russian episode, and a lot of other important matters. He offered, as a chief inducement why we should stay in Denmark, the fact that Danish Television is at present out of order.

Later, perusing a book on Danish government, I found his name—his real one—listed as a member of King Frederik's Cabinet. But I still won't tell you that name, for fear a Danish policeman might read this and discover that Bo Bojesen thinks that Danish policemen think they are vain. I wouldn't want my friend, a truly Great Dane, to spend another winter in a summer house, or to leave town in an ambulance. Those ambulances make an awful lot of noise.

THE DAILY HERALD
COLUMBIA, TENNESSEE
FRIDAY, JULY 11, 1952

Country Woman Abroad—She Continues Optimistic

BY LERA KNOX

I just LOVE this Europe. To be sure, having part of my family over helps a lot; but I don't think it would be too bad to try to tackle the entire continent alone, especially when one's spirits are high and digestion is good. A great many of the people with whom tourists come in contact speak English, and almost anyone can learn to make gestures or point to maps. But that's the hard way.

I have wished many, many times that I had paid more attention to European geography while I was in school. Although two wars have shuffled countries and boundaries around considerably, wars haven't yet moved the Kattegat or the Skagerak Sounds, or the Mediterranean.

Sometimes I feel so ignorant over here I feel like sending myself back to grammar school and standing me in a corner in "Granny" Mitchel's room.

And I feel that I should like to send myself to Mr. Duke's office and beg him to let me study Danish, Swedish, Spanish, German, Italian, Greek, and Cockney—instead of letting me skip French and Latin classes.

Languages over here are somewhat like clothes when you come out of a swimming hole: you feel embarrassed if you haven't got 'em.

My friend, Bo Bojesen, "The Great Dane," whom I have quoted before, said that one difference in people over here now is that after the war the optimists studied English and the pessimists studied Russian.

I said: "Well, judging by your excellent English, you must be an optimist?"

"Oh, but I have learned one sentence in Russian."

"What is that?" I queried.

He jabbered something, then interpreted it as: "Don't shoot me!"

I'm optimistic enough to appreciate my English, but just the same, I'd learn a little Russian, too, if I had to. And I'd always try to keep my hands free for gesturing, and my feet free for running.

Speaking of "The Great Dane" reminds me of a bit of conversation during the dinner that "the poet" (as he likes to be called) and Meg and Stan and I were enjoying a Coc d'or, popular little restaurant.

We had run low on subjects for conversation, when I brought up the topic of weather—a daring thing to do. It had been unusually cold and rainy for June. And I had been wearing my coat and sweater throughout the trip and wishing every day that I'd brought raincoat, umbrella, and overshoes.

"Oh, this weather is beastly," he exclaimed. "It's nasty!"

Those expressions and their accent can be accounted for when you remember that his wife came from Manchester, England.

"Well, I am wondering what it is like in winter?" I suggested.

He gave a sort of French-ish shoulder-shrug, and said, "Oh, so-so!"

Then he went on. "It is at least different. For example, my wife-to-be was here in August when we became engaged. When she came back as a bride in December, she was not sure she was in the right country."

"I imagine you have a great deal of skating and skiing during the winter?" I ventured.

"Well, yes, when we can import enough ice and snow from Sweden. All of our ice and snow, like our raw materials, have to be imported, you know."

Then it popped into my head, something I had read or heard about one terrible winter recently. "Well, I imagine that importing ice and snow from Sweden was very easy during the recent winter when the entire Sound between Sweden and Denmark was frozen over!"

That was a dreadful thing to say to a Danish host. I might as well have donned a fur coat in Miami—if I'd had a fur coat and had been in Miami. One thing Europe has in common with Florida and California is that any weather that is unpleasant is "unusual."

THE DAILY HERALD
COLUMBIA, TENNESSEE
SATURDAY, JULY 12, 1952

Country Woman Abroad—
Finds Danes Apologetic

BY LERA KNOX

The Danes seemed slightly apologetic about three matters: first the weather, which admittedly has been rather cool and damp during our visit. But imagining what the weather in Tennessee must be like at the same time, I simply drew my coat closer around me and was thankful that I can do so. My Danish hostess, however, Miss Jennie Buhl, gets up every morning, looks at her own private weather observatory, a thermometer and barometer, and is "so, so sorry" that she can't do right by me so far as weather for the day is concerned.

But to her amazement I never let the weather slow me down. I even took a boat-ride (in an open boat) in the harbor, on one of the drizzliest days we've had. It was just about the dampest I ever got, what with mist and fog and drizzle, too—except of course in the French bath tub when the ocean came up on me and the shower came down, but in the French bath I didn't have on my only coat, shoes and hat! I got along very well, however. Two ladies from England had two umbrellas, and they loaned me one which I shared with a bald-headed, bare-headed gentleman from Sweden, and a good time was had by all.

Another matter the Danes apologize for is the fact that their country is so small. Now that, of course, depends on the point of view. Looking at a map and comparing Denmark with say, Brazil, it does seem rather a small spot on the map. But riding backwards on a crowded European train for about six hours, from the German border at Flensburg to Copenhagen, after having had already ridden 12 hours in Germany previous to that, I felt sure we must be at the far end of Siberia before the train finally stopped at Copenhagen. I assured all apologizing Danes that the country is quite large enough for me.

And I am sure that the mythical goddess, Gelfion, who is reputed to have changed her four sons into bulls and with their help to have plowed the whole great island of Zealand, on which Copenhagen is located, off the southern end of Sweden, and all in one day—I think that Gelfion thought at least the Island of Zealand is large enough. Gol-lee! That was a whopping big day's work for one country woman even though she was a mythical goddess.

All right, here to prove that the Goddess Gelfion and I are not alone in thinking that Denmark is no small "skimshion," I'd like to note a few statistical lines from a little book I purchased from my friend Mr. Kaj Worm, the Boghandee. The book *This Is Denmark* was edited by Knud Gedde, and was published in 1948, by Jul. Gjellerups Forlag. (I'm very glad I can copy those names for you and don't have to pronounce them.)

Mr. Gedde declares, "Before World War II Denmark was the country with the greatest per capita foreign trade. If a world map were drawn with the total area of the globe distributed among the various countries in relation to their trade, one would get quite another idea of Great Powers and small nations than is the case with an ordinary world map. On such a map Denmark would occupy more space than e.g., Brazil, though the area of the latter country is about a hundred times that of Denmark and its population eleven times larger. Denmark would, indeed (according to 1938 figures) occupy a little more space than the Soviet Union, which covers nearly one sixth of the globe and has one twelfth of the population of the world."

So much for Gedde's statistics. He, also, seems to think that little Denmark is big—commercially, at least. The Danes are not braggarts. They are just proud, and furthermore, they've got the butter and eggs and bacon and ceramics, and diesel engines and ships to prove that they are good producers and good promoters, despite their small acreage. The whole country is about the size of two of our smallest states, not including Tennessee. And from what I've seen and tasted I'm glad to brag with them.

The third and last, so far as I know, topic for apology, is that of mountains, or lack of them.

I think, perhaps, that Denmark is sort of semi-consciously waking up to the fact that tourists are abroad again, and that tourists' dollars and traveler's checks can be changed into Danish kroner to a good advantage.

I think, also, that Danes are looking, with just about one fifth of an iota of an atom of jealousy to Switzerland with its enormous influx of tourist business because of Switzerland's good food, friendly and honest people, and marvelous mountain scenery.

Now I haven't seen Switzerland as yet, but I believe I'd stake Denmark as second to none so far as honesty, friendliness, and good food are concerned. However, I believe they say that the highest hill in Denmark is not much more than 20 feet above sea level—and even as much as I like the country, there is little I can do about that.

The Danes, however, have done something about it. In their tourist propaganda leaflets they call attention to the fact that "in Denmark there are no mountains to hide the beautiful scenery."

On one of the conducted tours through South Zealand, the guide very graciously offered to do anything for the guests except give them a mountain to climb. But he added, "That would make you too tired."

Moving pleasantly along through the picture-book countryside in a sightseeing bus, he called our attention to the modern model farms; the ancient castles, or ruins thereof; and then as we crossed a tiny stream, no bigger than Helm's Branch, which he told us was once a "raging river during the glacier age," he dramatically announced, "Now we are leaving the Island of Zealand, the Country of Denmark." Everyone seemed astounded, of course. I began looking down the highway for a jumping-off place—then he added "we are now entering the Land of the Fairies!"

For hundreds of years, he explained, the King of Denmark dared not cross that raging river (3 feet wide), for fear he might meet the King of the Fairies in yon Fairy Hills (the hills must have been 12 or 14 feet high) and thus promote a war.

At last, however, one very great, brave, (and curious), king did venture across the stream in the middle of a bright moonlight night.

"He did not meet the Fairy King, however. He met only a beautiful girl!"

"But that," he concluded, "is another story." And having delivered this dramatic oration, he sat down.

I, sitting directly behind him, couldn't have noticed that he probably had his tongue in his cheek. So I bit, just as I was supposed to, I suppose.

I touched him gently on the shoulder, and queried, "But aren't you going to tell us the other story?"

"That, Madam, I must leave to your imagination."

I suppose he meant that anyone who didn't have imagination should never have crossed the raging river (3 feet wide) and entered the Kingdom of the Fairies amid the Fairy Hills.

THE DAILY HERALD
COLUMBIA, TENNESSEE
MONDAY, JULY 14, 1952

Country Woman Sees Tivoli

BY LERA KNOX

Try to imagine a combination Centennial Park, State Fair, refined street carnival, opera house, flower garden, music festival, and general gala, taking in five or six city blocks, perhaps. Fill it with fountains, gardens, music halls, lights, merry-go-rounds, Ferris wheels, little lakes with safe little boats, cute little ducks and swans, more flowers, more bright lights; three or four grandstands with home-town bands playing classical, popular, jazz, and all sorts of music.

Throw in a game parlor; a fairyland, brilliantly lighted dance halls, concert stages, pantomime plays, shooting galleries, singer's pavilions, dozens of delightful restaurants, souvenir shops, playgrounds, scooter-floors, parading bands of little boys dressed exactly like the King's Guards; little trains that anyone can ride, old millwheels, houses; more fountains, flower gardens, bright lights and ducks. All that together, thickened up with happy people from eight years old and under, to 80 years old and over—and you have what Copenhagen calls her amusement garden, "Tivoli."

Tivoli, owned partly (51%) by the city and partly by fortunate individuals, was opened in 1843 and, to prove its success, the gate receipts show that more than 10,000,000 people had entered the gates before it was 100 years old.

It opens at 9 a.m. and closes at midnight, and on Saturday nights and special occasions you get fireworks, also, for 5 cents to 10 cents admission that you pay at one of the four or five entrances. Winners of "Wheels of Fortune" and other games and contests are paid in special Tivoli coins, which can be used to buy souvenirs or to pay for other amusements. But like a big world's fair, which it rivals, the best things at Tivoli are free.

As for people, you are likely to meet the King and Queen and the three little Princesses; a group of Australian sailors on leave from their ship in the Atlantic; half a dozen GI's on a weekend pass from Frankfurt; a group of tourists, or a typical Copenhagen family. You'll see, also, couples from the city's "Old Peoples' Homes"; children from nursery school or orphanages; the richest, the poorest, and all the rest—and unless your bifocals are stronger than mine, you won't be able to tell who is rich and who is poor.

Denmark thrives on being a land "where few have too much and fewer have too little."

From before he is born the Danish infant is treated like a king. And an expectant mother is sort of a queen for a year.

She is provided free milk, free medical care and advice, service of publicly employed midwives; doctors when necessary, a visiting trained nurse during the first year of the baby's life; milk for the baby and mother until he is a year old; nursery and kindergarten for children of working mothers; in fact when Denmark adopted the stork as its National Bird, Denmark meant business.

And she sees that whatever the stork might choose to drop is going to get proper and adequate care, food, training, and education right on through the university; or through trade school, or in whatever trend his talents direct—and free at that!

There are more than 4,000,000 people in Demark, and I am sure I saw several hundred thousand of them. I noticed a smaller percentage of cripples, fewer ill or unhappy-looking people in Denmark than in any place I have ever visited.

There are two great breweries in or near Copenhagen, and it is said that by going out for a visit you can get all the free beer you can drink. A large percent—in fact all of the net profits from the breweries—are dedicated to arts and sciences, but I saw no alcoholics, and apparently no drunken people anywhere. To be sure I noticed one old man talking to himself, but I'm afraid I also could have been found talking to myself when no English-speaking people were around. And I hadn't been to the breweries.

Throughout the years of the Danes' working lives, or from the time they finish the compulsory school courses at 15 years of age, they pay a small sort of social benefit or insurance which entitles them to be ill and have hospital and medical care for not much more than a dollar a day, or less. Until they earn more than 10,000 kroner a year. And when the women are 60 years of age and the men are 65, they are provided with perfectly lovely, little, modern, model apartments for not much more than $4 a month, with meals out at about 20 cents each. Elderly married couples have two-room apartments with kitchenettes; and single persons have single rooms with kitchenettes.

And all have congenial neighbors of their own age. Those are the people I meant when I spoke of the people from the Old Folks' Homes being at Tivoli. I saw some of those cute little apartments, and believe me they are worth living 60 or 65 years for.

I'd say that the Danes are "soaked in culture" from cradle to the grave (or crematorium). And they like it. They can get sick; get old; go to school; work; and have fun (at Tivoli or elsewhere) cheaper and more pleasantly than any people I know. But of course I couldn't learn all about the Danish social system in just the short time I could be in Denmark. The main thing is that the Danes all seem to like it.

To give authority for my one woman's opinion, I quote from the booklet *This is Denmark* by Knude Gedde:

"In all cases the benefit societies provide free medical attention, often combined with allowances toward medicine, dental treatment, massage, bandages, and the like. Hospital treatment is always paid for in full, and as a rule a benefit society will also wholly or partly defray the cost of special treatment in clinics or convalescent homes. The major societies, incidentally, are owners of such homes."

So you see, Denmark seems to be an excellent, and pleasant, as well as an inexpensive place in which to enjoy ill health —if you can get it.

But Tivoli, just around the corner from the courthouse, is so much more fun than the hospital, convalescent home or clinic, and besides it is so reasonably inexpensive, that Danes just stubbornly seem to stay healthy and live to a very ripe old age, just to enjoy those cute little apartments.

THE DAILY HERALD
COLUMBIA, TENNESSEE
TUESDAY, JULY 15, 1952

Country Woman Learns Of Danes vs. Nazis

BY LERA KNOX

Standing at the bier of the late King of Denmark, His Majesty Christian X, at Roskilde Cathedral, where his casket is waiting for its marble sarcophagus, being made like those of many other royal rulers entombed there, I noticed among the wreaths left by Very Important Persons and faded little bouquets of field flowers evidently contributed by neighboring farmers' daughters, a small faded scrap of blue-and-white ribbon that seemed to be given a place of honor.

Curious as usual, I asked about it.

"Oh that," said the guide respectfully, "shows that he was the leader of our Danish Underground Movement."

I felt rather shocked. I had supposed that "underground movements" were something that should be kept under cover. But I remembered the information.

Looking over a magnificent collection of Christmas Plates cherished in the Museum of one of the great porcelain factories in Copenhagen, I had asked about the significance of the Christmas plate designs and the years they represent.

The plates for the years of World War I were especially noticeable: with their crosses and helmets they made me think of the poppies that grew in Flanders Field. But the most significant plate of The World War II years showed merely a narrow avenue with a castle at the end. I asked about that.

Our host explained: "That one little picture meant a great deal to the Danish people. That is the castle where the Nazis kept our King a prisoner."

From then on I began to make more inquiries about what is more properly called in Denmark, "The Resistance." The stories I heard compare well with the stories we have heard of our own "Confederate Resistance" of a few years back, except that they are fresher—and more horrible, or at least some of them are.

Many of the stories naturally carry a twang of the Danish wit. For example, one that goes the rounds, is that one day early in the uninvited occupation, 71-year-old King Christian was out horseback riding alone as was his habit, when a German guard noticed him and asked a nearby Dane,

"Isn't that the King?"

"Yes," was the answer.

"Who is guarding him?"

"All of us Danes are guarding him," was the reply.

An officer in one of the porcelain factories told us that a high dignitary in the Nazi realm ordered a magnificent and large piece of pottery to be made for his private collection. He inquired several times whether the pottery was finished.

"We have no coal to fire our kilns," was the answer.

The German dignitary sent coal, but the factory decided that the Danish people needed the coal more than the kilns did.

Again the Nazi inquired about his porcelain. Again the reply was "No coal." And again they brought more coal, and for another winter the Danish people were warmer as a result.

I know for a fact (for I saw it) that the enormous piece of porcelain was finally fired, but not until the man who ordered it had already gone to a place where, in the opinion of many, the heat might be so intense as to melt the porcelain even if it could be delivered to him.

In the Shell Building, the Gestapo are said to have had their offices on the lower floors and to have kept their Danish prisoners on the upper floors, as a protection from Royal Air Force bombing, just as they always put their prisoners in the front coaches of the trains as a protection from railroad saboteurs. But the Danes were clever enough to arrange with the R.A.F. to skip-bomb the lower floors of the Shell Building without too much damage to the upper floors.

The Shell Building and all other buildings that were damaged seemed to have been repaired in good order again. But not the hearts and memories of the people.

It is probable that my best source of information about the Resistance Movement might have been my landlady, Miss Jennie Buhl, for when unperturbed Miss Jennie speaks excellent English. But at almost any time the war is mentioned her English and her emotions are so upset, what she says is almost incoherent.

"They killed seventeen of my young men," she exclaimed in tears. By her young men, I knew she meant the University students who boarded with her.

"They came to my door one night, put their guns in my chest, and shouted: We want Hans Buhl. We want Hans Buhl."

Hans, her nephew whom she had reared, and who also was studying at the University, heard the commotion, from his back bedroom shouted "Farewell Aunt," and scuttled down the narrow little circular back stairway that leads to a blind alley.

It went all the way the four floors to the ground. They didn't know, also, that Miss Jennie makes a practice of leaving all her empty milk bottles at the head of this little narrow stairway. Of course it was dark. Hans knew about the bottles, so he escaped and got away to Sweden. The Nazi's and milk bottles evidently tumbled all the way to the bottom. I could imagine as they didn't know that it was circular, very narrow, and that she told me the story and showed me the stairway, that I could still hear echoes of Nazi profanity from the lower floors.

WARNING: To any other aggressors hunting Danish youth; Miss Jennie still keeps milk bottles on her back stairway.

And Hans—well, he was the blond young man who showed us to our room the night we arrived. He is the one who carried my typewriter and 3 1/2 bags down the four flights of front stairway when I left. And at 28 years of age he graduates this month from the University of Copenhagen as a doctor of veterinary medicine. He is one of the finest, most wholesome young men I ever met. And his handshake is truly Danish.

Because 21-year-old Hans' resistance was of apparent value to his country, Miss Jennie and the entire family changed their prominent and honored name for the duration of the aggressive occupation. She removed the beautiful and well-polished brass name plate "J. Buhl" from her door and apparently moved away.

A cousin, who was a prominent priest of a nearby parish, was not so fortunate as Hans. He was captured, tortured to insensibility, and left for dead. A good Danish neighbor, however, found him, revived him, hid him in a cave until he was recovered enough to be slipped away to Sweden. "Underground" brought word to his weeping family that he was still alive, and to encourage his friends they put a notice in the papers that he had been suddenly called out of town.

The Nazis inserted a notice in the papers that he was dead. That evening from a Swedish Radio Station he talked to his people. I didn't meet him, but saw several of his pictures in the family album.

A Danish newspaper man told me of how the Danish press was controlled and censored. There had been a terrible bombing attack on a nearby city. The Nazis demanded that the editor state in his paper that a bomb had been dropped but had only killed a cow. The editor did as he was told, but he added:

"The cow is still burning."

That's the Danes for you.

It is not always the big things, but sometimes the smaller things that a person or a people do that expresses them best.

We in the United States do homage to "An American Soldier Known Only to God." The French burn and guard their "Eternal Flame" in the Arch of Triumph to honor their unknown Soldier. But what did the Danes do? They brought the ashes of an Unknown Concentration Camp Victim and gave them a place of honor in one of their most revered cathedrals.

Again, that's the Danes for you.

THE DAILY HERALD
COLUMBIA, TENNESSEE
TUESDAY, AUGUST 5, 1952

Country Woman on French Train

BY LERA KNOX

(Now in France)—

That French porter knew how to put me in my place on the train. I followed him down the 20-inch aisle, on one side of the coach, and at his behest wedged myself with seven other people into a compartment built for four while he shoved the bags into a little rack over my head. I was lucky in one way, however—I got second seat from the window riding backwards. I figured that from there I could probably see just as well, and by the law of gravity, would probably get fewer cinders than the man who was in the seat next to the window riding forwards.

I was glad it was still daylight so I could enjoy the scenery, for I felt I couldn't look forward to much conversation from all those foreign—what was I saying? Those people weren't foreigners at all. They were legal (I suppose) French citizens. They were in their own country! They were at home; I was the foreigner.

If you have never felt the feeling of being a "foreigner," you won't be able to imagine how I felt just then. For one thing I think I shrank up several sizes—even my tam was too big, it must have dropped down over my eyes far enough that I didn't have to hunt for a handkerchief.

Of course, I wasn't a bit homesick, but I would have liked at that moment to pick up the telephone and call up Alex or Mamma, or Elsie, or Mrs. Evans, or Mrs. Petty, or Mrs. Lavender, or Jane, or just anybody, and I'd liked to have been able to buy a *Herald* from the train butcher; or perhaps as much as anything else being as it was well past 7:00 p.m., I'd have liked to sneak into Knoxdale Café or Hines, or Masseys, or just about anywhere and pick up a hamburger and a coke.

Much of what I could see of Le Havre was docks and more docks, then ruins and more ruins. It wasn't a very consoling sight at first.

But soon I saw some dirt—really good old fashioned dirt of the roadside and common garden variety. And all along the railroad tracks were the friendly faces of field daisies. Hothouse roses, even those with 4-ft. stems, never looked so good to me as those little wild French daisies—just exactly like those in James Napier's field next to our garden at home.

Next I noticed wild ferns among the daisies. Quickly my thoughts were back on the north side of Stone's hill and in Neely Hollow.

In a little ravine beside the tracks I saw a dozen or more small gardens, none of them larger, it seemed, than my 12'x16' living room, each as neat as a parlor carpet, and each bordered with rows of flowers—why bless those Frenchmen! They weren't foreigners at all, they were just jim-dandy good gardeners. And I really didn't feel so much like a foreigner after all. I felt like a citizen of the World and a fellow flower-lover with the French people.

A hill covered with locusts in bloom, elder bushes, Lombardy poplars, walnut trees, berry vines, also in bloom; sheep, already sheared; an old sow, monstrous and dirty-white, scratching her bacon on a pole fence; after all that ocean for six days that old sow, and those sheep and trees—I think even Johnson grass would have looked good to me at that moment!

More little gardens, neat and flower-bordered. Except for their lack of size and weeds they might have been our own garden back home, although they looked a lot more like Mamma's garden in town, especially with those rows of white and red and pink flowers.

Why, French potatoes were not much farther advanced than Alex's, especially the ones he put fertilizer on. The cabbages were bigger than ours, but maybe because the Frenchmen had ordered "frost-proof" plants from Georgia—then I realized that could not likely be. They had grown their own, perhaps, just as we did, but they planted sooner than we did. That tall stuff couldn't be onions, not even in France. It must be French garlic, or maybe leeks. They seemed as tall as a man. Peas were tall, also, and white with blooms. A gardener and his wife waved pink peonies at the train. I felt better. I wasn't so hungry, either.

Cows in a pasture, red, and black and white spotted; more sheep; a square pond on a hillside—it looked funny shaped like that. A bunch of milk goats; a little graveyard covered with flowers. I might decide to like these Frenchmen after all.

On the whole that bit of French landscape might have been what Maury County would look like after someone had given all the weed fields and fence rows a sort of close shave and crew haircut. I could very well fancy I was in Tennessee until I saw a house. It was the houses and barns that were different from what I might see at home. They seemed all built of brick or tan stucco and all wore either tile roofs or thatched roofs. They were really pretty among all their bright green surroundings.

I think God must have made Tennessee and France very much alike; it was what Man has done to them that made them different.

Another huge white hog scratching his back. More goats and cows. Barley ready to cut. It would be the same at home—except the barley fields in France were just about the size of farm gardens in Tennessee! A neat orchard. Fruit trees, loaded with ripe cherries all along the roadsides and even along the railroad tracks. Bicycles on every road we passed. No automobiles, trucks, or even wagons that I could notice. A family bringing in a hay crop on pitchforks. A small farm so patched up with different crops it looked for all the world like the experimental plots at our own Middle Tennessee Experiment Station.

A tall Church spire (God is in France, too), with little tile-topped houses clustering around it like little chickens around an old red hen. That was a village. A big city, pitifully ruined with bombs—was God there, also?

More garden-sized grain fields; a little donkey pulling a cart. Cows staked out in the pasture. We went through a town that reminded me of the way they do towns in Georgia—run the railroad right down the main street. That gave me a closer look at shops and people. The French are really friendly. Everybody waves at the train. Even the baby sucking his thumb waved with his free hand. But they are probably selfish, too. He never did turn loose that thumb—or offer it to me.

I forgot to mention that the trees all looked like well-trimmed French poodles. When I noticed those I remembered hearing that the fuel shortage was so acute in Europe that the French trimmed every little extra twig off their trees for fire wood. That thought kept the high-trimmed trees from looking what I might otherwise have thought of as funny.

A life-sized monument of Christ on the cross in a neat, flower-covered cemetery. Perhaps some of our own soldiers were in that cemetery, too. Yes, definitely God is in France.

This sort of sightseeing and self-conversing went on for 2 1/2 hours, then the buildings began to get bigger and blacker, and it was beginning to get dark. The few dim lights that were popping out seemed to make the dark look darker. Tall gray-looking apartment buildings—could people be happy in those? Yes, there were flower pots in the windows.

Then an immensely long, black shed, with only a few dim lights strung along it. It was not until the train stopped, however, that I really felt astounded. Here I was in Paris! Gay Paree? Bah! There was nothing whatever gay about that train shed!

Then I realized that there I was in the middle of 20,000,000 Frenchmen with 4 bags and two hands. I really felt "bagged" down. If I took out two, I would have to leave two! And I'd heard that Frenchmen weren't any too honest. I might as well let them have all of them, so I picked up pocketbook, camera, and typewriter, and stepped off the train. I've never felt so alone in all my life.

What was the name of that hotel? A porter with a cart came along, and jabbered something. But it was so dark he didn't look too dependable. However, he seemed a drowning man's straw to me. I wondered how you say Franklin Roosevelt Hotel in French. Just then another man's voice came over my left shoulder: "Can you use a little help?"

I turned around into the bosom of a brown tweed suit; raised my eyes to a stubby black haircut; and under that crew-cut was a grin that could only belong to Stan Morgan!

The only reason I didn't fall into his arms is that he is so tall. I jumped!

His next words were: "Meg is waiting at the gate, stationed there to catch you in case you got off the other side of the train."

My prayer to God and the United States Army had been answered. Stan got that leave.

It was a long, long way to the gate; but there stood Meg grinning in brown gabardine. Brown quickly became my favorite color just then.

Suddenly I wasn't even so hungry anymore. My knees weren't so weak. Why, I believe I could even have toted the bags, camera, typewriter, and 10-quart shoulder-bag all by myself. But they had taken all my load except the pocket book.

Paris began to look a lot better. And right at that particular moment I felt that backed by brown tweed and flanked by brown gabardine, I could conquer the Continent—especially if I could get a hamburger and coke to go on with.

THE DAILY HERALD
COLUMBIA, TENNESSEE
TUESDAY, AUGUST 19, 1952

'Country Woman' Is Back Home; To Tell About It

Mrs. Alex Knox is back home!

"The Country Woman," whose articles in the *Daily Herald* about her trip to Europe this summer attracted much attention, arrived Friday night at her Knoxdale home, her arrival a complete surprise to everyone, for she had originally planned to sail from Europe on September 21.

Mrs. Knox said she just suddenly decided to come back—and visit Europe again next year—when she visited Paris and saw, among other things, the American flag flying above the U.S. embassy. That did it!

She rushed to the steamship office, got her tickets changed to Aug. 6, and with only the clothes she had for her Paris week-end—and without her beloved typewriter—she bid her daughter goodbye in Paris, and took the train for the boat.

Result: she arrived in New York August 12 and was here two days later, tired but happy.

She begged off from writing an article about her return until she had rested up a bit, but promised one next week, "A Country Woman Returns From Europe."

[Note: The follow-up article was apparently never written.]

A NOTE FROM THE TRAVELS EDITOR

On this first trip, from the passenger list of the *Liberté* Mother had ferreted out a fellow passenger, Monsieur Jean Desses, a fashion designer of international note. She interviewed him. She was still full of excitement over the incident when she arrived at our apartment in Germany. She announced that I was going with her to see the Paris fashion shows! I explained to her that getting into those shows was roughly comparable to going through the eye of the needle. She countered with the explanation that that would not be a problem because M. Desses had told her how to do it. Never one to turn down a trip to Paris, I agreed to go.

We attended the shows as they came up on the roster, and, each time, Mother remarked, "That was a good show, but that was nothing compared to what M. Desses' presentation will be. Just wait until you meet him!" I finally felt the need to warn her that she should not expect too much of that designer, or to expect him to remember her. His was one of the last presentations of the show and on that near last morning we walked into the building where the presentation would be held. The building was beautiful, appearing to be almost all glass, and had been owned by the man for whom the Eiffel Tower was named.

As we entered the great glass doors, a man at the front of the entryway broke away from his conversation and rushed over. He exclaimed, "Oh, Mrs. Knox! I'm so glad you could make it! And this must be your daughter from Germany! I'm so glad that you are both here! I hope the two of you enjoy the show."

And enjoy it we did. When the presentation got underway we saw the M. Desses' designs were not only classics that day, but they would be in great style ten years hence. Mother was too much a lady to say "I told you so," but I never did attempt to tell her anything about fashion or human nature after that. This leader in the international fashion world had recognized the woman who had sat on mules' heads to keep them from hurting themselves on that farm hillside back in Tennessee.

After the fashion shows Mother happened to pass the American Embassy in Paris, saw the American flag, and became instantly homesick. She returned home to writing for the *Banner* and the *Herald*, to working in the Knoxdale Café. And was very happy until we wrote that we were going to brave the post-war reconstruction and the food restrictions in London and try to see the Coronation of Queen Elizabeth II in 1953.

Margaret Knox Morgan

PART IV

Country Woman at the Coronation

PART IV

Country Woman at the Coronation

THE DAILY HERALD
COLUMBIA, TENNESSEE
SATURDAY, APRIL 25, 1953

'Country Woman' Off To Europe, To 'Cover' Coronation for *Herald*

FLASH—HERE'S BIG NEWS!

Mrs. Lera Knox is going to write for *Herald* readers again. In fact, she's gonna cover the coronation for them. And besides that, she's gonna write a whole flock more of those popular "Country Woman Goes to Europe" articles, because she's going to Europe again real soon.

How do we know? Here's How.

We just got this letter:

Dear Mr. Finney:

Snap! Snap! Snap!

It happened like that!

A letter from Margaret, our daughter in Germany. A wave of homesickness (in reverse) to see her and Stan and the people I saw and the places I enjoyed so much last summer; a phone call to Mrs. Keaton's Travel Bureau in Nashville, and the good and astounding news that she really could get a berth for one person, tourist class, aboard the grand new Liner *United States*, said to be the "greatest American product ever to go to sea."

If I could sail from New York May 8, I would arrive in either England or France May 13—and thirteen, bless it, has always been my very lucky number.

That would be just about 18 or 19 days before Elizabeth II officially dons her crown, and who couldn't use that much time scouting around England, Scotland, and Ireland? Besides, I felt sure that the Queen would be right proud to have somebody from Columbia at her party.

Next, went off a letter—telegram to Margaret and Stan that I could meet them in London if they wanted to see me; and also one to Mr. and Mrs. Leonard Briggs. He is the foreign editor of the *London Daily Herald*, whom I met on board the *Liberté* last summer. And then I began to wash out my nylons and brush off my typewriter.

So it was just like that: Snap! Snap! Snap! And in thirty minutes from the time the mail carrier tooted his horn with that letter from Margaret I was ready to start packing for another trip to Europe. Guess that other trip got something Continental into my blood, or at least under my skin.

Now the point of this letter is this:

Would readers of the *Herald and Democrat* like to get a slant on the Coronation through my bifocals?

Would they like to jog along with me on some continental bus tours?

Would they like to rattle around on some of those very rattley international trains?

They won't have to bother about passports, shots, reservations, customs, and sore feet; that can all be included in the price of their *Herald and Democrat* subscription if you think you'll have room to print some more of that country woman sort of stuff like you used last summer—and please do 'cause I suspect I'll need the money before I get through paying for my part of the Coronation inflation.

Of course, it's that Old Impulse operating again, the same impulse that sent me scooting home last summer right in the middle of the most wonderful trip I ever hope to have.

I was walking down that Big Main Street in Paris, on my way to one of the Big Main Fashion Showings, when Snap! I must have been passing the American Embassy, for I just happened to look up and there was what the French call "them Stars and Stripes" waving at all the world in general, but at me in particular.

I did a sort of solemn inside salute and said under my breath in Hill Billy American (without French accent):

"Doggone it, you're the prettiest thing on this whole Continent, and I'm going back where we both came from!"

I turned right around, forgot French fashions, and went down to the Steamship office to swap my September 23 ticket for soonest sailing date on any ship going west, which was August 6. And that was July 31. Paris and I got along very well for the next few days, but I didn't miss my boat. I had made a promise to my Flag.

> Of course, I had left most of my nylons and my typewriter in Germany. But Margaret mailed them home, and they arrived in time to be packed up to start again. Overseas mail is sometimes somewhat slow. But I'll try to get the Elizabethan Coronation articles back to you, before time for them to crown Bonny Prince Charlie—of course, that is if you want the stuff.

Now, isn't that letter just like Lera Knox?

And how do you think she got the letter to the *Herald* in a hurry? Why she got an English girl and a Japanese girl to bring it in—in their Austin. But more of that later.

Meantime, Sure, Mrs. Knox—we KNOW that the 7,700 families who subscribe to the *Daily Herald* will want to read what our own Maury County "Country Woman" sees and hears in Ireland and England and then in Germany and the rest of Europe this summer.

So—Here's your letter of credentials, and good luck and Bon Voyage. And don't forget, Lera, we want those first letters to start just as soon as you land—and Oh, Boy, how we are looking forward to those letters—especially that one titled "A Country Woman Sees the Coronation!"

(Oh, we almost forgot about the English girl and the Japanese girl who brought the letter in. It's this way. It seems that just after Mrs. Knox made the big decision, and wrote us the letter, a weather-beaten little Austin drove up, and out stepped Miss Priscilla Hele of Cambridge, England, and Miss Sana Mil of Osaka, Japan—to get a swig of cider at Knoxdale Café.

(The girls were returning from a Southern tour, to Madison, Wisconsin, where they are students at the University of Wisconsin. Lera Knox is a talker, and so were the girls, so they were still talking into the wee hours. They left for the North this morning with a real insight into the South—the kind of first hand insight into Ireland, England, and the Continent of Europe that Lera Knox is going to give *Herald* readers this summer.)

THE DAILY HERALD
COLUMBIA, TENNESSEE
WEDNESDAY, APRIL 29, 1953

Where To Rest My Weary Head And Cool My Swollen "Dogs"?

BY LERA KNOX

WANTED: A bed, a bunk, a cot, or even a hammock somewhere in the British Isles between May 13 and June 5.

I'll probably be glad to get a bench in Hyde Park with a *London Daily Herald* for a pillow, or maybe a cell in London Tower, if the Coronation crowds are as big as expected.

Lacking those, I'd like to borrow, beg, or buy a pair of good strong field glasses so I can watch the proceedings from the top of Eiffel Tower in Paris, if I can't get any closer.

The other day I heard a British girl, who has been in America a short time, say:

"I don't know why so many people are so crazy to see 'Lib get bopped on the bean!"

I don't know either, but I'm just so crazy that I jolly well will.

I'm leaving Columbia on that 5:45 bus next Monday, May 4th. Expect to sail from New York on S.S. *United States* at noon May 8th, and arrive in South Hampton sometime May 13th.

Meanwhile I've got to get my tourist court, restaurant, and grocery ready to be rented out while I'm gone. I've got to gather me up some "Coronation Robes," but most of all I've got to get me up some good Big Comfortable Coronation Shoes!

Shoes will probably be as important to the spectators as the two crowns are to the Queen.

At least she won't have to wear the Crowns so long, nor stand in line for the Parade. But I'll probably be trodding cobblestones for days hunting that bed, bunk, or park bench. I'll probably have to sleep on my feet, so I'd like my Coronation Shoes to be comfortable enough to sleep in.

News is that "absolutely nothing is available," and my British friends, the London editor and his wife, are leaving town for the Coronation. Margaret and Stan applied for reservations seven months ago, and they won't be sure of confirmation until May 15th.

So really (and I mean this), if any of you homefolks have any kinfolks or friends over there who might be able to spread down a Baptist pallet (or even a Presbyterian or Methodist one) in the attic I shall be eternally grateful. (And I'm not a bit particular as to the denomination or the pallet).

Or if you know where I could get some field glasses I'll be just as grateful. I promise to take a few winks on the pallet for myself, and several glimpses at the Coronation just for you.

Just call me at 2846-J, or drop me a line here at home, or at Paramount Hotel, New York, between May 5-8.

Meanwhile, I'm not packing a pup tent. But I'm learning to hum "Mister Can I Sleep In Your Barn Tonight?"

And if I don't find a Mister or a barn, I'll just hunt up a neat cozy kennel, and whine "Move over Fido, please."

I can't let a little thing like lack of a cot, or a cell, keep me from seeing 'Lib get bopped on the bean, and get kissed nine times!

THE DAILY HERALD
COLUMBIA, TENNESSEE
SATURDAY, MAY 2, 1953

Country Woman Leaves Early Monday for Coronation Trip

BY LERA KNOX

Well, there are folks and folks; good folks and bad folks; tall folks and short folks; fat folks and thin folks; but the best folks of all, as you know, are HOMEFOLKS!

We all know this all the time, but sometimes something will happen that emphasizes and clinches the fact just a little bit tighter. This proposed trip I'm planning to make to Europe, starting next Monday morning at 5:54 (I mustn't forget the time that bus leaves) is one of those things that reminds one of how nice some folks can be to some other folks.

Just a few examples: My neighbors, Fred and Frances Evans realized how badly I'd need some comfortable Coronation shoes to trod cobblestones in, to sleep in, for fear I don't get a room, and to die in (if I should be dead on foot), and offered expert assistance.

Paul Erwin offered to lend me those big, red, air-conditioned, rubber-soled "accommodations" of his. I tried them but they seemed a little large; after all, I really didn't need a yacht and baggage coach! (Please pardon me, Paul, I couldn't resist that.)

Meanwhile, George Knox is half-soling my old ones—I'm too smart, I hope to start out on so long a trip with new shoes only; and those old re-treads will come in handy for a change. But don't you think for a minute that because I've got two half-soles I won't be able to make a whole-soul trip. I do hate puns, really.

Speaking of souls and soles reminds me of another good soul, Solon Pryor. He has promised to send me some Poke Sallet, a big Maury County Special Leaf, with a copy of the *Rambler* attached. If you do that, Solon, I'll strictly promise to spread that Leaf right down in the middle of Pall Mall or Whitehall, for the Queen to ride over—just as Sir Walter Raleigh spread his coat down for Elizabeth I, to walk over. And that copy of the *Rambler* column—well, I'll hunt up the Rambling Duke of Windsor and present that to him. After all he does deserve something out of this Coronation, seeing as it's all his fault, and Wally's, that Elizabeth II is Regina. I understand that he says it's not customary for ex-kings to be present at coronations of other kings, but that he'll probably be viewing it from a window somewhere.

P.S. I hope he has better luck getting binoculars than I've had.

But back to homefolks! I was in the bank getting my Traveler's Checks when who should come striding in but Tillman Moore. He was wearing one of those comfy looking, ventilated jockey caps that men wear with such smugness.

After the usual howdydoo's I said, to make conversation and because I meant it, "I like that cap." He replied, "Thanks, I'll let you wear it sometime. Or better, I'll buy you a new one for 98 cents." So it went.

That night he called me on the phone and said: "Lera, I think I'd like to let you wear my own cap if you will. It's just six days old. And I'd like for it to see the Coronation."

Now think of neighbors like that. Not the shirt off his back, but the cap off his head, and a nearly new one at that. Of course, being a little on the Scottish order, C. T. will want that cap back when I return. It's just a loan, of course. But I don't suppose he'll mind if I get it sort of messed up with autographs of Very Important People I might meet; nor will he mind, perhaps, if I get on it a few ashes of Sir Winston Churchill's big cigar.

But, now I'm giving you fair warning, dear readers, if anything in articles to come sounds a little bit "top cap," it's all because I'm wearing Tillman's Thinking Cap. And if in the movies or TV reports of the Big To-Do you see a ventilated khaki cap waving "God Save the Queen," you'll know at once that it is that borrowed Moore Cap, autographs, ashes, and all.

And speaking of loans: I was passing the Elks' Club Stage line innocently enough when I was abruptly accosted by a portly gentleman who exclaimed; "Stand right where you are and wait 'til I come back." He then dashed inside and came back with a quarter in his hand, a marked quarter, with a big W scratched across the face. I don't know whether he borrowed the pin or the quarter, but with a flourish, before all the Elk's Club Grandstand as witnesses, "Dr. George" ordered me to take that famous Williamson Marked quarter with me wherever I went, and to bring it back with the W and all.

(By the way, you may notice in the coming articles that if the English language gets in my way when I've got something to say, it doesn't stand a chance, and neither does punctuation, but I will state this, I am in no way responsible while I'm gone for the policies of the newspapers this stuff might be printed in.)

But back to homefolks again. In addition to the Moore Cap, which might not be formal enough for the Coronation Social Events, I have a hat, not that four-year-old tam you've seen me in so much, but a brand new black ribbon-hat that I can fold up and put in my bag, or wear without knowing it's on.

Sweet little Miss Orna Colquitt fitted me up in that, and said she wished she could be a little flea and ride in that hat all the way. I wouldn't mind a flea like you, Miss Omy, but I plan to go to Scotland, and I'm sort of afraid Bobby Burns might rise up from his grave and write a poem entitled "A Flea on a Lady's Bonnet." And he'd never know at all that it was you.

Even as long as you've been putting bonnets on ladies, Bobby Burns didn't know you, I imagine.

I have heard that a new hat has been known to reduce a woman's blood pressure, and mine always needs to come down. But just to be sure, one of Columbia's good doctors and a good druggist fixed me up with some bottles of pink and red and green pills. I hope those colors will harmonize with the official Coronation Colors.

And a good foot specialist trimmed my corns and gave me some powder to make my Coronation shoes more fitting.

Ray Burt loaded up my camera, and Buster found me a nice oversize camera bag. It was so oversize I had to think up something that would fill in the extra space. Both Nature and I abhor a vacuum.

That night about 2 a.m. I happened to think that if I should be quartered in a doghouse, lacking hotel room, Fido and I might enjoy listening to BBC broadcasts of the Coronation. I called Mrs. Stanley next morning, and she said she'd find me one and even bring it out. She did just that. A 3-day battery set, just about as big as a Collegiate dictionary, and it fitted perfectly, with room for a few Kleenex and even my raincoat and camera, in Buster's big shoulder bag.

It just looks like the Lord intends for me to make this trip. He's making everything work out so nicely. I am sure that only He and Mrs. Keaton could have arranged for me to get that one Tourist berth on the S.S. *United States* at this late date.

There are dozens of other people who have called, or written, or done nice things for me in a Bon Voyage way. The *Herald and Democrat* couldn't possibly have room for all in this issue, but I'm grateful just the same, and will mention them later.

To make a long story short, everybody's trying to get me off with a bang and in a hurry. Maybe they just want to get rid of me. But what they say is "Hurry off, so you can soon be writing back." And that is just what I'm trying to do. Now you all behave yourselves while I'm gone.

And Solon, send that poke sallet leaf c/o Capt. Stanton Morgan, 0465219, 2nd Bn. 8th Regt., APO 39, c/o P.M.N.Y.C.

THE DAILY HERALD
COLUMBIA, TENNESSEE
MONDAY, MAY 11, 1953

'Country Woman' Off To Homesick Start

Lera Knox Finds Leaving Home Painful

BY LERA KNOX

Enroute Overseas, by Bus—

Dear Folks at Home:

When that bus pulled out of Columbia last Monday morning, May 4, at 5:45, the lights were still shining on the used car lots, and the weatherman was sifting out samples of what English weather may be—and me with no raincoat or overshoes. I had vowed in starting my packing that those would be the first things I'd put in.

It is surprising how many forgotten things one can remember after the bus door is closed. From the time Smith Dodson slammed that door until we got to Pottsville, I had thought up a whole trunk full. But I'll try to struggle along without them—I never use these things at home anyway, and probably would never unpack them. They were mostly "just-in-case" items.

Sitting there looking at the back of Mr. Dodson's head I felt particularly placid, even though he didn't have the toothpick he used to always chew. Back during the War Years, and for many years before, I have rushed many times breathlessly to catch that early morning bus to Nashville.

Those were the mornings when he picked up school children for Franklin, and older students and business people for Nashville. He always had that pick between his teeth, and perhaps, others in reserve. The more children he took on, the harder he chewed. And I don't believe one splinter could have held up under all that tension. I wondered if it were children, toothpicks, or merely years that account for Mr. Dodson's "store boughts" now; but strongly suspect that years have played an important part in that loss or gain. I don't like to admit it but my platinum streaks among the auburn witness the fact that Mr. D. has been jiggling the wheel of that bus for a long time. It must be nearly 25 years. That would be nearly 10,000 mornings, and there must have been times when he made more than one trip a day, perhaps or most of the time, and I have never heard of his bus having a major accident! And that's something!

I was very happy that Smith Dodson was the one who helped me get started on this long trip to Europe. It seemed a good omen. And there is, and always has been, something family-like about that early bus. I thought that morning, as we rode along in gloom, if that bus only had a fireplace it would be completely homey.

Hay! What's the matter with me? Am I getting homesick before I get to Franklin? Ah well, France will be different! You bet it will. But France, with all its man-made art, won't be any prettier to me than the Bear Creek Pike was that morning with dew-diamonds on the cedars and a chiffon veil of fog over all.

However much motorists may cuss "That Detour," we all must admit that it has a lovely way of meandering.

It is just too bad that we can't move some of the scenery off that road over to the New Highway, especially the Dr. Porter Curve—but I guess the insurance companies would object, unless we straightened out the curve, then it wouldn't be itself.

Of course Big New 31 Highway has her own beauty, her glamor, her wide and sophisticated vistas, but 99 has her charm.

I could write a poem about Highway 99, if I could write poems. I wish somebody would.

In fact I think I'll stick my neck out and make a promise that to the person, or persons, who present the best poem, prose or whatnot about 99, I will bring back a miniature of Eiffel Tower right straight; from Paris itself. I'm perfectly willing to leave details of contest and the judging to the *Herald* staff or someone selected by them. I just want to prove that

I'd give the Eiffel Tower for a true word-picture of one of our Tennessee treasures.

Of course a fast poem written about that ancient horse-and-buggy course might have a joggley meter, but it should also have a rugged individualism.

Oh they say it's rough, and all that, but starting out on a long journey like I am, I only hope that the Atlantic won't be any rougher; And I pray that I won't get any homesicker on the S.S. *United States* than I did that morning on Smith Dodson's bus, even though the bus didn't have a fireplace.

THE DAILY HERALD
COLUMBIA, TENNESSEE
TUESDAY, MAY 12, 1953

'Country Woman' Rides To New York With Columbian

BY LERA KNOX

Dear Mr. Finney:

It's just like you said:

The darndest things do happen to me!

I felt like Mrs. Astorbilt's assistant chauffeur, having reserved Seat No. 1 on the New York Express bus from Nashville. It was the seat right behind the driver so I could shudder at every turn and put on brakes going down the mountains.

I'll admit I've always been a Front Seat hog. But that old front seat ain't what she used to be, not on a New York Express. There was a wide stainless steel bar right across behind the driver's shoulders and it entirely blocked my line of vision. I had to either look over or under, and by the time we got to Murfreesboro my head had been stretched up and down so much, like a jack-in-the-box, my neck was sore. Finally I got tired and disgusted and just slumped down to relax and let the driver handle the job as best he could by himself on in to Knoxville.

When we changed buses there I very graciously let another woman have Seat No. 1 and I moved across the aisle. At Bristol I moved farther back, hoping I'd have a double seat to curl up in for the night. I didn't. Had to sleep straight up like everybody else, or not sleep. I didn't. There were three babies behind me, and two yackety women in front.

When we changed again in Washington, and left the station at about 6:00 a.m. I was on a front seat again, but not behind a rail. I'd learned to ride on the right of the driver if I were to be any help to him.

The driver seemed to be doing very well, however, so I turned attention to my seatmate. We discussed how we had or had not slept the night before, and where the coffee had been, or had not been, good. Then I asked where she got on the bus.

"Nashville," was the answer. "Do you live in Nashville?" was naturally the next question. "No, I live in New York; I've been visiting relatives and friends in Nashville and Columbia."

When you're umpty-odd miles north of Washington that word "Columbia" sounds mighty good. I perked up in my seat.

"Oh, Columbia, that's where I live. I wonder if I know the people you visited."

"Well, there was Mittie Elam—"

Miss Mittie's name never sounded so sweet. I almost rose straight up from my cushion, and left the driver entirely to his own devices.

"I adore Miss Mittie," I said, "I'm Lera Knox, was Lera Ussery."

"I'm Alice Carpenter, John Carpenter's widow."

It's a good thing the bus had a baggage shelf over seat 3 or they might have had to patch the roof!

The heroes of my childhood were not "Buster Brown and his dog Tiger" not Mule Maud and her owner Si, nor even the Katzenjammer Kids and their long-suffering Captain—but were John Trotwood Moore, and John Carpenter!

I used to try always in Church to sit on the same seat with Mr. Moore, or at least as near as I could get within worshiping distance. And I used to stand on the sidewalk near where the Magnolia tree is now on Kroger's parking lot, look through the fence and marvel at the John Carpenter House. I had heard, when they built that house, that every brick in it cost a nickel. I would stand and count the bricks, when The Racket Store could accumulate so many nickels, and then spend them for bricks when The Racket Store with its toys and dolls, and Sharp's Fruit and Candy Store were not much more than a block away (where McClellans is now).

We discussed Miss Mary Carpenter whom I admired so much because she could not only speak foreign languages but could teach them at Columbia Institute. I used to stand on the porch at the old Athenaeum and envy the girls who could be in Miss Mary's classes, for "she had been to Europe" and often told her girls about her travels! I'd have given my most prized possession, (whatever it was at that time) to be in her geography class just one day.

We also spoke of Rebecca (Mrs. Myron Millice) and Ed, whom I knew only by sight, and Virginia, whom I didn't know at all, but learned that her daughter was married to Secretary Sinclair Weeks; and John, Jr., who wore the neatest kneepants of anybody in my recollection; and dainty, frail, little Rachel, who wore very short skirts, frilly poke bonnets, and looked like a Dresden doll.

I didn't know the first Mrs. John Carpenter, but I remembered very well her dear parents, the Rev. and Mrs. Dinwiddie, of the South Columbia Methodist Church.

Mrs. Alice Carpenter told me of her home in New York, at the corner of Fifth Avenue and 98th St., which was one of the first cooperative apartments in the city. Mr. Carpenter, it seems, introduced the idea of Cooperative apartments to New York.

"He was years ahead of his time," she said.

We discussed the scenery along the Turnpike, but she declared, "It is not nearly so pretty as our Tennessee." I agreed.

In fact, I was so enthralled in conversation, I forgot that my clothes and typewriter had been checked only as far as Philadelphia. I had intended to stop off in Philly and talk with Bud Waldo of *Holiday* magazine about a possible assignment. But I was so much interested in Mrs. Carpenter's conversation I passed the city right by, and had to phone back for my baggage to follow me two days later. If I meet many more people like Alice Carpenter, I may never see the Queen of England.

THE DAILY HERALD
COLUMBIA, TENNESSEE
SATURDAY, MAY 16, 1953

Country Woman Sees New York, And TV

BY LERA KNOX

I traveled so fast from Nashville to New York that I out-ran my baggage, leaving all but my purse, camera, radio, spy-glasses, coat, and "thinking cap" in Philadelphia. The baggage master at 34th St. station phoned back to Philadelphia to have them sent up on the next bus, and suggested that I might enjoy looking around Macy's just across the street, or Gimbel's just down the street, while waiting for clothes and typewriter to arrive.

Walking into the big front door at Macy's, I thought that I must have wandered back into the Smokies themselves, except that the mobs I encountered could not have been our dear mountaineers—yes, every nationality was there except Hill Billies, so I decided to try well to represent us.

It was Macy's Gigantic, Colossal, Stupendous, Spring Flower Show, and at least half of New York and a large part of New Jersey were jammed in there.

The place was packed with azaleas, mountain laurels, dogwood trees as high as the ceiling, and many other plants all in full bloom, and as beautiful as a fairyland. The crowd seemed to get the spirit. But I soon saw I wouldn't have the heart to buy a raincoat in that beautiful mass of sunshine (artificial and) real flowers. So I pushed my way out and down to Gimbels. There in a gloomier atmosphere, I found my London regalia, a plastic raincoat, hood and overshoes. Those are probably what I'll be wearing at the Coronation.

Back to the bus station, but typewriter and suitcase had not arrived. I decided to leave their arrival up to Luck and the Greyhound, as there was little else to do, and go up to the hotel and see if I'd find a place for the night. I did, right next door to the room I had last year, but higher.

Everything in New York seems higher this year except perhaps the Empire State Building, and I didn't check on that.

I'd had orders from Mrs. Keaton to go, as soon as I arrived, to British and Irish Railways, 9 Rockefeller Plaza, about reservations for a tour of Ireland in case I couldn't find room to lay my head in Britain in this pre-Coronation rush. After much rambling around and getting into a dozen wrong places I finally found the B.I.R. office.

The man at the front desk took my name, looked through the files, and could find absolutely nothing in the way of correspondence about Knox, and nothing from Keaton.

Were the Irish going to reject me, too?

I turned around to walk out, and I must have looked like I felt, for he added, "I'm sorry, Mrs. Knox."

As I opened the door to go out onto the street, I heard another man at a neighboring desk say, “What did you call that lady? Hey, lady, what’s your name?”

I told him, and he exclaimed, “Why Mrs. Knox, I’ve been looking for you all day. I have your file and Mrs. Keaton’s file right here on my desk waiting for you. It just happened that Mrs. Keaton added a postscript to her letter asking me to look out for a room for you in London for the Coronation period, and just this morning I had a message that Charing Cross Hotel, on the Strand right in the middle of the celebration has a single room, due to a late cancellation. I’ve had four chances this afternoon to let the room go at any price, but something told me to wait for you!”

I could have hugged that man, except there was a wide desk between us. It all made me surer than ever that a very important and interested Someone or Something, be it God or Gremlin, has intended for me to take this trip.

Would I take that room in Charing Cross Hotel, just off Trafalgar Square which the procession would pass three times? Well, he could just bet I would.

I hadn’t especially relished the idea of snoozing in London Tower even though more illustrious heads than mine have ached there, and I didn’t particularly want to crowd a poor old English bulldog out of his kennel, even though I was carrying a portable radio to listen in on and a pair of James Dugger’s binoculars borrowed to look through.

I really do believe that this Coronation is going to be actually the Biggest Show on Earth, and probably the last one of its kind that will ever go down in history. All the British people with whom I have talked, and all the information I can gather seems to point to that probability. I still feel that the Something or Someone who is directing me on this trip intends for me to see that show and tell you as best I can what it is like. I shall still feel that way until the fishes or the Bobbies get me!

Rambling on around Rockefeller Center, I found I was lost again. Rounding a corner in The RCA building, or somewhere in the maze, I ran smack into the very large face of "Mr. Television" himself, Milton Berle, painted on the wide white wall.

I stopped right in my tracks, began to count on my fingers the days I had missed. Why this was Tuesday, and surely my Guiding Somebody intended me to see the Berle Show that very night. I back tracked to the nearest information desk.

Information sent me to Guest Relations; Guest Relations sent me to Press; Press called back to Guest Relations; but nobody had tickets, and nobody seemed to know how tickets could be had. It was just another one of the many impossible things in New York—to see Milton Berle, Ezio Pinza, and Rosalind Russell.

Finally, Milton Brown of the Press Department wrote a little note for me to take to a man at the theater. The man at the theater wrote another little note, and I passed that on to the

Head Usher, and she told me to tell the page at the front end of the aisle to seat me in the center section!

And that's exactly where I was when the curtain went up, and Mr. TV bounced out onto the stage and down the runway into the center of the "front and center section." Lucky for me that luck, or Something, can do things that good looks can't.

Instantly after Mr. Berle appeared on the stage, I could understand the reason for the Big Star on his dressing room door. He has a personality that is almost ELECTRIC! That's the only way I can describe what he does to an audience. He is much more handsome and younger looking than his pictures imply. The whole cast seemed to feel his influence, just as did the audience, who went almost wild with applause. When he was on stage things were definitely snapping. I had never noticed that before on the screen.

The announcer estimated that more than 35,000,000 people were looking in on that show. But I'm sure not one of those millions enjoyed Berle and Max more than I did. Ezio Pinza, also, was glorious. And when the show was over, Berle, Pinza, Russell, and Max came down the runway and we could almost have spit on each other. But I'm glad we didn't—the law of gravity would have worked against me.

THE DAILY HERALD
COLUMBIA, TENNESSEE
MONDAY, MAY 18, 1953

"Country Woman" Gets Big Thrill from New 3-D Movies As Seen In New York

BY LERA KNOX

(Written May 10 on board S.S. *United States*)—

Two things there are in New York that people never seem to tire of: one is the Automat with its excellent coffee for two nickels a cup, and its good but inexpensive food; the other is *South Pacific*. Both New Yorkers and tourists seem to want to go to these places over and over again.

One can go into the Automat at any time, but not *South Pacific*—that seems always to be sold out, even to standing room.

The play was leaving New York May 9, for a month in Boston. That is probably why Rosalind Russell's *Wonderful Town* was sold out for the entire month of June. I doubt if even a Press Personality could be wedged in sidewise to that show until it gets a lot older than it is.

During the short time I could be in New York I tried to soak up as much of Broadway as I possibly could. I had seen *South Pacific* and *Guys and Dolls* as well as several others last year.

I saw *My Three Angels* (See last *Life*); *The King and I*; *Time Out for Ginger*; *Moulin Rouge*; *Hans Christian Anderson*; and the *Cinerama*, that Lowell Thomas version of Third Dimensional movies.

As you may imagine, I wore out almost half of my half-soles trying to see all those, get some shopping done, find my lost baggage, and make some European reservations during the three days and nights I had in town. Oh yes, I also made another tour of Radio City—that's another feature of New York that is always new to new-comers. Was in the studios from which *Pepper Young's Family* and *The Doctor's Wife* originate. And caught part of the *Bob and Ray* show.

That *Cinerama* is just about the craziest seeming thing that has ever been invented so far as I can find out. Mr. Thomas calls it "a new adventure in sight and sound." But Lowell, that's putting it really mildly.

You get your ticket and go in and sit down just as you would in any other movie house. You have a complete explanation of the Thing, how it works, and are warned not to get excited, not to hoop and holler, not to stand up or get excited. But when the whole theater and everything around you begins to roar and rock and roll, and to screech and howl, you can hardly hold onto your seat or keep your hat on your head or your feet on the carpet.

Lights are out, then they are on: and you are right in the middle of a tremendously large Roller Coaster, in a Thundering Noise; like fifty million cyclones; you are zooming up and over and down and around steep inclines. You are sure that the whole world has gone star crazy; you are breathless, seasick, scared to death, completely bewildered, and yet above it all, you are mostly amused that you'd let yourself feel like such a fool.

Mr. Thomas says, in explaining the phenomenon, that you become a part of the picture. And brother, he is so right.

The picture takes up the whole view before your eyes, it is on a circular screen. That's what makes it seem all around you and gives such a very lifelike-ness to the scene. The sound, also, comes not from the screen or the control box, but from all around you. The loudspeakers are on all the walls, and seem also to be under your chair.

After the violent Roller Coaster ride, you settle down again to catch your breath and wish you were home; then appears a magnificent ballet in extremely rich coloring, and you feel that you are on the stage right in the midst of the "Rockettes." You feel almost that you could touch them. Yet you know all the time that it is merely a movie. But what a movie!

By the time you have blinked your eyes twice the ballet is over and you are in a white marble church, and service is beginning beautifully. The white robed choir walks slowly down the side aisles near you. A minister big as life and twice as natural reads in tones that sound as though he were speaking from the seat next to you.

On the whole, the production gives you a tremendous sense of realness, a feeling of being better than on the spot. Whatever happens in the show is happening to you!

Next, you are in Venice in a gondola, listening to the softly singing boatman, and you sit all scrunched up and very still to keep from rocking the boat.

A blackout, sudden change, and you are before Edinburgh Castle at a meeting of the Clans. Colorful plaids, swinging kilts, and piping bagpipes almost make you start marching and singing with them.

Shortly you are in Austria, right in the midst of a beautiful Boy's Choir; from that to a bull fight in Spain, where you can hear the audience in Spain and the people around you sigh and cheer in unison.

A quick hop and you are helicoptering over New York City. Then over Niagara—there the film almost adds a fourth dimension. You can practically feel the dampness of the spray.

Another quick change and explanations and you are flying over the waterfront in Chicago, then over the geysers in Yellowstone. You catch your breath and duck, or at least I did, when the pilot dared to fly us under the Golden Gate

Bridge. Over Yosemite Falls, back and quickly across the Grand Canyon, and I swayed with the plane as the pilot banked and turned, and I was sure he'd clip his wings in his daringly close flight along the cliffs of the canyon and almost down to the river below. The *Cinerama* way of seeing the Canyon is a lot faster than the Donkey way down Angel Trail.

After those chilling and thrilling sights in the Canyon I thought sure that the pilot would bring us back by Knoxdale so I could see if the hollyhocks at my house are in bloom yet, and then perhaps by the Hermitage. And I wouldn't have been surprised—in this miracle of sound and sight—to see Uncle Alfred chopping wood there in the back yard, or to hear the darkies singing at "My Old Kentucky Home."

But not so. We were on to Washington, back to New York, then we got instead an explanation of how it was all done. It was like a magician explaining his tricks after the lights were on again.

It seems that Fred Waller, and friend Lowell Thomas, have worked untiringly for fifteen years and have spent millions of dollars in research and experiments developing *Cinerama*. They say it's all done with a three-eyed camera, taking front and side views at the same time, a huge concave screen made up of hundreds of overlapping vertical tapes (to kill the flatness of the picture); and a battery of semi-directional microphones.

Now if you know what those things are and how they could all be put together, you know how *Cinerama* is presented.

On my way out of the theater, after I'd gotten my sea-legs and perspective straightened out, I couldn't help but think of an incident that had happened just before I left my hotel for the show.

Mrs. Cecil, of Mt. Pleasant, on her way to *Casa Blanca*, had called from her hotel wanting me to tour the town with her that night. I already had my *Cinerama* ticket which I didn't want to waste, so I asked her instead to go with me.

She said, no, she really didn't care to see 3-D, that they had already had that in Mt. Pleasant about three weeks ago.

Well, what I said to myself after that show at Broadway Theater was this. "Well, I never do know what is going on around among my neighbors, but if Mt. Pleasant has had an "attack" of *Cinerama* like I got it that night—well, poor, rich, Mt. Pleasant!"

THE DAILY HERALD
COLUMBIA, TENNESSEE
MONDAY, MAY 25, 1953

Country Woman Sails on Sea-Going "Pot"

Mrs. Knox Enjoys Safety, Meals and Speed

BY LERA KNOX

(Special to the *Daily Herald*)—

Perhaps the World's Biggest Aluminum Pot, she is the S.S. *United States*—990 feet long; 101 feet 6 inches broad; 12 stories (or decks) high; capable of carrying about 2,000 paying passengers and a crew of 1,000 for 10,000 miles without docking to replenish fuel and supplies; and weighing a mere 51,500 tons, whereas her big rival the *Queen Elizabeth* weighs 83,673 tons and is 2 1/2 feet shorter—truly a big vessel!

And can she go? Boy, when that big pot "boils" out across the Atlantic, all the fishes, the other ships, and even the unknown monsters of the deep, had better mind the waves. What her exact capacity for speed really is, few people know. That might be an essential military secret someday; but it is known that she can do 30 to 35 knots or better (a knot according to my nautical information is 1 1/6 mile). It is a matter of record that she crossed the Atlantic last summer on her maiden voyage in a little more than 3 days. And the Atlantic is a lot of ocean to be kicked under the stern of one big floating city in the span of a long weekend.

And modern, every inch of her! When I tell you that her cooks roast their good meats by radar, what more can I say? Television? Well, not exactly, nor 3-D either, so far as I learned; but I shouldn't be surprised to find even those and other newfangled gadgets when I see her again, Sept. 24, on my return trip. Whatever that ship does won't surprise me in the least. She's so much like the United States—without Congress!

Perhaps the Powers That Plow Her Through The Waves won't like to know that I compare her to a "pot," but to me that is the nearest word I can think of, and not having a thesaurus among my luggage, "pot" is the word I'm stuck with. Albeit, she is a most magnificent, ultra modern streamlined, rakish, beautiful, and altogether lovely and pleasant air-conditioned Melting Pot.

She is so much like the United States you really don't realize that you are out of New York until you look out and see the waves, or until you feel the decks and corridors rock beneath you. The sidewalks of New York are a bit steadier and they do have shops, shows, and neon all around instead of stateroom doors; but as for the people you meet in the passages, and the crew that work around you, they are like the great admixture of nations you see in the big city, only more concentrated, therefore perhaps more noticeable.

It must be like a real U.N. As a German steward remarked, of himself and his fellows—Chinese, Spanish, French, Finish, American Negro, English, Floridian, and what-not—"We work together, fight together, drink together, sleep together, and have our good jokes together." And I find that altogether they are a pretty good lot, and typically American.

It takes a lot of stewards to "stew" a big vessel like the S.S. *United States* and to keep her on even keel, believe me it does. And it is perhaps for their own protection that they are union to the "bone." In fact, that seemed to be the passengers' main bone of contention. The Union was always getting in our way.

When I wanted my suitcase from the baggage room so I could wash nylons and go to bed, I had to wait for Union Regulation. Stewards were "off" at that particular moment. Next time by golly, I'll try to get a union card and tote bags myself. I can't let Unions keep me out of my pajamas. Or maybe, I'll tuck a "union suit" under my arm, or smuggle it in my shoulder bag.

The poor ship owners, it seemed to me (and I can so easily be wrong for you see I had only a glimpse in passing) cannot sift and select, hire and fire the crew as they please. Instead they take what the Union sends. And the Union, perhaps, cannot be too particular either, seeing that dues are dues. That's just the way it seemed to me, and I'll gladly swallow my impressions if they are wrong. But these seemed to have been the impressions of other passengers too, so a lot of folks will have to do a lot of swallowing.

We were only too thankful that the Union permitted us to get out of the port, which is more than could be said for the poor *Ile De France*, a lovely ship indeed, if she is like her big sister the *Liberté* which I rode and loved last summer. The *Ile* was struck to the docks by a strike of some kind, I understood; and passengers on the S.S. *United States* had to double up on an already crowded ship to make room for 75 of the more urgent French Line passengers.

Next to stewards that didn't "stew" exactly as passengers would have always liked them to do, the only other criticism I could hear of the S.S. *United States* was that her decks did rock, more perhaps than if she had been a heavier, fatter, slower Old Lady of the Sea.

Being so tall, so slim, and so fast, she made many of the passengers, including me feel that a bunk is man's best friend—and woman's too. Seasick—well, not exactly. You know I'd hate to admit that. I ate well, slept well, rested much. I seemed always deliciously tired. Especially did I eat well. I've heard that seasickness is worse if you've got "nothing to lose." And I resolved that if I were obliged to feed the fishes I'd see that those fishes would be well nourished.

Where else on land or sea could one find such an excellent and varied assortment of foods other than aboard a great "melting pot" such as the S.S. *United States*?

Each menu truly had an international flavor; for instance, French meat salad; stuffed Philadelphia chicken; baked Idaho potatoes; King cake; Queen olives; Pumpernickel; H-O oats; Pate de Foi Gras on toast; baked tuna fish steak; prime ribs of beef au Jus; American breakfast bacon; broiled kippered herring; Camembert cheese; Zwieback; Amlettes a la Reine; Julienne of Yorkshire ham in cream on toast; country sausages; California fruit cocktail; green gage plums; Neapolitan ice cream, huckleberry pie; fresh lobster (perhaps from Maine); Royal Ann cherries; Vienna Mocha layer cake; Swiss, Gorgonzola or Luxembourg cheeses; Maryland turkey with giblet gravy and cranberry sauce; and believe it or not, New Orleans chicken gumbo.

The only things I can think of that they might have missed would have been some good old Tennessee turnip greens, hog jowl, "poke sallet," black-eyed peas, and hoecake. But I forgave this omission. Even those indescribable delicacies would not have tasted good after the gala dinner we had on Monday night. And I didn't give a swallow to the fishes!

As to the navigation and general management of the ship, I felt satisfied, after the first afternoon aboard, to leave those more or less minor items to the seemingly very efficient Commodore John Anderson and his mates. I will say that the matter that came to my attention most of all on board was the utmost precautions taken for safety. We met and experienced Sensations of Safety on every hand.

I liked the air-conditioned cabins and the tailor-made temperatures all over the ship. I liked the fresh sea breezes, and the good company of other passengers. But most of all I liked to lie down on my bunk and feel, "Thanks to God and a good Captain, I never had it so safe." The fire drills were really thorough, even on this gigantic all Aluminum Pot.

THE DAILY HERALD
COLUMBIA, TENNESSEE
TUESDAY. MAY 26, 1953

Country Woman Writes Letter to Editor of London Paper

Mrs. Knox Learns British Ways Quickly

BY LERA KNOX

(Between Hotels in London,
13 days before Coronation, 1953)—

Dear John,

I thought I might as well write to you this morning, as that is the way I feel, and explain my actions and inactions of the past several days.

I arrived in this Big City a week ago last night, expecting to go right into a Conducted Tour of Ireland and one of Scotland so I would be sure of room reservations for at least two weeks. But my boat train from Southampton, the harbor town, arrived in London two hours later than my train for Ireland was supposed to leave. So there I was, in a full town with no place to go.

I had the names, and names only, of two hotels: The Charing Cross, at which I had been promised a room from May 29 to

June 4, and the Victor, where Margaret and Stan expected to stay during the Coronation.

I thought I might also appeal to the British Travel Agency or to a kindly policeman in case of desperation. But I started my Taxi toward Charing Cross. That seemed the biggest and the bestest. The hotel was full for the time. But the clerk phoned the Victor, and they took me in.

I've been very comfortable, despite no tub or shower, which I didn't expect anyway, for the whole week. And today Charing Cross will have room for me, according to agreement. So I'm moving there at noon today.

I'm still believing that my best way of making this trip is to turn my hunches loose and follow them, though dear knows where and to what they may lead. That's a great part of the fun of it.

On the morning of the third day I waked up with the idea that I should perhaps write a little note of thanks to London, telling her just exactly how I felt about certain situations. I did just that.

Then, how to present it to London?

Through a newspaper, of course. Everybody seems to read every newspaper here. It is seldom you see a man or woman here without a paper in hand.

I had heard that Fleet Street is Newspaper Street in London, so I asked the conductor of the big red double-decker "Doodlebug" bus to put me off at Fleet Street—a big order.

The first office I wandered into was the *Edinburgh Express*, or something like that. But they all seemed too busy to notice me, so I ambled on down the street to another big and impressive street to another big and impressive-looking black building. The *London Express*, it said. I'd heard that is Lord Beaverbrook's paper, and as I remember, a much-quoted one.

The man at the door might have been Lord Beaverbrook himself, or he might have been a porter, or a doorman, or what they call an inspector (which I don't understand), or he might have been Mr. Scotland Yard, or one of the Queen's Guards. At any rate he was much-dressed-up and he looked important, and wanted to know my business. I told him, frankly, that I had a letter to London.

He sent the letter somewhere upstairs, and I sat down to wait. Meanwhile, I chatted very pleasantly with a London visitor from Virginia.

Shortly after, Mr. Uniform called me to the telephone, and a very pleasant lady's voice told me that the person who would see me is the Feature Editor, but that she could not make an appointment for me to see him before three o'clock the next Monday. Would that be agreeable?

"Agreeable? Well, of course! And Certainly! And Thank you very much!"

And then she asked me to turn the phone back over to the Commissioner, and she would explain matters and procedures to him. So that was his title. Mr. Uniform was not Lord Beaverbrook nor the doorman, but The Commissioner.

Therefore, I've marked in my book of Things-to-be-remembered that I must put on my best nylon bib and tucker, and my gloves, and next Monday afternoon at 3:00, I am to call on the Feature Editor, Mr. Hern, of the *London Daily Express.*

After this appointment was made I heard that the *Express* is the largest newspaper in the world, with a circulation of 4 1/2 million! And that it seems primarily a feature paper. So I've got four days to tremble in my half-soles.

It will be a great experience to receive "Regrets. Space limitations" from a man like that. (The lady kept the letter. I'll enclose you a copy.)

Now as to why I haven't written, or why I haven't sent you an article yet.

I wrote one about the trip over on the S.S. *United States.* But while I went out for lunch, leaving my papers and notes on the table that I use for a desk, my very clean little Italian maid came in a cleaned up the room, confiscating all my thoughts and ideas to the London Scrap Paper Drive, which was probably a proper place for them after all.

As for London, well I can hardly see the city for the decorations. They cover everything, even the street names and numbers. But I'm getting around, perhaps as much as the Londoners did in the Great Black Fog of last winter. And I'm stuffing all my future notes in my bosom, for maid-protection.

As soon as I get moved to my more permanent address at Charing Cross Hotel today, I'll try to send something else.

THE DAILY HERALD
COLUMBIA, TENNESSEE
THURSDAY, MAY 28, 1953

Country Woman Sees the Tower Of London

Mrs. Knox Learns History Firsthand; Sees Crown Jewels On Last Day Shown

BY LERA KNOX

Any story, or group of stories, about London, or England, should certainly begin, it seems, with a story of "The Cradle of the Empire," the Tower of London.

Never had I imagined that such a stack of stones could have such an important and thoroughly interesting history until I visited, then revisited, that place. And I think I shall go back again.

In the eighth grade, English history was merely a red-backed book which I carried to class, crammed for exams, and got uncertain grades in.

But standing on Raleigh's Walk, looking out over the busy Thames, or down, at a corner of an old Roman wall, built 1,900 years ago, or up at the spires of The Great White Tower, and the palace-prison which William the Conqueror had built of stones

This is not London Bridge coming down but Tower Bridge going up, to let some big ships come through to unload in "The Pool" beyond which the big ships can't go. It is one of the 13 of 19 bridges that an aviator recently flew under "to make a fitting finish to 41 years' of flying," he said. It nearly scared Londoners as bad as the blitz. I snapped this picture from The Traitors Gate, which I didn't enter.

imported from Normandy in 1078; and imagining a parade of ghosts led by Sir Thomas Moore, including Anne Boleyn, Katherine Howard, and the two little murdered Princes, Henry VI (stabbed at prayer), Lady Jane Grey and her beheaded husband, Sir Walter Raleigh, hundreds of others, and ending (I hope) with Rudolph Hess, the Deputy Fuhrer—I gained a tremendous new respect for, and interest in English history.

Our well-informed guide, and the well-uniformed Yeomen Warders (known as beef-eaters, which they don't do so much now), with the famous Tower Ravens thrown in for atmosphere, together with the stocks, and racks, and dark prison cells, with walls 15 feet thick, and a very efficient looking beheading block, and other such "props" gave us all some spinal prickles that Hollywood could hardly produce.

"In truth, there is no sadder spot on Earth" is what Macaulay said of The Tower. And I'm not in a mood to argue with him.

Looking down at Traitor's Gate, which was the entrance where prisoners were brought in from the river, I could imagine why they left all hope behind. I could chuckle, however, over how the princess, later Queen, Elizabeth I refused absolutely to enter by that gate, because, as she said, she was not a traitor. But how, shortly after, she entered the gate in order to escape one of those famous London rainstorms. Weather can sometimes accomplish what guards and soldiers can't. How like that same Elizabeth, eccentric as she was said to be, to insist on entering The Tower later by that same Traitor's Gate—after she became Queen.

I can imagine her having tea in what is known as the Queen's House, where her mother Anne Boleyn was a prisoner, and looking out on the Tower Green where Anne's head was hacked off with a French sword, as she insisted, rather than with the regular executioner's axe.

It's a gory business, but so is most of the history of the Bloody Tower. I could imagine Lady Jane Grey, for nine days Queen of England, and only seventeen years old, tripping and stumbling over those stones I stood on, to have her own head chopped off. The record says that she stumbled because her shoes were raised (in other words, high heels). But having just seen her husband beheaded, and being the young thing that she was, her nerves were probably not too steady anyway.

I could understand that *The History of the World*, written by Sir Walter Raleigh in such a cell as the one I saw, couldn't be too cheerful; and I wonder how he could get so much information, and how he did his research surrounded by walls like those.

One cheerful aspect however, was the narrow, walled, ledge on which the author could walk and I noticed that it was near enough to the River that though he couldn't jump in, he could at least call back and forth to the sailors down on the wharf.

For other stories of the Tower of London you can dust off your old red-backed English History book, or turn to *Encyclopaedia Britannica*. But you won't get the real-life feeling of history that I got standing there scared, on the sacred spot. It was marvelous.

And while we were touring the castle and looking over the gruesome objects from such bloody, by-gone days, a group of soldiers were drilling out in front. Clap, clap, clap, their feet beat on the cobblestones. The shouts and howls and yelps and "orders" given by a rough-and-gruff voiced sergeant made me feel all the more nervous and creepy. I looked about more than once to see if somebody had been left in the racks, stocks, or dungeons.

A palace; a prison; a fortress; a mint; a chapel; a banquet hall; a menagerie for British lions; a knight's barracks with stables attached; a place regarded with love, hatred, foreboding, fear, yes, and even a certain degree of glamour—that's the Tower of London. And I was glad that I got a comfortable hotel room and didn't have to apply for a night's lodging there.

But it has its beauty, too; not only in its architecture and its antiquity, but in certain of its contents. It is there, in Wakefield Tower, one of the thirteen towers that have later been added, that the magnificent collection of English regalia, or Crown Jewels, is kept.

I walked up some steep and narrow tricky stairs to come face to face with the greatest array of gold and gems and glitter that is to be found anywhere in the world, perhaps.

They were all to be taken out the next day to be made ready to use at Westminster Abbey, June 2, but with the exception of the two very important crowns (their absence marked by the presence of two empty velvet pillows), they were all there in magnificent array.

Again it was my good luck to visit The Tower on the very last day they could be seen. I stared goggle-eyed at the real genuine Royal Scepter, bearing the Great Star of Africa, a diamond that seemed almost as large as my fist, weighing, they said, 530 carats, and the largest cut diamond in the world. If the Tower had not been so dark inside we would have probably needed shaded glasses to look at it.

Many of the jewels are comparatively new, dating only from the 17th century, all because of that Cromwell fellow who didn't like kings. He put most of the old royal heirlooms, including even Alfred the Great's crown, into a melting pot and turned them all into money or something for the common people, or so they say over here.

But there's much left, or made within the past 400 years, to give plenty of glitter to the Westminster Episode, soon to take place.

Despite scepters and crowns and maces and rings and orbs and trumpets, and such the two little objects that interested me most were the little Gold Eagle bottle, or Ampula, from which the Holy Oil will be poured into the ancient Anointing Spoon, and used to anoint the Queen in the form of a Cross on her forehead, her breast, and in the palms of both hands.

If I don't get any closer to the Coronation than that, I still have seen the Sceptre, the Rings, the Orbs, the Spurs of Knighthood, and the cushions that wear the Crowns more than the Queen ever will, and the Ampula and the Spoon that will hold the Oil that will make a Queen. And I've seen The Cradle (if not the Grave) of the Empire.

THE DAILY HERALD
COLUMBIA, TENNESSEE
FRIDAY, MAY 29, 1953

Country Woman Visits Kin on London Stage

Mrs. Knox Gets Chuckles from British Humor, Sees the Sights of London the Hard Way

BY LERA KNOX

Well, well, well, you never can tell what a day of adventuring in and around a city like London is likely to bring forth. Mr. Pepys was right. I agree that perhaps the best way to do London is by the dairy method. It seems that at least two newspapers here, and perhaps more, have sort of roving reporters, or general reporters, who do daily dairy columns.

Yesterday morning I waked up with an idea of writing a sort of little thank you note to my dear friend London to tell her how I feel about her and share with her some of the chuckles I've had here, but I'm not quite "sure-footed" yet as to how I tread around among the British sense of humor. I've heard however that the Britisher gets his laughs from understatement, while Americans howl over exaggerations. London is big enough for both.

I heard so much about be-headings at The Tower of London I'm afraid it was beginning to affect my photography by the time I got to Picadilly where I snapped this. Sorry to behead this old animal. Notice the scaffolds in the back. All London that is on the procession route is being scaffolded for seats for Coronation.

The Old Curiosity Shop is still doing a thriving business. Of course I had to buy a Dickens book here for the grandchildren.

I stopped in Ye Old Tobacco Shoppe where Beau Brummell bought his snuff, but as I don't use his brand I didn't make a purchase there.

I wrote the note; put on my raincoat; gathered up camera, binoculars and a candy bar for lunch and started out, counting my errands for the day on five fingers.

First, to see Miss Elizabeth Andrews, Secy. to the President of the Association of American Correspondents in London to pick up my Scotland Yard Pass for the Coronation, and my invitation to the American Ambassador's party on June 1; and ticket for the General George Marshall luncheon on June 3. Those errands seemed important. They were all on one finger.

The address I had was c/o Columbia Broadcasting System, 26, Hallam Street, which seemed simple enough. I asked the conductor on the bus I boarded at the hotel door. He suggested that I get off at Victoria Station, which is centrally located, and ask an inspector to show me the right way.

The inspector suggested that I take either No. 16 or 38 and get off at Piccadilly. I took 16; asked the ticket man on that bus where to get off to go to 26 Hallam Street. He didn't know, but a lady across the aisle suggested that I go to the Marble Arch and turn left. I did, and found myself walking the entire length of Oxford Street to get back to where I should have gotten off at first.

To make a long story less painful—couldn't shorten the wandering, for I rambled from 9:30 a.m. until 1:30 p.m. hunting Hallam Street and asking anybody I saw who wore an official-looking cap—I finally found a little boy with a messenger's cap, and told him my story. He looked at the address on the letter I'd had from Miss Andrews, and said.

"Oh, what you want is Alum Street."

There it was. I'd forgotten again. All that four hours of walking and being lost, just simply because of one little "H" which I 'ad'nt dropped.

The boy showed me right to the door.

Next I had to find Thos. Cook & Sons office on what I had heard pronounced as Barclay Street. But when I found the place, it was on Berkley Street. After so long a time I will remember that Derby is Darby, so Berkley would naturally be Barkley. I thought, too, that I had studied the King's English in school.

But it seems that the Queen's English is not exactly the King's English. Or maybe I'm the Johnny who is out of step. I just must remember my "er's" and "H's" if I don't want to do a lot more unnecessary stepping.

There were some pictures I had to pick up near Piccadilly Circus, so I rambled back there enjoying the crowds and the magnificent decorations that are going up on every hand. One particularly was impressive, so I stopped and waited for a little sunlight to make a picture.

The sun is very obliging that way. It will peep out every now and then as though just to see what we're doing, and if you are quick you can snap a picture before it winks back into the gloom again.

Then you put up your umbrella again. The greatest activity in London, I would say, besides putting up scaffolds for decorations, is putting umbrellas up and down, and folding and unfolding raincoats.

But the particular decoration I especially liked was a large figure of Queen Elizabeth II on a horse, beside a huge picture of the first Queen Elizabeth in a picture.

On the other side quoted from Elizabeth II, evidently, was: "...with a new faith in the old and splendid beliefs given us by our forefathers, and the strength to venture beyond the safeties of the past, I know we shall be worthy of our duties. 1953"

With a queen like that I think that the British people will get along very well.

But by that time I could find several good reasons for a cup of tea, two of the reasons being my feet.

It is a wonder what tea will do for tired feet and a limp disposition. I was soon out looking for more London to conquer. Remembering that Margaret had suggested that I must visit The Old Vic Theatre, I caught a Waterloo bus, and got there in time to get the last seat in the house, so box office said, and which I didn't doubt judging by the crowds around.

It was still a couple of hours or so before show time so I decided to take in another museum, The Imperial War Museum, where I saw original Rockets and buzz bombs, and planes, and hosts of murderous stuff, then started back to the theatre by a short cut through the slums. All would have been well, I supposed, if I had been minding my own business, but I couldn't resist asking a little boy pushing a pram if the baby inside was a little brother or a little sister. Promptly he shouted up at me, "Shut up!" And with what emphasis.

I did, and took even a shorter cut to the theatre, stopping only for what the British call, with characteristic understatement, a Coca Cola. "Slop" would have been a shorter and more accurate word for it, I thought. But perhaps it was my feet-affected mood.

They were to play *Henry the Eighth* by one William Shakespeare, which seemed a very appropriate play for these times in England, seeing he was the father of Elizabeth I. I got into the theatre after the lights were dimming, so I didn't notice my program until intermission.

Imagine how I felt to read that the person playing Cardinal Woolsey so excellently was one "Alexander Knox." There was something strikingly familiar about that name, being as I've been married to an "Alexander Knox" long enough to have two children.

I explained the matter to an usherette, and gave her my card to prove it. After the show, she asked me to go backstage. Imagine appearing at Stagedoor of "The Old Vic" in London saying, "Mrs. Alexander Knox to see Mr. Alexander Knox." There's something very homey about London.

He's a charming person, even half out of grease paint, and very friendly and gracious. He's living in town now, but trying to get outside where the five-year-old son will have a place to play.

I was trying to think what films I had seen him in. He said, "Was it *The Wilson Story*? *Sister Kenny*?" He named several others, and movie-ignorant that I am, I had to shake my head. Then at last he struck it.

I'll Climb The Highest Mountain. That was it. I remembered very well then.

And he remembered best, "the beautiful hills and valleys in Tennessee, and the excellent fishing." I did, too, especially the hills and valleys, but I'm not a fisherman. So maybe we are not such close kin.

London (UP)—

It would take 13 trucks and trailers to carry all the principal characters from the novels of Charles Dickens, coronation pageant organizers have found.

The organizers will include a Dickens display in their pageant at Southwark—where Dickens once lived, and where he set the scenes of several novels.

The 13 trucks and trailers will be headed by "Dickens" himself, seated at a writing desk.

Nearly all the Dickens' characters in the procession will be portrayed by the Dickensian Tabard Players—a group of amateur and professional actors who play excerpts from Dickens' novels in their spare time.

THE DAILY HERALD
COLUMBIA, TENNESSEE
SATURDAY, MAY 30, 1953

Country Woman Gets "The Leaf" From Home

Poke Sallet to Be Real Part of Coronation

BY LERA KNOX

Written at Charing Cross Hotel, 6:30 a.m. May 28, 1953—

Dear Solon Pryor, and Everybody Else Back Home:

The will of you people shall be obeyed. The "Poke Sallet Leaf" (Spell it Polk if you want to, but it is still poke to me) arrived in due time and in good condition (after going to Germany and two London Hotels). In fact I think it is "fit for a king" and I shall place it carefully in the pathway of the Royal Couple.

> (Editor's Note: Mrs. Knox had requested some local friends to send her something to "remind her of home," so Mr. Pryor of the *Herald* and others mailed her a single leaf of 'poke sallet' and a clipping of a current *Rambler* column.)

In watching on television you may not be able to distinguish it exactly, but, as I think now, I shall place it on the one spot of all the Processional Route which the Queen will pass over three times. That is Trafalgar Square, which isn't a square at all, but a sort of traffic circle around the huge Nelson monument and column with four enormous lions around it.

It is the meeting place of The Mall which Her Majesty will travel coming from Buckingham Palace, and Whitehall, over which she goes to Westminster Abbey. The two streets make a V meeting at Trafalgar. Making a base for the V is Northumberland Avenue, leading down to Victoria Embankment which is a whole street reserved for children. So she will cross Trafalgar there too. And returning from the Real Crowning, wearing all the glamorous Regalia and Robes, the "Undoubted" Queen will again crush the lowly Poke Sallet Leaf of Maury County for the third time.

By that time, I would judge, it will be as thoroughly a part of the Coronation as the Shamrock Leaf of Ireland, The Daffodil of Wales, The Thistle of dear old Scotland, and the wild pink Tudor Rose of England. Being as it was a young and tender leaf to begin with, it probably wouldn't cost much to return the Leaf to Maury by air mail, but I won't try to find what's left after this Biggest Mob in the World tramples it.

Incidentally, this piece of Freakish Luck which sent me over here, giving me the last berth on the S.S. *United States*, the last available room in one of the best Hotels in London, the last seat at the Famous Old Vic Theater to see my "Cousin-in-law"

(Alexander Knox) play Cardinal Woolsey in *Henry VIII* is now seeming to do some other peculiar tricks.

My hotel window is closer to Trafalgar Square than the *Herald* is to the Courthouse at home. But some thoughtless characters of history (or commerce) (or both) have carefully or carelessly put up a lot of tall buildings between me and Mr. Nelson.

It's one time I'd like to be a pigeon. The pigeons of Trafalgar Square really have it grand. They seem to have a longtime lease on the whole place, including the monument, and they are given all the honor and all the food that pigeons could possibly consume.

Or a cat! I'd be even a Cat for a Day. Londoners really like their cats. I haven't seen one in a delicatessen window as I did on Sixth Avenue, in New York, but there are plenty here, and they seem to have full sway.

I haven't noticed a one of them carrying a yellow Scotland Yard Press Card, such as I have, with the official stamp of London's "Metropolitan Police New Scotland Yard" spread right across the nose and most of the chin on my passport picture. But the cats get by. Can I resist chanting "Pussy cat, pussy cat, where have you been?" And do you suppose that the answer would be, "I've been up to London to look at the Queen." It might well be.

To me it seems that the whole world, or at least a large part of it, is here. It's like the biggest Mule Day we ever had multiplied by four figures.

If ever a place could be said to have a tremendous attack of DECORATE-ITIS, this is that place. You've never imagined so much bunting, flags, and flowers in all your life. I only hope that Highway 31 will be as pretty when the Garden Clubs get through with it as some of these streets are here.

One business man told me that the places on his little street, which is not even near the route, had spent an average of 40 pounds, about $100 each, on their places. And that much money will buy a lot of covering for a small storefront in England.

The fact is that visitors can't see the city for the decorations. The fact that street names and numbers are covered up doesn't help much. And the fact that the town is laid off like a patchwork quilt still doesn't help. But somehow we all manage to get around, or seem to.

But I started to say about my hotel room being so close to the main point in the route, Trafalgar Square, and about the way my erstwhile Luck is serving me. My situation is like this: I applied for my pass, and paid my money for my ticket, and now the news comes up that my seat will probably be in Stand 5, East Carriage Drive, which is somewhere between Hyde Park Corner and Marble Arch.

In other words, it's like this. My room is just in behind the *Herald* Office, which is fine. The procession will cross the corner of West 7th and Garden three times—but I'm blocked off by the Woldridge Building. Now the Procession will go out Pulaski Pike, by good old "Knoxdale," and through the Metropolis of McCains, turn across to the Borough of Bigbyville, and back the Campbellsville Pike. And to the Woldridge corner again and back to Courthouse which I am imagining as Buckingham Palace.

Now the thing that the Gremlins (or Luck, or What-not) have done to me has been to assign me a seat somewhere between Mynders School and Bigbyville store porch. And I must be there before 6:00 a.m., and the parade won't pass until 4:00 p.m. or thereabouts.

Now if you had to go from the *Herald* office to Bigbyville before 6:00 a.m. and take your lunch, your camera, your raincoat, cushion, umbrella, radio, typewriter, et cetera, and through crowds of people as thick as Johnson Grass in a river bottom, just how would you arrange it?

Well, I happen to have a friend among the powers that "pull," a taxi driver whose son I complimented on a television program, and I do believe he is my friend. I have his telephone number, but whether he can get to me in my distress I don't know. That remains to be seen.

And now news comes to me that there will be a dozen or more television sets in a dozen or more lounge rooms right here in the hotel, and I could stay right here in an easy chair and watch and hear the whole proceedings—but I won't do it, at least I don't think I will.

Me and that Poke Sallet Leaf have come a far piece to see Queen first hand, and we are going to be found trying.

The highest priced lumber that history has ever known is what we've bought for this coronation; and I'm going to get my money's worth. For some of the seats I understand that people are paying 50 pounds, or about $150, to occupy 15 inches of hard rough oak board for 7 hours or more. Mine being a "Press Seat," it is only about $11.20, but I'm going to press that seat all that day, I think. Of course I'll place The Leaf carefully in a place of Honor on Trafalgar Square, if there is room for it to be wedged in between so many people. And it is a question of which will look worse after C-Day, the Leaf or I!

THE DAILY HERALD
COLUMBIA, TENNESSEE
MONDAY, JUNE 1, 1953

Country Woman Tells London It's Her 'Tea'

Mrs. Knox Writes about Her First Impressions

Editor's Note: Today we present, on the eve of the Coronation, the first impressions of Mrs. Knox on landing in London, as written by our correspondent to a London Newspaper, the *Daily Express*, and giving in her own inimitable style a capsule resume of the views of a Tennessee woman on first seeing London—designed for the reading of Londoners.

BY LERA KNOX

May 19, 1953

Hello Britain:

I am a Tennessee farm woman enroute to Germany to visit my daughter, and my son-in-law who is with the American Army near Frankfurt.

Without special invitation I stopped here to attend your Big Party, and I am having a wonderful time.

As I said, I came in without invitation, but what seemed worse, I barged on in without reservation, knowing only the

Coronation Traffic Jam

LONDON—This aerial photo, taken Saturday, shows cars streaming under coronation arches on the Mall as they make their way towards Buckingham Palace (background), during coronation rehearsal. (United Press TELEPHOTO)

names of two hotels in all of London, and doubting whether those or any hotels or homes might have room for me, or for any unexpected guests.

I confess I had visions of a stone pillow in the Tower of London, or of a newspaper pallet on a Hyde Park bench or I thought that if worse came to worse, I might "go to the dogs" and plead, "Move over, Fido, please."

Rather a silly stunt, to start out alone for a strange country not knowing where I'd lay my weary head and bathe my aching feet, but prospects of seeing my children and attending a Coronation made me too reckless to turn down the one available ship berth for an Atlantic crossing.

From Nursery Rhymes I've heard of your sovereigns; and from school days I've read of heroes. And I had the impression that your sovereigns wore robes and crowns, and that your heroes had turned to dust and monuments.

But not so.

The impression I have now, after being here a few days, is that your real sovereigns, the men and women on the street, wear raincoats rather than robes, and that your heroes are too damp to be dusty.

Putting my predicament and impressions Biblically, "I was a stranger and you took me in."

To realize the full impact of those words you would have to be a foreigner, a country woman, getting off a boat train in Waterloo Station rather late on a rainy night, besieged by what might seem like (if you were scared) a wolf-pack of taxi drivers.

But they really were not like wolves at all, once you got your American ear tuned in on the particular brand of English they drawl.

The one to whom I finally trusted my destiny and destination took only nine of my mysterious shillings (I offered him a hand full of metal coins), when the meter read six. But he insisted that he would accept American dollars, about two would be right, seeing as how I didn't as yet understand English money. I paid in shillings!

But be it redounded to my honor and glory, by the time I paid for a cup of tea the next afternoon, I could count even pence.

Whether this precocity was due to some few drops of British blood exported on the Mayflower, and passed on to me through some particular ancestors, or whether it comes from a bit of the Scots that I acquired by marriage (name Knox) I'll never know, but now I know the difference between the big pennies and the little ones, and I can distinguish between a sixpence and a dime, I think.

Next, what do I think of London? After being here a few days I'd say that the most of your city people are like the best of our country people.

And believe me, Friends, that's GOOD!

Confusing? Yes. The abundance of your traffic is astounding. But the fact that it is all going the wrong way, according to my standards and experience, makes me rub my eyes and wonder if I'm dreaming—and with my head at the foot of the bed!

And your way of pronouncing what I suppose is the Queen's English, is also a maze to me.

When the man-in-the-cab at the station told me to take the "Mine Line" I wondered if I had wandered into a coal producing section. But I soon discovered that "mine" is "main" which I pronounce to rhyme with lane.

Also I've learned that "go straight and take the lift" means take the "elevator" and not "turn left."

But all in all, Folks, I'd state that at this particular moment, in spite of rain and bread and taxis and shillings and traffic and the Queen's English, Jolly Old London is My Cup of Tea—and I'm liking tea better every afternoon.

After a day of stomping your pavements I see that there is a lot of reason for a cup of tea.

And thank you for everything.

I love you all.

LERA KNOX
(Mrs. Alex Knox)
Columbia, Tenn.

(From May 21 to June 5, at Charing Cross Hotel)

THE DAILY HERALD
COLUMBIA, TENNESSEE
TUESDAY, JUNE 2, 1953

Country Woman Sees Colorful Coronation

Mrs. Knox Gives Impressions of "Big Show"

BY MRS. LERA KNOX

(By Cable to the *Daily Herald*)
London, June 2—

Mount Everest climbed. Elizabeth crowned: Britain's big show greatest on earth—magnificent, stupendous, colorful, gay.

Crowded millions had been sleeping on the sidewalks since Sunday to see the royal procession along its tenuous line of march.

The parks are packed with children on dad's shoulders, bells ringing everywhere, people singing. It's thrilling and spine-prickling, military and noisy.

The crowds are variegated and good-humored, tense and expectant. The colors glittering and sparkling. All is perfect except the weather.

Profile Study—The Queen smiles as she poses for a profile study in the Green Drawing Room of Buckingham Palace. The diamond diadem, which is of great age, was reset for Queen Victoria.

Many of the people are prayerful. All are respectful and patriotic. An international flavor, people from all over the Empire of all races, creeds, and colors come to honor their queen.

Some have periscopes the better to see. Many are bundled up, the better to keep dry and warm.

Now it is all over.

It was a magnificent spectacle. There were tremendous crowds. The rain poured, and we all got wet together, laughing, shouting, and singing.

Here in London tonight there are 20 million tired feet and 10 million sore throats.

But the undoubted Queen has been crowned and not one of us who saw it will ever doubt it. All hail good Queen Elizabeth II!

It was a "great show." Everyone was gay. But it rained. That is England, and London, and Coronation Day.

I've got Coronation indigestion, sore feet, an aching back, and cold hands. But I was right in it, and it is a spectacle a Country Woman from Maury County, Tennessee, will not soon forget!

P.S.—Having a wonderful time—wish you were here.

[The following United Press articles further describe the coronation of Queen of Elizabeth II.]

THE DAILY HERALD
COLUMBIA, TENNESSEE
TUESDAY, JUNE 2, 1953

'Priceless Gown' Worn By Queen

London—(UP)—

Queen Elizabeth II wore a priceless white satin gown, heavily embroidered in gold, silver, pearls and rhinestones with the emblems of the far-flung empire she rules, for today's coronation ceremonies.

Designed by Norman Hartnell, the gown was cut on the simplest lines to display the queen's 23-inch waistline and pinup figure.

There is not a diamond on the 12-pound dress. But the 27-year old monarch wore a diamond necklace and her favorite diamond tiara, which once belonged to Queen Victoria.

The gown is short-sleeved, has a low-cut neckline and a full, flaring skirt with a straight train—designed so as not to interfere with her climbing in and out of the golden state coach or kneeling in Westminster Abby.

The dress hugs the queen's figure almost to the hipline where the flare begins. The skirt is lined with a layer of crinoline

LONDON—Held in complete secrecy until the last minutes before Coronation, the gown worn today by Queen Elisabeth II is revealed in this sketch by designer Norman Hartnell. The regal dress features the Commonwealth emblem in its design, with gems and embroidery worked into a scalloped pattern across the full skirt. The two crowns at left and right are drawings of those worn by the Queen during the ceremonies. (United Press TELEPHOTO)

and paper-weight silk taffeta. The queen also wore a stiffened petticoat of white net.

"The gown is priceless," Hartnell said. "We couldn't begin to estimate its cost."

Into it went 15 yards of British-made satin and the embroidery alone took six seamstresses eight weeks.

The neckline was cut square over the shoulders, then curved into a heart-shaped center. Bodice, sleeves, and extreme hemline of the skirt are bordered with an embroidered band of golden crystals, various sized rhinestones and pearls.

Queen Dedicates Life to People in Ceremony Largely Religious

BY LAURENCE MEREDITH
United Press Staff Correspondent

London (UP)—

Queen Elizabeth dedicated her life to her people today and she was solemnly anointed for her task.

The coronation is essentially a religious service, though it is bringing London its gayest celebration in many a year.

It is completely non-political. Prime Minister Winston Churchill and the members of his cabinet were in Westminster Abbey as guests only—the service had nothing to do with them.

The 1,000-year-old ceremony has become sacred to British religious instincts. The sovereign is head of the Church of England—corresponding to the Protestant Episcopal Church in the United States.

By her coronation, the queen becomes for her people "God's anointed."

The coronation service centers on two of the holiest sacraments of the Church of England, the communion service and the anointing of the queen with holy oil.

The enthronement and the actual crowning are solemn and impressive. But they are largely symbolic and to some extent incidental to the anointing of the queen by the Archbishop of Canterbury.

With the anointing, every British sovereign becomes something more than a mere mortal in stature.

The coronation service is set in the framework of the service for the administration of communion.

Authorities differ as to what, exactly, the service confers upon the sovereign.

Under the tradition which has grown up over a span of more than 1,000 years of crownings, the coronation does not exactly confer upon the sovereign the quality of priesthood. But it confers something more than a purely secular quality.

Prelates of the Church of England hold that the service is an expression of the unique quality of the monarchy as an office which, while it is not exactly spiritual, is not wholly secular.

The service, they say, will confirm the queen as having the supreme power of temporal jurisdiction in all causes which arise from her combined roles of head of the state and head of the church.

A Beautiful Princess Was Crowned Queen

Once Upon A Time—

BY HARRY FERGUSON
UP Staff Correspondent

This story should be written by Hans Christian Andersen and like the fairy tales we hear in childhood it should begin:

So once upon a time there lived a beautiful princess who married a handsome prince of the royal house of the far-away land of Greece. After passing through the dark days of a great war and the sorrow of the death of her father and grandmother there came a happy time when she rode down an ancient road to a medieval abbey. There she was crowned Elizabeth II, by the grace of God and of the United Kingdom of Great Britain and Northern Ireland and of her other realms and territories queen, head of the Commonwealth, defender of the faith.

Once upon a time was today.

From the time the first procession started through the streets this morning everything that happened here was centuries removed from the age of the atomic bomb and the internal combustion engine. It was all cut of the story books and the long age when knights were bold, when all ladies were fair and when fabulous jewels flashed from priceless crowns.

Elizabeth, like Cinderella, rode in a golden coach drawn by handsome horses. Like Cinderella, she was gowned and jeweled in breath-taking style and escorted by a tall prince. But Elizabeth, unlike Cinderella, had no dream of midnight; for when Big Ben proclaims the hour tonight the great ball will just be getting under way and people will be telling each other that everybody is going to live happily ever after.

The gray old city named London put on her party clothes early for the coronation. She sparkled with golden crowns suspended above the streets. Her war wounds were bandaged in red, white, and blue bunting. Her bomb cars were covered with paint or scarlet and gilt.

Two million persons lined the streets. They were packed into specially built grandstands and jammed into every inch of sidewalk space. Thousands of them had stood patiently through darkness and rain for as long as 40 hours.

All of them had retreated from the present into the distant yesterdays. Their mood was that here was a fairy tale being enacted before their own eyes and they were determined to make the most of it before the magic spell was broken.

The population of London was going about its business of buying and selling, working, eating and sleeping. They will heed the ancient admonition engraved on the sun dials—"It is later than you think"—and return to reality and to work. But today they all feel the same way as does Sam Kalis, who runs a tobacco shop in a weather-beaten building at the corner of Wine Court Lane.

"I shan't miss one second of it," he said.

His store door is locked. He is not worrying about food, money or the routine matters of daily existence. He is on a magic carpet for a 24-hour flight back into England's long, rich history. And every Briton the length of this island is aboard as a fellow passenger.

Some persons have lost their names and identities for this one day. Sir George Bellew is a typical upper-class Englishman who on ordinary days wears a derby hat, a dark gray coat, striped trousers, and black shoes. He carries a tightly-furled umbrella over his left arm.

But today his name is not George Bellew. He is "King of Arms of the most Noble Order of Garter." He has put aside his derby hat for a plumed bonnet. His gray coat has been replaced by a tabard of gold and velvet and a crimson mantle. Knee breeches, black stockings, and gold-buckled shoes have taken the place of his striped trousers and conservative boots. Instead of an umbrella, he carries a glittering staff of office.

The chair in which Elizabeth was seated to be crowned today was constructed almost two centuries before the French began building New Orleans at the delta of the father of waters. Westminster Abbey was erected in 1043 at a time when Pasadena was a beautiful wilderness. Some of the paving over which the queen rode today covers roads laid down by Julius Caesar's legions at a time when Fifth Avenue was a battle-ground of Indian tribes some 14 centuries before Columbus sailed westward.

The sense of the past was everywhere along the line of the great procession. As the queen's coach approached Westminster Abbey the clop-clop of the horses became hoof beats of history. William the Conqueror went to this same place for the same purpose on Christmas Day in the year 1066. The crusader king, Richard the Lion-Hearted, took the same journey in 1189. And in the year 1559 Elizabeth the first walked across the same abbey floor-stones to be crowned in the same coronation chair.

White-Clad Prince Sits in Wonder as All Pay Tribute

BY JACK V. FOX

London—(UP)—

Elizabeth II, beautiful but tremulous, was crowned Queen of Britain and the commonwealth today.

At 12:33 (5:33 CST) in Westminster Abbey where for 900 years British sovereigns have been crowned, the Archbishop of Canterbury gently lowered the jeweled crown of St. Edward to her dark hair.

Then with a great roar, the 7,500 peers and peeresses and heads of state in the Abbey, cried:

"God save the queen."

The guns of Hyde Park, Windsor Castle, and the Tower of London boomed 41 times. As the sound echoed throughout London and was relayed around the world by radio, in Britain, the nations of the commonwealth and the colonies, the same shout went up among many of her 600,000,000 subjects:

"God save the queen."

It was the climax to a religious ceremony, part of which goes back to the days of Solomon.

In a setting of breath-taking beauty in blue and gild, she had sworn to govern her peoples according to their laws, to govern with justice and mercy and to uphold the laws of God.

She had received the sword of state, been anointed with holy oil poured from the eagle-shaped Ampulla into a golden spoon, touched the golden spurs, been invested with the bracelets of sincerity, and had received on the fourth finger of her right hand the emerald ring which "wedded" her to the empire.

She had received the orb, oldest Christian symbol of monarchy, and she had held the scepter, sign of power and justice, and the rod with dove, symbol of equity and mercy.

A few minutes before the supreme ceremony of the crowning, a small boy in a white satin suit was led by his nurse through an entrance to the Abbey at Poet's Corner and then to an alcove looking upon ancient King Edward's chair. It was Prince Charles, four and one-half, brought to see his mother crowned as he, one day, may receive the same crown of the world's oldest existing monarchy.

Charles sat in wonder, his eyes transfixed on his mother.

In the great abbey where William the Conqueror was crowned on Christmas Day, 1066, Elizabeth betrayed only by a slight huskiness and the tremor in her voice the emotions moving her as she dedicated her life to her people.

Of all those statesmen and soldiers, princes and ladies gathered there, it was Elizabeth whose poise was supreme.

As she took the oath, Elizabeth's voice was tremulous, not the self-assured, high-pitched voice so often heard. But her poise was magnificent.

Then came the moment of the crowning.

A hush fell over the abbey as the great crown of St. Edward was carried on the deep red cushion to the archbishop.

He grasped it, and, for a moment it seemed to slip in his fingers. He tightened his grip, turned to the queen, and settled the crown upon her head.

The archbishop pronounced the benediction and then came the moment when breaths were held in suspense.

The five-pound crown seemed to perch perilously on her head. But, with the rod and scepter in her hands and the heavy garments brushing her feet, Elizabeth walked with a calm grace from the coronation chair and mounted the steps of the dais to her throne.

She never faltered nor swayed. She turned on the dais and graciously waited until the bishops and great officers had gathered to hold her arms and "lift" her into the throne—a ceremony going back to the day when sovereigns were enthusiastically hoisted on the shields of their soldiers.

The archbishop knelt before her, placed his hands between hers, and as all the other bishops in the abbey knelt with him, pledged himself to be faithful and true.

Then Philip came before his wife. He removed his ducal coronet and handed it to his page, then ascended the steps and knelt before Elizabeth.

Glancing at a printed script held by a bishop, Philip said: "I, Philip, Duke of Edinburgh, do become your liege man of life and limb, and of earthly worship; and faith and truth I will bear unto you, to live and die, against all manner of folks. So help me God."

His voice was clear and unwavering. Then he rose and bent over his wife, kissing her warmly on her left cheek. But man and wife were very solemn; there were no smiles and Elizabeth looked straight ahead.

The Duke of Gloucester, the queen's uncle, followed, and then the 17-year-old Duke of Kent, shy and in a hurry, paid homage. The senior peers of each rank came then and, as each knelt, all the other dukes, or earls, viscounts or barons, knelt in his place in the abbey. Prince Charles was reluctantly escorted from the royal alcove then, as the communion service began, with Elizabeth and her husband kneeling together and partaking of the bread and wine.

Duke Prays

Paris—(UP)—

The Duke of Windsor fought back tears in a darkened room today and prayed silently beside his duchess for his 27-year-old niece, Queen Elizabeth II, as she was presented the crown he renounced for love.

[Mrs. Knox continues the account of her experiences in London for the Coronation of Queen Elizabeth II.]

THE DAILY HERALD
COLUMBIA, TENNESSEE
FRIDAY, JUNE 5, 1953

Herald Correspondent at Tower Of London

Lera Knox Shows Dixie Flag to Beefeater

Country Woman Fights Crowds to Place Leaf before Crowning

Editor's Note: Mrs. Knox had told us about the London Travel Association photographer having taken this picture, in a note with one of her earlier articles but had expressed doubt that it would ever reach us amidst the Coronation confusion. However, the British Travel Association came through in a big way—for which our thanks.

Mrs. Knox Tells of Recording for WLAC Sunday

BY LERA KNOX

London, England—7:30 p.m. Monday, Pre-Coronation—

This is the night before the "big show" and already the crowds are tremendous. But I will try to wedge my way through to the post office across the street to mail this and tell you I'm still pushing.

LONDON, ENGLAND—Pictured showing her wallet, which is stamped with the Confederate flag, to one of the Yeomen Warders, or "Beefeaters," at the Tower of London, is *Daily Herald* special correspondent Mrs. Lera Knox. She is in Britain to report the Coronation.

[This air mail letter was written the night before the cable in which Mrs. Knox gave *Herald* readers her impressions of the Coronation, the last word from our *Herald* correspondent.]

One catering firm, Lyons, plans to feed more than a million. The crowd is estimated at 10,000,000. I don't know who will feed me and the others. But all are good natured, happy and well-behaved—adoring their Queen.

Incidentally F.C. Sowell of WLAC asked me to make a recording for his *What's Happening* program for Sunday, 9 a.m. (my birthday) and it took me four hours to get to the broadcast studio here to make inquiry. But arrangements are made to record the tape Wednesday at 2:30 p.m. but I've got to be at a luncheon for General Marshall at 1 p.m. Guess I'll have to "helicopter" across town to make the tape.

Pan-American Airways will pick up the tape recording here and take it to New York, then another airline to Nashville by Friday they say. So if all goes well I'll speak to you with my newly acquired British accent Sunday morning.

Will place leaf (poke sallet) on Trafalgar Square early tomorrow morning before the "big show" if I have to push down the Lions and Mr. Nelson's monument to do it.

The Leaf must go before the Queen.

The news editor of the *London Sunday Express*, largest newspaper in the world, heard about the leaf and sent a reporter for an interview and said he would use the story of the Maury County Poke Sallet Leaf That Came to Do Homage to the Queen, probably in his Coronation Extra Supplement, or somewhere. Anyway, he sent a smart reporter, a Mr. Ellis.

Love to all, I've got to get ready for tomorrow's battle of the crowds, so I may see the Queen and all the notables.

THE DAILY HERALD
COLUMBIA, TENNESSEE,
MONDAY, JUNE 8, 1953

Country Woman Sees Queen Third Time

Mrs. Knox Tells Of Recording, To See Fair

BY LERA KNOX

London—June 4—

It is now 42 hours (and 53 aspirins) after the Coronation. People are packing and leaving town in droves. But not me. I've become so attached to the British soil (I don't mean stuck in the mud) that I'm going to stay in and around England at least until after June 11.

Margaret and Stan leave for a few days in Scotland tomorrow, but I want to get out and dig among the "grass roots" of rural England to see what the real and actual soil-tillers are doing and thinking. I'm going to do the big Essex County Fair, as guest of the Farmers' Union, on the 11th, and dear knows what else. I may even see the Derby.

I hope the recorded tape (for the WLAC broadcast on *What's Happening* Sunday) reaches Nashville in time, for Sunday is my birthday.

How did I ever get the tape made in time? If I hadn't been lost so many times in London and if I hadn't stumbled upon BBC (British Broadcasting Corporation) in my four hours of rambling around hunting Hallam Street, and if I hadn't wanted to hear a nightingale sing and stopped at BBC to ask to hear a record of such a song, I might never have had the grit, nerve or guts to ask aid from so busy a corporation on the eve of the Big Event.

But BBC was most gracious, although the earliest date I could make for a recording was last Wednesday afternoon.

I'd hate to tell you how early I got up on Coronation morning, but the mobs were already in their places before I got there, so I had to have practically a police escort through Marble Arch, waving my Press Card, compliments of Scotland yard, above the heads of the crowd.

And I'd hate to confess how late I got to bed that night, but even then I left the fireworks going and the crowd still cheering.

Wednesday morning I was convinced that my $10 a night bed was the best place in all of London, but I had to get up and go read the newspapers. So actually it was noon before I got down to the typewriter to think what I'd say to you folks at home on June 7.

After several interruptions, I was putting on the last paragraph at 1:45 p.m., when the maid came in and told me that the Queen would pass before the front windows of the hotel at 2:00 on her way to visit the “Little Streets” in East End. I was still in pajamas and due at the studio at 2:00 if possible, certainly not later than 2:30, or at least 2:40, because the Airways would pick up the tape at 3:30.

I stamped a hasty period on my script, jumped into a suit and rushed for a front window. The Queen was 15 minutes late because she stopped to greet some children and old people in the Mall (pronounced Mell.)

At 2:20, I stuck the unread manuscript into my 10-quart shoulder bag, grabbed up my umbrella, and rushed for the nearest taxi stand. The mob was thick as flies on three-day-old fly paper in a dairy barn in July.

I sneaked through the subway under the hotel, out to daylight, and trotted three blocks back to Strand, thinking I'd get out of the crowd to another taxi stand, but the mob was packed there too. Finally, I appealed to a policeman and a taxi starter, telling them I had an emergency situation and a broadcast to make. They found me a taxi, but he had to go through all the jam to Strand and Trafalgar to get to Piccadilly. I was exasperated.

But we made it, even went through Leicester Square, with all its mob. We crossed the Queen's route twice. I couldn't have picked a worse time to get to No. 6 Whitehorse Street, nor a better taxi driver. When I gave him ten shillings and jumped out, he called me back to get my umbrella; I stuck it under my arm, and rushed into the studio, not noticing until after the tape was made that it really wasn't my umbrella at all. I'd had mine hanging on my arm all the time. So after recording I walked out into the London sun with two umbrellas. One dishonestly, if ignorantly, acquired.

The girl in the studio asked if I had rehearsed it and timed it. I said, "No, I haven't even read it."

She said, "Well, we'd better time it, so we'll know what length tape to use."

My typewriting is awfully hard to read, but I stumbled through it in 15 minutes and 8 seconds.

Then it was time to do the Real Thing (or is that the REEL THING?). The studio was a sort of temporary emergency affair, with no signal lights and not much light of any other kind, but I blundered along through it, filling in with what I thought and felt, when I couldn't read the typing, and finished it at 3:28. The Pan American van was due to pick it up at 3:30. You probably heard my sigh tacked onto the "Goodbye."

But the van, like the Queen and I, was also tied up in traffic, so the manager asked if I'd like to hear the tape run through while we were waiting. I'd never heard myself talk before, so I thought it might be at least an experience, so I consented. He punched some buttons.

Then I heard what I thought was a rather nice voice come out of a box in the wall, and make some remarks that sounded like my sentiments. And the sentiments sounded true and reasonable, too. I even dropped a few more tears on my pocketbook. (We just don't have enough tissue to go around over here.) But I still believe The Gremlins did that recording.

P.S. It's 2 p.m. Thursday. I just saw the Queen again, the third time in three days. She is wearing a black suit and a white crown-fitting hat today, and looks lovely, as usual.

THE DAILY HERALD
COLUMBIA, TENNESSEE
FRIDAY, JULY 31, 1953

Country Woman Changes Her Mind; Poke Sallet Is Back

Editor's Note: Followers of The Country Woman will remember that Mrs. Knox had written she was planning to place the leaf of Maury "poke sallet" sent her by Solon Pryor of the *Herald* and others, in the pathway of the Queen on Coronation Day. Herewith is what happened.

BY LERA KNOX

London—Two days after Coronation—

Dear Solon and All:

I have a confession to make, (but not an apology). I did not place the Poke Sallet Leaf, Product of Maury County, before the Queen.

First, I could not get into the crowd at Trafalgar Square Tuesday morning, by any means except perhaps by "hoverplane" (helicopter to you), and the Duke of Edinburgh has a sort of monopoly on 'overplaning over here.

Second, I thought I'd place the Leaf under Marble Arch. But there just wasn't room for even so thin a leaf to be wedged in among that crowd there. I verily believe it couldn't have reached the ground even if it had been dropped. Except in the middle of the street you couldn't see the mud for the people.

Third, I hid it in my bosom, to keep it out of the rain, and keep it warm, until the procession started, then I took it out, opened its envelope, and my erstwhile determination failed me. In other words, like a woman, I changed my mind.

That little Leaf looked so tender, so frail, so delicate, I couldn't place it on that sloppy street, even for the Queen to crush.

After all, the Maple Leaf of Canada, the Shamrock of Ireland, the Daffodil of Wales, the Wild Rose of England, and certainly the Thistle of Scotland, were not being trodden underfoot. They were waving high.

And I resolved that the Leaf of Maury County should do the same. So, sheltering it in my hand (to keep the rain off) I stood on tiptoe on top of my bench (and cushion) and waved it at the Queen as long as she was in sight.

Maybe the will of the people was not entirely obeyed. Maybe it was. Anyway, I am returning it to you, crumpled, but intact.

THE LEAF THAT LOOKED AT THE QUEEN!

Also enclosed a bit of moss from the Bank of the Thames beside Cleopatra's Needle.

THE DAILY HERALD
COLUMBIA, TENNESSEE
WEDNESDAY, JUNE 10, 1953

Country Woman Tells of Coronation Jam

Mrs. Knox "Takes Her Stand" The Hard Way

BY LERA KNOX

Everyday can be See-day in London; but it is unlikely that there will ever be another C-day such as we saw June 2, 1953, not in London, not in any other place—not even in Columbia, Tennessee, (I hope) nor even in Hollywood, the unbelievable.

There were, and are, several ways of seeing C-day; namely, The Hard Way, The Harder Way, and The Hardest Way. And then there is The Best Way. But you choose that from among the aforenamed.

I saw it first The Hard Way: That is sitting and standing on a very small piece of very hard oak board, in a cold downpour of rain for eight hours, a $12 seat in the stands. I was assigned Seat 10, Row N, Stand 5, and getting there was no cinch, I can promise you. Taxis, buses, and even subways were cut off from the area. The only way to arrive was to travel to your destination as early as you could the night before by whatever means of public or private transportation you could beg, buy, or borrow, then make it the best way you could by that old method known as "shank's mare"—namely, your own two feet.

When I tell you that the route was eight miles, and the taxis were charging or asking 6 pounds or $16.86 to take you a few blocks, we were glad to rely on "shank's mare."

I caught a subway to Baker Street Station, which I had heard would be only about five minutes to Marble Arch, where I wanted to go. But it was more than 45 minutes of hard going before I got there. When I finally reached Stand 5, Row N, Seat 10, I sighed fervently, and plopped down, breathing "On this stand I take my seat."

But when Her Beautiful Majesty, in the golden, grey, and glass coach, with its eight grey horses, and coachmen and footmen in gold and scarlet, came into sight, my determination was changed to "On this seat I take my stand."

That was the hard way, sitting, soaked, for eight cold hours. But my daughter Margaret, and her husband, Stan, had it a harder way. Even though they made hotel and railroad reservations last August, they failed somehow to reserve seats. I got my seat six days before C-day, thinking that they had surely taken care of that major or minor item for themselves. But fate decreed that they would stand—they did, for 12 long, cold, wet hilarious hours in one spot, but a good spot, on the steps of the Duke of York (whatever that is) in the Mall, which is really the main and most beautiful avenue of them all.

That's the one that leads right up to Buckingham Palace from Trafalgar Square, and looks like one great solid pin cushion of people in the pictures you'll see of C-day.

Yes, their way was the Harder Way, but the poor people who most certainly had had it The Hardest Way were the ones who took their places on the hard concrete of Trafalgar Square, or other such places of supposed advantage on Sunday and Saturday, stood, slept (but not rested) there, for two cold, windy, rainy nights and days. They, I think, really proved either their patriotism or unabated curiosity.

The people who saw C-day in comparatively The Easy Way were the ones who had either covered, or enclosed seats, at a cost of up to $150 each, including lunch and champagne. But theirs were not necessarily better views. Some of them had access to television during the Abbey program. Those who probably had it easier were the ones that stayed at home, and from the warmth of their own fireside and tea-tables, watched the whole thing on television with perhaps a little, or a lot, of radio thrown in.

But it is probable that The Easiest Way of all, and it may be The Best Way, is the one that still is to come Your Way—by movies in Technicolor.

That is what I saw today. It's just out. In fact I stood in a mob last night for two hours to watch the Crowd-of-the-Fortunate file into the Odeon Theatre to see the Premier, or first showing anywhere.

Today the color film was shown at four more theatres, in one of which I saw it. Monday, it will open up at more than 200 cinema houses in London. It is sure to reach Tennessee before long.

The *London Evening News*, Friday, June 5th, announced "1000 Sleepless Men Get Colour Films Through for Tonight."

It also states that Sir Gordon Craig, British Movietone News chief, has proved his statement the "Colour newsreels are just around the corner."

"Sir Gordon, working day and night since Tuesday, had one of 39 hours without closing his eyes, but was able to see for the first colour print of his picture in less than 12 hours after the Queen returned to the palace after being crowned."

The News reporter further states that the three rival color film companies will have more than 1000 reels on screens by Monday, "the greatest film race ever known."

Names of some being opened here are *Coronation Day: Elizabeth is Queen*, and *A Queen is Crowned*. The latter is the one I saw today, and it is remarkable.

It is very comprehensive, very clear, considering what weather did for film folks on June 2, 1953. And it is narrated by Sir Laurence Olivier, who I saw going into the Premier last night to hear his own narration.

So you folks at home will see the "reel" thing in the Easiest Way. But I still am sure that seeing the Real Thing was worth getting wet six times. And if I had to do it over, I still would take my Stand. And every soaked "see-er" I've heard says that C-day was the greatest See-day that the world has ever known, and probably will be the greatest that will ever be known. It was still a great experiment and a great experience.

THE DAILY HERALD
COLUMBIA, TENNESSEE
THURSDAY, JUNE 11, 1953

Country Woman Sees Bright "Blitz" And Many Blisters

Mrs. Knox Tells Of London after Crowning

BY LERA KNOX

Hello Homefolks:

London and I just can't get over this Coronation "Blitz."

It's bigger than both of us, as "Miss Television" (Max/Ruth Gilbert of the *Milton Berle Show*) would say.

I still can't have any idea of how much Coronation stuff you've had, and of whether or not you've got a sort of Coronation "colic." The newspapers here, and radio, have been constantly proclaiming highlights and sidelights and bright-lights ever since I arrived here May 13, but I'm not tired of it yet, and when I leave June 12th, I'll wish I didn't have to go.

Dr. Johnson, one of the most Britisher of them all, is quoted as saying long ago something like this: "When a man is tired of London, he is tired of living, for London is Life."

Of course the Honorable Doctor Esquire could not speak for woman, so I'll have to do that. I think when a woman is tired of living she still wouldn't be tired of London. But of course that's just one woman's opinion. Rather more drastic, perhaps, than Dr. Johnson's, but then he wasn't here on C-day.

But as I was going to say, I don't know whether the papers in U.S. and radio and television have given you all you want. And I don't know really how much stuff I've sent you, nor how much has arrived at your door through all this congestion of mail and telegraph. But if you don't mind I'm going to keep sending stuff.

The best way I can describe the whole of it would perhaps be to say that it is much like some of the fireworks displays; it all went up in one brilliant column to the Crowning Moment, then it burst into millions of balls of brightness that scattered and slowly descended upon the gasping millions of the "pin-cushion" crowd below.

Being just one small "pin" of the pincushion I could catch only what two hands, two eyes, and one small head could hold.

But if the Crowning Moment was brightness all above; and certainly it was, the Coronation Week, or weeks as it promises to be, has been something else down in the regions of our knees and feet. I must admit that. Human bodies just aren't built to take so much on foot.

There are certain items of merchandise that can hardly be bought in London any more, namely corn-plasters, aspirins, and camera films.

Going up some stairs in a restaurant yesterday, I noticed that half the ankles I met coming down were strapped, and shoes had adhesive plasters sticking out above what I judged were Coronation blisters.

So it has been Blitz above, and Blisters below.

I've been surprised at how well my erstwhile clod-hopping "dogs" have been able to take it. The fact that I had nothing to wear but old shoes has helped, and the fact that I've kept a bottle of Vaseline handy to rub my corns after encounter with sidewalks, has helped.

But with knees it has been different. I steadfastly refuse to strap my knees. With the Gremlin luck I've been having, I never know when I might come face to face with Her Majesty, then I'd want to do a complete low curtsy; and I'd never be able to do her justice with stiff knees.

So I get around rather wobbly, but so does everyone else. If a great waltz or dance step should ever evolve out of this great celebration, you'll notice that there is a decided knee-weakness in the step.

And crowds! There just aren't words in English-English, nor in American-English, that are big enough to describe these crowds, nor what they do to the people who are part of them.

It just happens that my little hotel room window looks out only on roofs. But the bathroom which I attend looks down on the street, The Strand, to be exact. Well, when I go to that bathroom I always close the window, because every time I look down on the heads of those millions, I want to run back to my room, jump into bed, and pull the covers tight over my head—even then I dare not go to sleep for fear I'll dream of crowds.

When it is absolutely necessary for me to go outside I just shut my eyes, dive in, and push. That is about the only way to get about.

I have made some very good friends over here. One is a woman I met down in the offices of the *Sunday Express*, a Mrs. Church, whose husband is a Captain in the British Merchant Marines. She has a dandy little Ford car and is very lonesome until her husband comes back at the end of this month. She has invited me to drive around with her every day for the rest of the time I am here. But do you know I'm not even taking advantage of that wonderful opportunity, not much that is.

Driving in Britain is safer than anywhere else, I believe. And she says that London is certainly the "City of Undamaged Mud-guards," and so it is. But even in a car, one is still in crowds.

She begged me to go to the Derby with her and some Canadian friends. It would have been a wonderful experience, especially as we expected to see the Queen lead in her colt, Aureole, as winner. But I stayed in my little back room looking out on roofs and heard Sir Gordon Richards on Pinza go past the Queen's colt, through the wireless of BBC. It was easier.

Besides, I'd have hated to see the Queen's face turn red when Aureole came up second, just ahead of the Frenchmen's Pink Horse, and of Aga Kahn's Shikampur, the fourth horse. It must have been a wonderful spectacle, but I've reached the point where roofs and brick walls are a peaceful sight to behold after the Coronation crowds.

However, there is one thing of which I am proud. Everybody else I have heard of has had to take 48 hours in bed to get over "Coronation Indisposition." But I took only 36 hours, though I must confess I'm not over it yet, and probably will bring some buckling knees home with me in late September. But I'm still able to go—when I have to.

The one person who will stand out in the minds of the millions longer perhaps than anyone else but the Beautiful Queen, is The Big Queen.

She is the only other reigning queen in London, Queen Salote of Tonga. And Tonga, I believe, is a little island somewhere off New Zealand. I had heard of her before she arrived. A little news story that said an American hosiery company had sent her a dozen pairs of Nylons for the Coronation, when word got around that she couldn't find any her size.

She stands 6'3" inches (out of nylons) and is truly a queen, every one of her 75 inches. She would weigh, I'd guess about 250 pounds, and she is every pound a queen.

The stunt that brought more cheers than either Sir Winston or the Queen Mother was the fact that Queen Salote, from a semi-tropical area, sat in an open carriage, in an evening dress, and took on her bared head and broad, bare shoulders every drop on that cold London Coronation Rain. When this brave and unwrapped body passed our shivering stand, the crowd yelled, stood up, and threw off its raincoats! She was superb.

Then we watched the papers for the announcement that "Queen Salote Has Chill." She did miss one important function, but she declared that the reason she didn't go was just "tiredness."

That's what we've all had. Just tiredness. But we're not yet tired of London. However, I believe that when these people shout "May the Queen Live Forever" they fervently mean it. We're pretty much like the little boy who got stuck in the brown-sugar barrel. For the present, and by the time this Coronation is over, we've "done got all that's good."

THE DAILY HERALD
COLUMBIA, TENNESSEE
FRIDAY, JUNE 12, 1953

Mrs. Knox Finds Much To Praise in Modern London

BY LERA KNOX

It is my impression that, generally speaking, the British people like to hold on to what is Old; whereas, we Americans usually are reaching for what is New.

Why, these people actually seem to be holding on to the Ten Commandments. The Commandments, they say, are Old, but not old-fashioned. They keep the good order by using them every day, and in almost every way. Of course there may be exceptions, but those get into the papers.

On the streets, in the hotels, in the crowds, and in every place you come in contact with the true Britishers, you'll find a fine blend of Courtesy, Common Sense, and the Ten Commandments in good working order.

A fine example of what I mean is expressed in the *Sunday Express* (one of my favorite newspapers over here) on the day after Derby day, when 750,000 people had been jammed into a small place to see the races. The *Express* said: "The general court which was held at Epsom on Derby night had only three offenders to deal with—a record low. There was a drunk, a 'suspected person' and a 'stealing by finding,' with not one pick-pocket, welsher, or gaming spiv." Now how's that for fair play and good sportsmanship?

Another thing which amazed me at first, then amused me, then pleases me very much, is the habit everybody has of calling everybody else "Dear." When the first street car conductor said to me "Hop on, Dear," I thought, "Well, you Fresh Thing!" When the cinema usherette showed me to a seat and said, "There you are, Dear," I didn't think she was trying to be fresh. When the taxi men, and hotel porters, and even the cops all called me "Dear" I didn't get offended. In fact I rather like it, and I believe you would, too.

However, I wouldn't say that this practice is altogether universal. One person I haven't heard of as "Dear" is Senator McCarthy. They only smile when he is mentioned. But I believe if he could have been in this Coronation Crowd, they would have pushed him along gently and said, "Mind your step, Dear." These people are just that way.

But just because they hold on to the Old doesn't mean that they are not also reaching for the New.

It was quite a concession for these staid old-timers to admit anything so un-ancestored as television into their Holy of Holies, Westminster Abbey.

And please don't forget the Comet. That is the jet plane that seems, at present, to be ahead of everything else overhead. I'd hesitate to make any statement as to its record, or the new records it is breaking, because it seems to be breaking its own records every day. I heard one Britisher say (and remember these people are not given to exaggeration), that the Comet "will be coming to the U.S. flying eight miles high at a speed of eight miles per second. So that if you eat lunch in London and board a Comet to New York, you will arrive in New York in time to eat a second lunch, and by New York time, this will be before you ate your first lunch." Now figure that out, if you can. No, England may hold on to the old, but she'll be right up there among the "firstest" with the new.

In talking with Mr. Jones, news editor of the *Sunday Express*, I ventured boldly to make a statement that I'm sticking to. I said, "I, for one, am glad that it rained on C-day." He didn't seem too shocked so I went on. "It gave me a chance to see under the skins of the British people."

And I meant just that. I don't know whether they have always been so brave, so patient, so calm, or whether the war did it to them. But the spirit I see in them is purely fine.

Call me pro-British, if you like, but that's the way I feel. And I'll confess that the "red coats" don't look nearly as bad to me now as they did when I studied American history. I wish George Washington could have attended this Coronation, and I'm sorry Senator McCarthy missed it.

Now you are probably getting around to the questions that I was most interested in finding answers for when, and before, I arrived. "What about war damage? And what about food?"

I was much surprised at what has been done about cleaning up, and covering up, the bombed out sections. I was told that anywhere I saw an open space, there had been a bomb-out or a burn-out. And there have been, and still are, plenty of open spaces. But they have been admirably cleaned up and made into parks or parking lots, or play-grounds for children; or have been covered up with reviewing stands for the Coronation; and the ones that have been covered have been so decorated with colored board and bunting and flags that you'd never guess that they were bomb-craters. It has been a magnificent accomplishment.

Not all, however. In the 25 days that I have been here I have done a lot of rambling in back streets and alleys, and into sections that are under a 99-year-lease, belonging to heirs that are gone. Some of these bear definite witness to the fact that there was war and that it was worse than terrible. However, trees are growing up in the ruins and Nature as usual is trying hard to cover the sins of man.

As to food, well we don't much talk about that. If you can eat tasteless fish, and also tasteless fried potatoes, three times a day for thirty days, with boiled cabbage, garden peas, and gelatin for variety, you'd get by on restaurant food. Fact is that it mostly tastes like sawdust, dry sawdust at that, but there is plenty of tea to wash it down. Fact is, I doubt if the English cooks will ever make a world record as cooks. But this is a place where one eats to live, not lives to eat. And with it all, I believe I'm gaining weight.

What puzzles me is that so many people can be so sweet, without sugar; so smooth, without butter; so generally calm and patient with a fish and potato diet. There must be some special vitamins in the fish—but I'll say this—you can't taste those vitamins. They, too, are like sawdust.

However there is plenty of "food for thought" in this situation. And there are many "white hyacinths for the soul."

THE DAILY HERALD
COLUMBIA, TENNESSEE
SATURDAY, JUNE 13, 1953

Country Woman on Towpath Tells Of Gardens and Murder

Tennessee Redbud Captures Her Attention

BY LERA KNOX

If anything good or bad happens to anyone in or around London anytime sooner or later, it might be blamed on the fact that so many people passed under ladders during the placing of Coronation decorations.

And you may remember that I arrived in London on the night of May 13, and am due to leave it on the night before June 13. And it is just as you say, the darnedest things do happen to me.

But when I tell you that just a day or so before it happened, I was on that very same towpath where two girls were so cruelly and insanely murdered, furthermore, that I have a most surprising witness of the fact that I was there—well!

It all started this way. Years ago I was guest of a farm women's encampment at Austin Peay Normal at Clarksville, and was particularly interested in the well-kept grounds. I got out early one morning and looked up the gardener, finding him to be Mr. Rolff, an Englishman, whose father was trained at Kew Gardens, near London.

Well, ever since meeting him and admiring his skill, I've wanted to see Kew Gardens, and as luck would have it, I set out to see Kew just a few days before the Coronation. I believe it was either Friday or Saturday.

Kew consists of 300 acres of people and plants, both from all over the world. So can you imagine a more enjoyable day than I had.

When lunchtime came, the sun came out in that bright and cheerful way it has of interrupting the usual London gloom, and I queued (or kewed) up with the rest of the folks for my buttered (I hoped) roll and cup of leafy tea.

As I came out of the refreshment tent, loaded down with the usual regalia, 10-quart shoulder bag, camera, raincoat, field glasses, umbrella, extra sweater, note-book, Kew catalog, etc., and with the tea and roll extra, I was glad to sit down at the first table I came to, especially as an unusually nice-looking young man made room for me and helped me set my burdens down.

Of course we couldn't help starting a conversation. The fact that the sun had come out was enough excuse for that. Then naturally we began talking about ourselves. He is with the U.N. in some executive capacity, has to do with fixing salaries, etc. He's on the 37th floor, and has invited me to visit the U.N. and get myself shown all around it by somebody who knows, when I get back to New York.

Oh, but I forgot, this article was to be about the famous towpath murder. And certainly he couldn't have been involved in that.

After lunch I got out my guide book and decided to walk down toward the lake and the boat houses. That sounded interesting. I started, and imagine my surprise, among the thousands and thousands of trees, to run across a Tennessee Redbud tree just coming into full bloom; also a bed of Jackson roses, or yellow moss roses, like Aunt Molly Barker used to have in her garden at Rock Springs. Kew certainly has everything.

I walked and walked, taking the grassy paths because after London pavements, they were a real relief. Finally I decided I must be lost, as usual. So I asked a woman coming toward me, "Did you see a lake down the way you came from?"

"Yes, it's just beyond that clump of trees. Do you know where the Judas tree is? I see it is advertised on the Bulletin Board."

Well, of course, I was delighted to show her our Tennessee Redbud, and thinking she'd never recognize it by herself, I turned around and went back with her to where it was growing, and at her exclamation, realized we had found the

"Judas Tree." I'm afraid she wasn't very much impressed, for I do admit it looked rather scrawny.

I told her we are planting our highways at home with redbud and dogwoods, but being from Australia, she didn't know very much about dogwoods, so I thought I might as well further her education along that line, and we rambled around through a complete park of azaleas and rhododendrons, looking for a dogwood.

Mission accomplished, she wanted to return the favor, so she took me to stare in amazement at a white wisteria vine as big as a house and in full bloom—magnificent, you can imagine!

Then I took her to see the Alpine and rock gardens, which were in their way just as remarkable. So we rambled around, each trying to outdo the other in favors to each other, and discovering a lot of things together.

Finally we decided that it might be a good idea to think about how we'd get back to London without getting into too much traffic jam.

She'd come down by bus, and I'd come down by subway, so neither of us particularly cared to go back the way we came, but we thought it would be rather nice to go back together.

I suggested that we try the river, which flows right alongside Kew, and supplies pleasure and passenger boats to London. A very nice little lady on the subway, who told me that her chief occupation is trying to make people happy, had told me when I left Kew to go out by the main gate, to cross the road, take a 27 bus, go to Richmond Bridge, walk up hill, and I'd see the prettiest view of England.

She said that from below the bridge, on the towpath, I could catch a boat on up to London.

Well, my friend, Mrs. Robertson of Australia, the lady-looking-for-a-Judas-tree, was the one person at that particular time with whom I would like to share the "prettiest view in England." So just as they were closing the gates to the gardens, we rushed out the nearest gate, caught a bus, and told the conductor we wanted to go to the bridge.

Well, that is where the Gremlins started working. In the first place the gate we went out was not the main gate. In the second place we didn't cross the road. And in the third place the bridge we reached was not Richmond Bridge, but Kew or some other bridge. But we saw the river below, the boats on the river, and the towpath alongside, so we wandered around until we found a way to get down to the river. She led the way and I followed. We came down near the Angler's Public House, saw the lock, which I judge now to be Teddington Lock, bumped into a sort of machine shop nearby, and finally ambled on down to the boathouse, caught our boat, and had a wonderful trip on up the river. Or down the river which ever way it was—for the life of me I can't tell which way the Thames is flowing, because it lets itself be bossed by the tide.

Well, there's the story. And that sharpened up file with which those two girls were so brutally murdered, before being tumbled into the Thames, might, of course, have come out of that very eerie looking path, all grown up in bushes, and we, seemingly from the schedule, caught the last boat up that night.

When I read of the finding of the girls; one on Monday morning, the other later, I confess I sort of shivered up my spine, and said to the Gremlins, "Well, fellows, we almost missed our cue that day at Kew Gardens."

But I can't leave this story there, although it is probably already long enough. And it may miss its point entirely if you haven't read in the papers of the murder of that 16-year-old-girl and 18-year-old one who were cycling on the towpath on Sunday night, or it may have been Saturday night. I keep getting my days so mixed up. Everything dates from before C-day or after C-day.

But I wanted to tell you about my pal Mrs. Robertson, the Lady-looking-for-a-redbud. She's an ex-teacher from Australia, mother of two sons, one a major who died two years ago of a rare jungle disease; the other, Capt. John Robertson, is commander of the Aircraft Carrier H.M.S. *Sidney*, and had brought his ship and quite a bunch of men to London to be, not only at the Coronation, but at the Spithead Naval Review, June 15th, when for once in her reign the Queen will review her Navy.

Mrs. Robertson will be on the battleship for the review, and asked me to be her guest, but ah those Gremlins again, they decree that I am to leave London for Holland and Germany on the night before the thirteenth. So, as important as it is, I won't be here on June 15th to see the Naval Review, from the decks of the majestic H.M.S. *Sidney*.

But I guess I'll stick to the Gremlins. If they could get us two lone women off that Thames towpath before that maniac murderer got there, I guess they're pretty good at that.

But then, neither Mrs. Robertson nor I, both being grandmothers, could possibly be as interesting as pretty girls. So we'll just jog along safely (I hope) on our way. But speaking for myself, my way won't be a Thames towpath any more for awhile.

THE DAILY HERALD
COLUMBIA, TENNESSEE
FRIDAY, JUNE 19, 1953

Country Woman Swaps a Match for a Fall, and a Good Meal

BY LERA KNOX

Editor's Note: In this article Mrs. Knox writes about England from Germany, where she arrived at the home of her daughter, Mrs. Stanley [sic] Morgan, last Saturday night after a 24 hour trip from London, reporting that it was a long, slow, bumpy trip and she was still rather sore from the fall she writes about, but "OK and going strong."

If life is just one thing after another, and if an interesting life is one interesting experience after another; then what I have been doing since I left home has been Interesting Living.

Really, I was not prepared for the number of interesting experiences I've had in England. It may be because my mind has been open and my digestion good—but it seems to me that the good qualities of England and the English have been presented to us in the same way that they derive their "humor"—with characteristic understatement.

I might say that the only monotony I have found over here has been in weather and in food. And ordinarily I just haven't cared to pay attention to either.

The poor overworked English weatherman really needs only two phrases: "Fine today, but it may rain." Or "Rain today, but it may be bright." As Mark Twain said, all they can do about the weather is talk about the weather, and they do. Much more so than do their visitors. The usual beginning of a conversation, if the Englishman starts it is, "This beastly weather!" But as I said, I don't really notice the weather very much, and I told them, "After all, we have weather, too. You needn't brag too much about yours."

But the food! That I tried not to notice, and tried not to mention. But it does seem to me that there are a lot of things that they really could do about the monotony of the food. The fact seems that they really don't want to do anything about it. They like the same old stuff fixed the same old way day after day—or at least that has been my impression from restaurant fare. And that fare, day after day has been cold, greasy, fried fish; cold greasy fried potatoes; stale tough dark bread; and very good tea—if it had the leaves strained out of it. I only sit and stare at my plate and wonder why sometimes they don't slip up and bake the fish and the potatoes and fry the bread instead.

Well, it seems that after so long a time, monotony can get so monotonous that it doesn't seem monotonous any more. In other words, one can eat fish and chips so much that one forgets that there is such a thing as Food, unless something happens to bring one up with a start.

It happened this way: If there is anything that there has been more of in London than fish and chips, it is people. I believe I have mentioned those before, how every time I look out of the window and see so many people I want to run jump in bed and cover up my head; but I don't always do that, because I fear that if I do I'd go to sleep and dream of people. Then one night I had a very definite conversation with myself.

"Lera," I said, "You've got to do something about this aversion to crowds, or it might get to be a phobia. You might just as well shut your eyes and ears and dive in, just like everybody else is doing."

I reasoned that there probably wouldn't be quite so many people out that night, for it seemed that everybody in Christendom had already been out to see the decorations, and the lightings on The Mall, and that might be just the night for me to take a lonely little stroll up to the Palace.

I hit the crowds on the Strand, my street. But I pushed myself on in and told my doubting soul that the crowd was mostly around the Strand Station, and they would thin out when I got to Trafalgar Square. But my soul soon knew I was lying. By the time I had reached the barricade around Mr. Nelson's monument, I knew I'd never reach the other side of the Square, much less The Mall, and furthermore I knew I couldn't get back to the Charing Cross Hotel. I was stuck like one strawberry in one big jar of overcooked strawberry jam.

And jam it was. The only thing I could do was to fold my arms in front of me and with my elbows to protect my inalienable right to expand my chest in an occasional breath.

I did the only thing I could do. Stood with the crowd, or moved with the crowd. I figured I would be there until the crowd went home which they probably would do about midnight, and it was 10:30 p.m.

At last I noticed some steps, and thought that if I could get my elbows over other peoples' shoulders I would at least have more space in which to inhale the fumes from the chuggingly waiting cars and buses. I gradually worked my way toward these steps, eventually arrived, and managed to climb up to a top step where I could not only breathe better, but could see better—not that there was much to see except people. Yet, I didn't see the persons next and nearest to me.

Finally I heard a sigh at my elbow and a woman say, "I wonder if by any chance anybody has a match that I can borrow?"

Well, I always carry enough stuff in my 10-quart shoulder bag so that I can open up a canteen or first aid station anywhere emergency demands, so I dug down among the credentials, pencils, rubber bands, powder puffs, chewing gum, paper clips, candy bars, et cetera, that I had packed in my bag at home, dug up a book of matches with Knoxdale Café advertising on it and passed it to her.

She said, "Oh, you're from the States?"

"Yes and those matches are to advertise our place of business. We have a restaurant." I replied.

"Oh, we have a restaurant, too. It's just up the street, next door to Garrick Theatre. I wish we could get out of this crowd. I'd like to take you up there and get you a cup of good coffee. Americans like our coffee. That's the best way I could thank you for the matches."

"I'll come up and collect tomorrow, if I may, and if I get out of this crowd by tomorrow, I could certainly use a cup of coffee. I've been tea-ed to a sufficiency."

"Well, you go up to 'Pip Inn,' and ask for Mr. E.I. Forbert. He's my husband, and he'll certainly pay you well for that match. I needed it."

We were too crowded to do anything else but talk, so we did just that. She and her husband had come from Budapest and had gotten out of Hungary just in time. They had brought their two granddaughters, but had lost their daughter, and practically everybody else. They were very lonely in London, but also were very busy, and thus were happy.

It was nearly midnight by the time we were able to climb stiffly down off our perches, and too tired even to go for a cup of coffee. I went on to bed, and frankly, didn't even give the matter another thought until late the next afternoon. I was scouting up on Charing Cross Road, happened to notice the Garrick Theatre, remembered Pop Inn, and sure enough there it was. I asked the girl near the door about Mr. E.I. Forbert.

She went downstairs and came up with a nice looking gray-haired man, and to my surprise he had in his hand that little book of Knoxdale Café matches.

"You're the American Lady? I've been looking for you. Would you like, perhaps, some American fried chicken?"

I know that my grin must have been wide enough to take in a turkey drumstick.

He led me downstairs to a darkened room, with just a little light on each table. It must have been "Bohemian atmosphere," but I liked it. The place didn't smell too much like fish either.

Well, such a meal as I had! I truthfully told him that it was the best food I'd had since before I left home, and that seemed like an awful long time. I finished up with a real apple strudel, the best I'd tasted since the Rotarians had a convention in Chattanooga, and Margaret and I stumbled into a kosher restaurant there and called for their specialty, strudel. If you can't imagine how good fried chicken and strudel can taste, you try eating fish and chips for a few weeks.

I had one regret, that there wasn't room for me to try the Hungarian Goulash mentioned on the menu. I asked if I might bring my daughter and son-in-law back on Friday, and try the Goulash. He was pleased.

So the first thing when Meg and Stan came in from Scotland on the following Friday, I promised them that they would have Goulash for dinner, even though it was then before breakfast.

We went our several ways for several hours and met back at the hotel at an appointed time to go for Goulash.

All went well. We went on up to Pop Inn, started down the stairs, me leading because I knew the way, and could show them how to get down. We reached the darkened landing, me cautioning to them to watch the steps, then I stepped out for the landing and it simply wasn't there!

I found my landing six feet farther down, on the dining room floor with my spine against a bench, and my head under the table.

That wasn't exactly the way I had intended to make my entry with my boasted guests. But somehow it's a practice of mine. I never miss stepping out for the step-that-isn't-there.

I think that the waitress was afraid I'd knock the table over. Meg was sure I'd break my glasses. And perhaps, slyly, Stan had ideas of what I could collect out of the management for not having a light on those dark and treacherous stairs. Men, you know, just can't always appreciate "Bohemian atmosphere."

My back was hurting pretty bad. My head really felt the bump. My neck seemed twisted six inches out of joint. But even though I lost my dignity and my hat, I didn't break my glasses—nor tear my nylons. And I think, considering everything, that was an accomplishment.

I said to the Hungarian waitress (Mr. E.I. wasn't there), "Well, I really fell for that Goulash, didn't I?"

But the poor girl, foreigner that she was, didn't appreciate the humor of the situation at all. She just wanted to rub me. Her hands were still trembling when she brought back our plates. Maybe she, too, was thinking about damages. But the real Hungarian Goulash made everything alright, except my back, neck, and head. And the Strudel—well, if I'd had another flight of dark stairs, I could have fallen all over again for that. Not to mention coffee "like Americans like."

THE DAILY HERALD
COLUMBIA, TENNESSEE
MONDAY, JUNE 22, 1953

Country Woman Sums Up Her Impressions of Europeans

BY LERA KNOX

Dear Folks at Home:

If my recent letters have given you the impressions that England can do much for your soul, but not much for your stomach, I shall not try to change those impressions; for fundamentally I believe they are factual.

Don't, however, take them as too factual, because of course I have had very little time to learn over here and very limited contacts in which to gather material from which to make impressions.

The situation is much like the conversation between the two old preachers. One stated very positively, "Dar ain't no such thing as heartfelt religion."

The other suggested, "Brudder, you might modify dat statement by saying dat dar ain't no such thing as heartfelt religion, so far as you knows of."

So please remember that the statements I make are "so far as I knows of." And it is obvious that I don't "knows of" much.

More and more as I meet more people and visit more countries, I recall that quotation "If I had two loaves of bread, I would sell one loaf and buy a white hyacinth for my soul." To me the person who made that statement had a fairly well balanced policy and philosophy.

It occurs to me that the same trait or measurement of character might be applied to nations, for example:

If we Americans had two loaves of bread, we might use one to make toast, or ham; or cheese, pork or roast-beef sandwiches. The other loaf we'd let get two days old, then throw it away as stale. We must admit that we are wasteful.

The Danes would swap half of one loaf for flowers and fun; then they would artistically smear every remaining slice with good Danish butter, fill an attractive silver tray with open-face sandwiches, or "smorgasbord," and offer the whole at reasonable prices as tourist bait.

The French would swap half a loaf for art; sell the other half to tourists at the highest possible number of francs; but the other loaf (and it must necessarily be a very long hard loaf), they would take home with a big bottle of good French wine, and with those they would practically fill the family larder.

But the English would swap almost all of their two loaves for flowers and culture, retaining perhaps only a slice or two for cucumber sandwiches which they would serve at High Tea. But ordinarily, they would prefer Afternoon Tea with hyacinths and cakes, even though the cakes might be few and very small.

Now which nations are right, I am not prepared to judge; but anyway, after four weeks in England with tea and hyacinths, I was glad to get back to my daughter's home in Germany where I could get a ham or roast-beef sandwich, even though I had to go out into the backyard and gather some dog-fennel for table decorations.

THE DAILY HERALD
COLUMBIA, TENNESSEE
TUESDAY, JUNE 23, 1953

Country Woman Succumbs To Fast Book Buying Spree

BY LERA KNOX

There are two institutions that I dare not go near: first, if I am out of the States, is the American Flag; second, if I am anywhere, is a second-hand book store.

So, because I reasoned that an American Flag would be flying over the American Embassy in London, I could not make up my mind to go anywhere in that vicinity—not even to a party given to American correspondents by the American ambassador on the afternoon before C-day.

I feared that if I should go there on Monday afternoon, and if I should see that Flag floating high in the English breeze, Coronation Day would find me swimming the Atlantic trying to get back home again.

But as it was, even though I didn't go to the Embassy, didn't see the Flag, didn't try to swim the Atlantic, I got wet anyway; but with C-Day rain, and not salt water.

As to bookshops; I had heard that Charing Cross Road is the "Street of Books," that its shops are stacked with literally millions of volumes, both new and second-hand. So I marked that street on my map as the street to miss.

Fortunately or unfortunately, the British never put things where they think you are likely to find them. For instance, Charing Cross Hotel, where I was staying, is not on Charing Cross Road, but a few blocks away. That helped. So I managed to avoid bookshops for 29 1/2 days, and was quite proud of myself.

That last afternoon, however, was my undoing. By that time I was so sure of my directions and so certain that I knew my way around my part of London, I discarded my map. Then I dared to try to take a shortcut across to the Strand, where I lived. I was really in an awful hurry, too. I had to meet Meg and Stan, eat supper and pack, and catch the boat-train to Holland that night. Then it happened: I looked up to a building that had its decorations removed, and there, staring right down at me was a sign which said "Charing Cross Road!" I knew I had to go through it. I knew also that my luggage was already too much, and far too heavy. But I knew also that luggage would be heavier, before I got off Charing Cross Road! But I conjured up an excuse.

In trying to tell you folks about this trip and about the Coronation I have been realizing more and more the inadequacies of the English language, or at least of the part of it that I have.

Even though I had used every suitable word in my vocabulary to describe the Coronation, you still would have been grossly cheated. And you are deserving of better than I could give you.

And after all, since I am using it, the English language is my business. And it is a poor workman, indeed, who doesn't at least try to learn his business. So I decided to make a more intensive and specific study of the language. And where better to study English than in England?

I had resolved that, for as long as I could endure it, my main hobby, and my bedtime reading, would be basic factors of fundamental English. Rather a large order, but I believed it would be an interesting one.

So with this in mind, or rather as an excuse, I entered two or three bookshops, rambled around, asked questions, but managed to get out with all my shillings. That is, until I came to Foyles!

Foyles was my undoing. If you ever found a place that literally has acres of books, that place would be Foyles. What a place to break both legs in!

I've always been saving up easy and pleasant things to do for the time when I shall break both legs and spend some time in a wheelchair. There's crocheting, tatting, hand-weaving, outline embroidery, and reading through The Bible, Shakespeare, and the dictionary.

But even though I didn't have my needles and tatting shuttle or loom with me that day, I put Foyles down on record as the place I'd like best to Break Both Legs In.

I managed to get away after buying five small books, three new and two second-hand, but all good and authoritative. But worst of all, I bought a big second-hand dictionary, a jim-dandy of a lu-lu! One of Skeats'. It's old and out of print, but delicious! I may hunt a wheelchair without breaking both legs.

THE DAILY HERALD
COLUMBIA, TENNESSEE
SATURDAY, JUNE 27, 1953

Country Woman's English Is Not Changed By Oxford, Nor By Eton

BY LERA KNOX

For a long time I have clung to the theory that if a person has been through Oxford, he doesn't mind saying "ain't."

And now I've been; but still I do.

Perhaps the theory is wrong. Or perhaps the course was not complete. It lasted about fifteen minutes. And that time was spent mostly in the courtyard of Christ's Church College, looking up at the architecture and listening to a conducted-tour guide telling of Henry-the-this, or Charles-the-that, doing this, that, or the other for the school in such and such a year, A.D. or B.C., or at least pre-war.

Anyway, I've been through the town that Oxford is in. I've passed the offices of Oxford University Press. I've heard some interesting anecdotes about people connected with the town or the college. But actually, so far as I am able to judge, I'm afraid that my going through Oxford is going to rest very lightly on my ways of using the English language.

As long as they live Eton Boys must not carve their names on walls or school furniture. But after they die, heroically, the Headmaster will carve their names in bronze underneath this colonnade. There are now 1905 names there from recent wars. This colonnade, or at least the north end of it, was recently restored after being destroyed by a delayed action bomb in 1940. Seventy boys were sleeping in the adjoining building but not a boy was hurt.

It is one of those places to which I'd like to go back, and in which I'd like to stay longer. But so far, I am afraid that any Oxford influence that there may be on my writing will have come from the dictionary of the same name.

And I am afraid that influence will be as slight for a long time as it has been in the past. Not that I don't have the highest respect for the English language. But the situation is this: When I get in a hurry, and if I've got something to say, I'm like Henry Ward Beecher: "if the English language gets in my way, it doesn't stand a chance."

It is not to the credit nor discredit of the guide, but probably because of my state of mind on the day the tour was made that the two items that stuck in my mind about the trip refer to a prominent and revered citizen of the town.

The guide told the first little story in a sort of off-the-record manner as we passed a very famous golf course on the route. She said that the presently very famous Lord Nuffield, the man who is to England what Henry Ford is to America, maker of the very popular cars, "Morris Minor," "Morris Oxford," and "M.G.," in the days before he was so prominent and so wealthy, wanted one day to play golf on this very exclusive course.

But for some reason, it seemed, perhaps because of his appearance or lack of prestige, he was excluded.

So what did this seemingly very determined Englishman do but buy the whole course, and throw it open to the public. A Nuffield course seems not so exclusive any more.

Another story I heard of Lord Nuffield came from a woman who claimed to be a friend of the family, one in a position to know that her story is true. She said that whereas Mr. Ford is reported to have driven a new car every night, Lord Nuffield has been driving the same old Morris for more than a dozen years.

When someone criticized him for not "trading," he replied, "Why I've gotten this car stepped up to where it will get 57 miles from a gallon of petrol. Why should I trade it off for another?"

So those are the things I learned at Oxford.

At Eton it was different. But not much.

Oh yes, I didn't tell you that I went to Eton, too. Well, I attended Eton after I had been through Oxford—which is a reversal of the usual procedure, I believe.

The word "Eton" has always given me an idea of something that is not quite complete. Perhaps the thought comes from the little short jackets I've always associated with the name. My course at Eton was like the jackets, little, short, incomplete, and without much of a tale. (I really do despise puns, but how else could I say that?)

I believe I did learn one weeny lesson which I want to pass on to you if you'd like to consider it.

There are two things I've always liked to do or see done: one is The Thing That Can't Be Done; the other, The Thing That Isn't Done. And it seems to me that the folks who dare to do the latter are most likely to attempt the former.

That, to me, is like the Eton boys.

But first a word of explanation about the school. "The King's College of Our Lady of Eton beside Windsor was founded in 1440 by Henry VI," says the guide book. I'd like to call your attention to the fact that 1440 was 52 years B.C.C. (Before Christopher Columbus). And the poor little preparatory school has been literally soaked in, and trounced by, tradition ever since.

From what I could gather, it seems that perhaps no school has ever been so strict, and no boys have ever been so completely surrounded by "The Things That Simply Aren't Done."

There is a question in my mind of whether it is because those boys have always been so restricted in school, that later in life, when they were turned loose in the world, they "expanded" so much that it is said of them, "The World is Their Playing Field."

At any rate they've carved their names in history more prominently than they were ever not allowed to do on their desks, the college walls, and other noticeable places about the school.

The guide book acknowledges that "Many names have been carved by the boys on the coping stone of the wall" and "The custom of carving one's name when elected to King's College dates plainly from early time; and it is mentioned by Pepys in his diary February 26th, 1666, as being a 'custom pretty.'"

At any rate the school authorities seem at last to have taken up the same practice. For underneath the colonnade is the bronze frieze bearing the names of 1,157 Etonians who were killed in the 1914-18 war; and to this frieze are now added the names of 748 Old Etonians killed in the recent war.

So it seems that the boys who dare to do The Thing That Isn't Done are often the ones who attempt to do The Thing That Can't Be Done. Indeed Etonians make the world their playing field, their fighting field, and the field of their many accomplishments.

Our conducted-tour guide told us a great deal about Eton and its traditions on the bus going to Eton. So I wrote all my notes in bus-hieroglyphics, and now, sitting in a straight steady chair I can't possibly read those notes—not at least until I can get on another bus.

I do remember this however in addition to the fact that boys under five foot four inches in height must wear cut away "Eton" jackets, striped trousers, "Eton" collars, and black ties; and boys over five foot four inches in height must wear tail coats and striped trousers, turned down starched collars, and narrow white bow ties tucked in beneath the ends of their collars. All must carry umbrellas, positively not rolled, unless one is of the privileged upper classmen. But under no circumstances, absolutely none whatever, is an Etonian to either wear or carry a raincoat.

This young man, I caught in the very act. Watch his future!

Then when I walked out of the college, I came face to face with the young man in the picture, a real Etonian absolutely and positively carrying a raincoat. In other words, the Eton boys are still daring to do the Thing That Isn't Done. And I say more power to them toward doing Things That Can't Be Done!

THE DAILY HERALD
COLUMBIA, TENNESSEE
MONDAY, JUNE 29, 1953

Country Woman Gets the News from Home, Now Wants Letters

Mrs. Knox Finds Much In Old *Heralds*

BY LERA KNOX

Surely it must be true that beauty is in the eyes of the beholder. I saw all sorts of beauty in and around London, everything from the lovely landscapes; the magnificent Chelsea Flower Show, surely the largest of its kind in the world; the resplendent Crown Jewels; to a lovely Queen in a gilded coach—in fact just about all that an empire could afford in beauty.

Yet, because beauty must be in the eyes of the beholder, when I got to Germany and received a bundle of dog-eared and tattered old newspapers that had spent more than a month crossing the Atlantic—well, I thought that those battered and tattered old *Heralds* were just about the prettiest things I'd seen for five weeks!

Really, just about the only way I could pull myself away from London was the prospects of mail I might receive when

I got to Germany. And did I revel in that mail! There were not many letters, much to my sorrow, so if I hadn't got the *Herald*, I wouldn't have gotten the news. I crawled into Margaret's spare bed, after supper, turned on the bed-light, and began to "get the news."

It didn't help much to turn to page one of the *Herald* for May 7th, and see a picture of the wrecked British channel steamship *Duke of York*, which had its stern knocked off somewhere between Harwich and the Hook of Holland. I had just come across that same channel the night before on a sister ship. And I could imagine, snuggling down among Margaret's wooly blankets, that the Channel waters could be rather cold. (It's 55 degrees here today.) I said my prayers all over again, and put in an extra "Thank You" for the safe journey, and for the *Heralds*.

It may seem like old stuff to you, for as editors say, "news is a very volatile substance," but to me that night it was all very newsy. I even read the want ads, and noticed that somebody had a Richmond piano for sale; I wondered if it could have been the one I practiced my scales on back in Mamma's parlor so many years ago, and so many miles away.

I was pleased to notice, in the *Herald*'s Forum, that F. C. Sowell has joined Mrs. Herman Smith, and others I am sure, in a plea for a Woman's Rest Room or a Ladies Lounge in Columbia.

May I put in my two-cents worth of pleading for the same cause? It has long been a positive need. We all know that. But it seems that it has been everybody's business, hence nobody's business.

Now let's see who will be the next to pioneer further into the field of promotion for the Ladies Lounge. Line form to the right, please! More power to Mrs. Smith for reminding us so forcefully of the need, and more to F. C. for reminding us of the reminder. I hope you all get it finished by the time I get back home in late September. You'll need it for First Mondays, anyway, and of course for every Saturday and all other days! And I'll need it when I get back home, 'cause I'm figuring on doing a lot of "resting" after this trip.

I noticed, also, that Columbia was preparing for Mother's Day. Why you old slow-pokes! That's over long ago! Then I looked at the date of that paper. It was May 8th, so maybe you aren't so slow after all. It's I that am behind times!

Then, "Washington is Closing Down 100 Weather Stations." That seems all right, but I don't believe we'll ever get rid of weather by legislation. We'll still have some of one kind or another, even when I get home, I imagine.

Congratulations to Josephine Kirk on her new book of poetry. She must truly be Columbia's Poet Laureate. I noticed that England's Poet Laureate ran out of words when he tried to rhyme up the Coronation. Maybe we have more words, or less to say. Anyway I'm proud of Josephine, and we all know that those poems were truly—written in "Crowded Moments."

In the May 7 issue, I was glad to notice that Mr. J. Amis Derryberry is sharing his "Meditations;" and in several issues of the *Herald* I was pleased with the way Home Demonstration Club members are telling of club activities and sharing good recipes. Those items are all news to folks away from home as well as to the members of the clubs themselves.

I was delighted with the well-posed picture of Maury's Miniature Beauty Queen, 3-year-old little Miss KaKay Thomas and her 3-weeks-old colt, Midnight Jubilee, both stepping out in front of their mothers. I'll bet we hear more of KaKay and Jubilee in the next dozen years or so.

I see also that College Hill, Culleoka, and Samaritan schools received Merit Awards for "tops" school attendance. I hope they will accept my congratulations along with others.

Although all these congratulations of mine may be coming in late, they are sincere. I'd like to offer more to Mynders Girls 4-H'ers and to their untiring leader, Mrs. Willie Hickman.

I was glad, too, to see a boat on Evan's Lake, almost in hollering distance of my home. I hope the fish will be big enough to fry by the time I get home, Fred.

I also see by the paper of May 11th that "Country Woman Got Off to a Homesick Start." As Mr. Peepers would say, "that's me." And that "homesick start," is not far from right,

Mr. Editor. And you notice that I'm not bragging much about getting over it.

By the way, I see that Columbia Woman's Club received a certificate of Merit from Tennessee Federation of Women's Clubs for achievements during 1952-53. That's fine. And of course I wouldn't be hinting, but wouldn't it be nice if one of the 1953-54 achievements of that hustling Woman's Club should turn out to be that Ladies Lounge we spoke of before.

I noticed "Woman Lay in Morgue 17 Hours Then Awakened." If that had been dated a few weeks later I might have thought that she had been to the Coronation. She must have been in what the *Rambler* would call the "Good Old Daze," or would it be "Doze?"

I could go right on spreading congratulations right, left, and center. And speaking of center reminds me to congratulate the *Herald* on that full front page of May 12. Starting off with the Texas Tornado, covering the Jr. Order Convention, and the Farmers' Institute, and topping it off with 100 lovely girls in the Beauty Review. Wow! What a Page One my paper can put out! Other papers please take notice, but you needn't try to copy. It's all old stuff by now, for news is volatile.

But I strongly suspect that you folks who have already read those papers are tired of having me re-read them for you. But if you don't believe old papers can be news, you get your accumulated *Heralds* all stacked up by your easy chair, or by your pillow, when you come back to "rest up" from your vacation. You'll see I told you so.

By the way, of course I could have had free medical treatment in England, and there are good doctors in Germany, but I just don't think those foreign doctors would have had any medicine that would help what seems to be ailing me.

I think what I need, if I may quote good old *Rambler* again, is some letters from "My Publick." If I have any, I really would like to hear from it, or him, or her, or them, or rather (if you are reading this) it means you.

I don't see why I should do all the writing when mail can cross the Atlantic both ways. If you don't want me to come swimming home to see what else is going on, you'd better sit right down right now, and tell me. An air mail letter comes in 4 to 10 days. Regular mail in 10 to 20 days. But newspapers more than a month. That's slow.

Address: c/o Capt. Stanton A. Morgan

8th Inf. Regt. APO 39, c/o P.M. N.Y.C., N.Y.

See you in September, I hope.

THE DAILY HERALD
COLUMBIA, TENNESSEE
TUESDAY, JUNE 30, 1953

Country Woman in Germany, But Heart Remains in England

Mrs. Knox Feels British Have Something

BY LERA KNOX

My self is in Germany, and has been for more than a week; but my soul seems still to be in England; and it seems determined to stay there until I go back to fetch it. Which I probably will do about mid-July or sooner.

Mary Martin might have put it this way, "I've gotta wash that land right out of my hair." I tried that but it doesn't work. I fear I've got a case almost equal to that of Rupert Brooke. Did he say something about, or to the effect, 'in whatever spot they buried him, whether on sandy beach or lonely peak, in whatever place they laid his heart there'd always be an England.' I wish I could think of how that quotation goes, but my portable library is inadequate for quotations.

To think that all last summer I avoided Great Britain, and for two reasons: one, I didn't want to be hungry, and people told me I would; two, I didn't think I'd like the British people because people told me I wouldn't.

Well, from now on I'll bet I keep an open mind. Because on the British diet I lost 10 pounds during the month I was there, and largely around my waist, and I've been trying ten years to do that at home. And also because I like the British people. They were as friendly to me as any people could possibly be, even though I've heard since that Britishers are reserved toward other Britishers. Well, maybe, but I like 'em.

Now if that be pro-British, make the most of it. Remember, also, that last summer I was pro-Spanish, pro-French, and pro-German; if I could go over to the Canary Islands I'd like to be pro-Canary.

Margaret is always accusing me of "throwing myself into a country too far."

But I guess I'm such a sponge I just soak it up. If I keep on gadding about I'll be a variegated pro-international.

And the Editor has always known that I'm a procrastinator.

Thinking back over the month in England and enjoying it in retrospect, I feel much like the preacher who said that the best parts of his sermons were the things he thought of after he got home and took off his shoes. So it has been with the Coronation.

I just wonder what makes people tick. What impression will be left on certain people by certain events? What influence certain people and certain episodes will have over certain other people.

For this reason I've been "analyzing" the effects of the Coronation on my homefolks here in Germany. I said to Stan and Margaret two weeks after the Coronation, "What stands out in your mind? As though I couldn't guess."

Margaret saw what I was thinking, and said, "No, it's not the sloppy food nor the rainy weather. I think Stan answered your question so far as he was concerned when he wrote to his mother and sister saying, 'The Coronation is the biggest thing I've ever seen.'"

I said, "Well, that answers for Stan very aptly. Now what do you remember best?"

"Battling the crowds," was the answer, and that, too, was apt.

Then I began analyzing my own recollections; I was in crowds, plenty of them, in crowds so thick and so large that even if I could have stood on tiptoes and looked ahead of me and behind me I could have scarcely seen anything else but people. Though I scarcely had room to stand on tiptoe.

But somehow I don't seem to think of the word "battling" in connection with those crowds. Of course if one had to get out of the crowd, or was trying to get through the crowds, that might have been different. But when I got in one I just stayed with it, and went where the crowd did, did what the crowd did. That seemed by far the easiest thing to do. To do otherwise would have been like one black-eyed pea trying to get out of a bag of black-eyed peas. And what a bag!

When I think through the whole of the Coronation—before, after, and during—it seems to me that the "Behavior of the Crowds" was the very top and outstanding factor that made the celebration most memorable.

I even had the nerve to tell a London newspaper editor, Mr. Jones, news editor of the *Sunday Express*, that I was glad it rained.

At first, he looked shocked. But when I explained that the cold downpour enables me to see "under the skins" of the people better than anything else short of a disaster, he seemed to understand, and to forgive me.

Having made that rather semi-shocking statement myself, I was somewhat prepared for what I considered a wholly shocking statement made by a woman I was talking with on a bus. We were discussing the recent war years when she said "They were the six happiest years of my life."

I know I must have looked astounded, for she hastened to explain. (And remember I knew so little about those war years, for I steadfastly avoided reading the papers during that time or reading war-books later.)

She said, "I was busy, oh so very busy! I worked in a hospital. And I really worked. I went on duty at 7 most mornings. And if I worked until midnight that was all right. And if I worked until 5 the next morning that was better. I still went back on duty at 7 that same morning."

"But it was the people I worked with that made the war years my six happiest years. They were so kind, so sweet, so absolutely self-less, so entirely lovable. I am sure I shall never see the like again until we have another war. I could almost say I'd wish for another war to show us how very fine people can be."

And that is where my curiosity, my propensity for curiosity, led me on one short bus ride. And that is why, where Rupert Brooke and I are buried, wherever our two hearts turn to dust, or mud, there'll be two lumps of clay that are "forever England."

I guess I do throw myself too far into a country!

THE DAILY HERALD
COLUMBIA, TENNESSEE
FRIDAY, JULY 24, 1953

Country Woman Finds Europeans Interesting

Editor's Note: This is the first of a series of articles in which Mrs. Lera Knox, the *Daily Herald*'s globe-trotting "Country Woman" reports on her trip into Switzerland—just before she reports on her next tour, a trip into Ireland and other parts of the British Isles.

BY LERA KNOX

On board the Basel Express, going from Frankfurt toward Switzerland, quite frankly I approached Southern Europe with all fingers crossed, with tongue in cheek, and with doubt stuck out all over me.

The reason for tongue in cheek was to keep me from arguing with the guide books and enthusiastic tourists who have been to Italy and Switzerland.

I always wanted to say: "It couldn't be that grand, that beautiful, that perfect."

I wanted to say further, "You've just had too much good wine."

So in starting out myself on the same type of tour I decided to stay sober, keep my spectacles clean, my viewpoint unprejudiced, and see things exactly as they are, according to my way of seeing them.

I've always been interested, also, in how other people see things, so I managed to make conversation on the train with anybody who would or could converse. It's a long and lonesome ride when you try to cross two countries on board a European train, and for me it wasn't too soft a ride, for in my poor German dialect, or absent-mindedness, or stupidity, or stinginess, I had bought 3rd class tickets. That means I was sitting most of the way on very hard, but well polished, wooden benches just three bumps less comfortable than a cattle car. But I discovered that if I could mix a little conversation along with the scenery I didn't miss the cushions so much.

Of course my mamma wouldn't approve of my picking up chance acquaintances over here the way I do, for really I wasn't brought up that way. But one of the comforts of my being a graying haired grandmother is that people don't seem to doubt my "intentions" so much. So I dared.

I could always start a conversation by saying innocently enough, "Do you speak English?"

Ordinarily the answer would be a slow, sad, shaking of the head, but sometimes the answer would be "Only a leetle." And that was good enough for me.

At one town a well-groomed graying man with very long nose and very long fingers and very long hair, sat down opposite me with a slim brief case. It looked too thin to be carrying the usually large bottle of wine and loaf of bread. So I wondered.

I asked the usual question. He sadly shook his head, but didn't even say, "A leetle." Instead he asked if I could "sprecken zie deutsch" or "parlez-vous Français." It was my turn to do some head shaking and look sad.

And how does one say "a leetle, a very leetle," in French or German? I just shook head and smiled. I didn't see any need of looking sad over my ignorance. Everybody has some of that, at least "a leetle."

But neither of us was deterred. Instead we began to converse interestingly, if not completely satisfactorily, in five different languages, not including "journalese," for I found that he was a political journalist for a Swiss-German newspaper in Basel. Our languages included what we each could muster of German, French, Latin, English, and fervent gesticulation. It was gesture-language that we both could understand best. But some things can't be said even with fingers alone. For instance, he told me "Mein Soeur habitat New York (hand up three times) anno."

That meant that his sister had been living in New York 15 years. Just as simple as that. We agreed that the scenery along the railroad was "shoern" in German, "Joli" in French, and also that it was beautiful in English. Then he said "Americas Vas Besser" and I agreed that if not better, it is at least very good.

A very portly gentleman in a very neat gray suit sat down across from me. His English was so much better than my German I let him take the lead in conversation, believe that or not!

He had just come out of Berlin that morning, was on the way to Switzerland to pick up his wife who was there for her health. He is a Berlin banker. And then I told him that I had noticed in the morning paper that the Deutschmark is now really "hard money," 99% as strong as the Swiss Franc, which is harder than the American dollar, he was very much pleased over my pseudo-intelligence as well as value of the mark. He said "America has done it." And it was my turn to feel pleased. So we liked and valued each other's opinions and a good time was had by all until the subject of Communism crept in.

I was curious, of course, but I dreaded to let the conversation get around to conditions in East Germany. His English was not complete enough for him to express his opinions in a manner satisfactory to himself. So he merely repeated over and over again, "I hate them! I hate them! I hate them! ! !"

He declared that if the East Germans could get guns their problems would not be so great. I wondered. For after all, the Russians, I understand, have tanks. He said further that the East Germans cannot possibly hold out much longer under what they are enduring, and he believes that there must be another war in less than two years. All of which made me feel not too good because my son-in-law is an army man.

But after all, I could take it if he could. His home and all his family are in Berlin, which he adores. I tried to turn the conversation to "Under der Lindens," but he sadly shook his head and sighed, "Der Communist under der Lindens now. How can we endure it any longer?" Then I said that the landscape going by the window was "shoern," also that it is beautiful. And again we reached a meeting of the minds.

But shucks, where am I? I started out to try to find something to knock about southern Europe, just to prove that guide books and other tourists could be wrong. And here I am rambling around about Berlin and "Unter der Lindens." It all goes to prove, I guess, that the mind is faster than the feet, or even than 3rd class passage on an international train.

I found Switzerland literally all wet, right in the midst of the rainiest and worst weather that the country has ever known. A man across the table from me at the lunch stop in Basel told me it had rained all the month of June. When I later got on the train to Zurich I could believe him.

I remembered that after the Coronation in England a great many people planned to fly to Switzerland (flying to miss France and the high tourist traffic there). It looked as though the famous Coronation Rain and the notorious London Fog had decided to do the same thing. One thing I can say for them, when they got to Switzerland they were the real thing, not sprinkle and mist, but downpour and pea soup.

The neat little gardens, some of them were barely sticking their heads above water, some were all under. The erstwhile small rivers were threatening to slosh over their highest banks. I saw a place where most of the roadway was under water, and a traffic policeman was directing the cars along the wide sidewalk.

Pedestrians were waiting in line until the cars had come off the pavement. Evidently the water in the highway was too deep for motors. Then I saw what could possibly be the most useless item in all the country at that particular time: An overhead irrigation system standing starkly over a flooded field.

Two men across the aisle, both speaking in very broken English, were telling each other all about women, and unconsciously paying me what I considered a compliment. Evidently they didn't think I looked "foreign" enough to be able to understand their conversation. I tried not to.

Then they discussed weather. But all either of them could say, or both together, was "Oh zis wedder, zees terrible wedder, ist terrible!" My opinion was that their opinions of weather were more correct than their conclusions about women. But I couldn't say a word, for by that time I knew too much. And if I opened my American mouth and spoke in English, they would know that I knew.

They went on to discuss wars. They said that the German soldier fights much like the English soldier. But the trouble is that the German soldiers now have no uniforms.

Then they went on into flying. One said that the reason he doesn't like to fly is that although it seems safe, it gets there too fast. He says that when he leaves his own country (I never did learn which it is) and arrives in another country and another climate so soon he feels as though somebody has hit him. I thought that he expressed the sensations of a flying passenger very well.

But I still didn't like all he thought he knew about women. I kept quiet however, because for one time in my life my English-speaking tongue kept still. My English-understanding ears had heard too much.

THE DAILY HERALD
COLUMBIA, TENNESSEE
SATURDAY, JULY 25, 1953

Country Woman Gets Wet Feet in Zurich

Mrs. Knox Saves Taxi Fare the Hardest Way

BY LERA KNOX

Zurich, Switzerland—

After a long, rather hard trip from Frankfurt to Switzerland on a long international train with rather hard 3rd class wooden seats, I was more determined than ever to prove to myself that guide books and previous tourists to Switzerland must be a little bit wrong. No one country, no group of people, could be as fine and kind and perfect and gracious and prompt and fair as the Swiss were reputed to be.

When I arrived, after several weeks of rain, the looks of the countryside were trying to bear me out in that opinion. Everything was really damp and dreary looking. The haze and fog from over the mountains hid everything except the railroad stations and grassy banks along the tracks.

However I must admit that the stations were neatly decorated with blooming geraniums and hydrangeas and the railbanks were as neatly trimmed as a young swain goes to his first dance. Even the crossties along the tracks were stacked like bricks laid by a master mason.

I noticed also that the "carcasses" of used cars in what would, at home, be a junky-looking used-car lot, were stripped and stacked in a pattern so perfect they made a pleasing picture. That's a fact. And a fact of Switzerland, I must admit.

I had taken a ticket to Zurich to get out of the beastly cold rain at Basel. But when I got to Zurich the rain seemed beastlier and cooler; and furthermore the afternoon was later and the fog was making dark come on earlier.

Margaret and Stan, my daughter and son-in-law, who love Switzerland so much that they trot off down there, or up there, at the slightest provocation (about six times to date, I believe), had told me a lot of things that a new traveler ought to know about the country, but I felt toward their advice like I had toward guide books and other tourists. All that they said couldn't be true all the time.

One thing they had specified was that hotels fill up really early in the afternoon, and that I had better find where I was going to spend the night before 3 p.m. And I had really intended to telephone from Basel and try to reserve a room for that night at Zurich. But after I heard in Basel that the very rainy weather had practically stopped all tourist business I decided that rooms would be a franc a dozen in Zurich that night.

However, when I went to Zurich hotel Bureau conveniently located in the Railroad Station, I found that Meg and Stan and the guide books and other tourists had been right about one thing. Every available room had been taken before 3 o'clock. Well, I felt silly and stranded.

Then, believe it or not, Florida came to my rescue—not intentionally of course.

A very much tanned and very swanky gentleman came up to the desk and asked the girl about a good room in a first class hotel. She was sorry but not a good hotel had a first class room available that night in Zurich. He himself was a first class hotel operator from Florida, he said. And he knew very well that Zurich still must have something to offer. And he was determined to have a first class accommodation if he had to go to another country to get them.

Then I got an idea. That's the American way, I thought, or perhaps just the Florida way. I'll just act like a Tennessee Country woman. And I told her that my accommodations did not have to be first class by any means. If I could just get room with a bed I'd be all right.

She chewed her pencil a bit, then said, "I wonder if the girls down at the tea room could take you in."

She made a call, talking in German, and found that they could. She charged me 70 centimes, about 15 cents, for the phone call and something else, and gave me a slip of paper with the name "Tea Room Burma," and the street and number of it. She told me I could either take a taxi, which would likely be very expensive, or take a tram which would be very inexpensive. If I would get on a No. 14 tram, in front of the station and show that slip to the conductor, he would let me off at the right place.

I stepped outside the door, wished fervently for the raincoat and overshoes that I had left in sunny Germany, but proceeded to try to raise the English umbrella that a taxi driver in London had given me by mistake.

It simply wouldn't go up. It was one of those neat little foldup affairs that you can put in your pocketbook. But it wouldn't be anything else but neat and folded up. Meanwhile I was getting soaking wet.

A news vender saw my predicament and offered to help. But he couldn't budge it at all. Then a hefty boot black added his assistance and main strength. It still was as stubborn as an Englishman is reported to be. Maybe it just didn't want to expose itself to a Swiss rain.

Finally a stander-by came to the rescue. He made me follow him, and with the umbrella. None of these fellows could speak a word of English but they knew a lady in distress, and very wet distress.

I followed the strange gentleman several corridors and to the door of Swiss Air. Well, I've heard that Swiss Air folks are some of the nicest in the world, but I never thought I'd have to ask them to raise an English umbrella for me.

The man in the office took the umbrella out his back door, leaving me all alone to take care of all his business for not less than 15 minutes. But he returned with the umbrella up. These people know how to get things done.

He showed me in very simple gesture-language that all we needed to know and do was just to press the little button in the end of the umbrella handle, and presto—it went up like a mushroom! That was all there was to it, but by that time it was pitchy dark outside and the fog was even coming into the door of the station.

I pondered a taxi. But remembered how much more I would have to spend for books if I could ride the cheaper tram. Then I figured that in all that traffic and all that dark and heavy fog the tram might stay on one tract better and be a little safer than a taxi weaving in and out tooting its horn.

I stood on the tram platform in the rain, getting wetter and wetter while cars No. 1, 4, 21, 28, 26, 27, 6, 7, and 13 went by. By that time I reasoned that when one is soaking and dripping one can hardly get wetter, so I still waited for 14. And finally it came.

The conductor, true to promise, put me off somewhere. It was in the middle of a block, and a very dark block at that. I stood in a doorway and waited a while, but not a human being, nor a cat, nor dog came in sight. I searched in vain for a sign that said "Tea Room Burma." But that wasn't in sight either. It was then after nine o'clock and everybody was in for the night evidently. There were no residences apparently. Just business houses and all of them closed tightly.

I sloshed along toward the nearest light, but it was a light, merely that and nothing more. I stood there shivering, however, until at last a scrubby looking scrub woman came along. I showed her my slip of paper. She said "Tea Room" and pointed up the street. I walked two blocks, but saw nothing that looked like Tea Room. However I did see a man half a block up get out of a car. If I could just get there before he hustled inside somewhere.

I really hustled myself, bag, baggage, and all. I made it, but he didn't know Burma Tea Room either. However he pointed up the street another block. I went up there, found two men, and learned that my tea room was four blocks back the way I had come and just around the corner. It really was. Right where I got off.

By that time my greatest fear was that the tea room would be closed. Having been for a while in England, I knew that any respectable "tea room" should be closed before 9:30 on a cold, wet, dark night.

It wasn't. It was open, had some customers, soft lights, soft music, and a lot of atmosphere—mostly smoky.

The girls were very gracious. Four flights up they showed me a room, not with one bed, but with two. And both beds had soft, fluffy feather beds, and warm-looking downy comforters, and a wooly looking afghan over a cozy chair under a soft light.

The girl apologized, seeing that I was an American, that the room had no running water. But believe me, that was all right. I'd had a gosh-awful plenty of running water for one night! It was, even then, running off my coat down into my shoes, and out of my shoes onto her nice clean rug.

I had proved to my own satisfaction that Meg and Stan and the guide books and the other tourists were not entirely right about everything. Switzerland is not entirely perfect in every way.

I spread my wet wardrobe out as best I could, hoping it would be somewhat drier by morning. But my shoes! What could I do about them? And they were all I had.

I wished for the man at Swiss Air to tell a woman how to dry shoes as simply as he had told me how to raise the English umbrella. But you don't push a button or rub a lamp to make shoes dry quickly.

Lamp! Ah that was the idea. The soft shining lamp happened to be the stand-on-floor type with a big wide dark shade. I perched one shoe up on each side of the lamp shade, wrapped myself up in the afghan, and sat in the comfy chair to wait until those shoes were dry before I could turn out the light to go to bed. Then I took the extra feather bed off the extra bed, put the covers of both beds on the one. Crawled in between the two feather beds, and didn't wake up with pneumonia! Nor even a sore throat.

Now I can't decide what kind of book to buy with the money I saved on taxi fare.

THE DAILY HERALD
COLUMBIA, TENNESSEE
TUESDAY, JULY 28, 1953

Country Woman Finds the Swiss Are Right

Rides in Rain and Finds Trains on Time

BY LERA KNOX

Zurich, Switzerland—

I caught Switzerland with her weather down, coming down in sluices. Which was all right with me, for I was entering the country in a sinister mood, with a made up bad disposition, and gray-colored glasses, and everything I needed, I thought, to prove that my children Margaret and Stan, the guide books, and the other tourists could not possibly be right in all the good things they said about the mountainous little country.

No place, I was sure, could be so beautiful, so perfect; no people could be so kind, so honest—except of course in Denmark! There has always been a sort of "Battle of Compliments" between my daughter and me regarding Switzerland and Denmark. She champions the former; and I protect and promote the latter.

The Danes, bless them, back me up beautifully (even as they do everything else), by agreeing that Denmark has everything that Switzerland has, except that they don't have any mountains to get in the way and hide their scenery.

But this story was to be about Switzerland, and it was intended to be a very gloomy, dreary description of a land and people who couldn't possibly be quite perfect. So I must start in and do an iconoclastic masterpiece about Switzerland. I dare not get started off talking about lovely, friendly, honest, hustling, beautiful little—I almost said it. But I positively won't. I must at least try to be fair to the people whose reputation I am trying to destroy.

"Ze Wedder," as the Swiss call it, had been so bad in Basel, I rushed over to Zurich, and got soaking wet for my trouble. But I did find a room with two feather beds, slept with one above and one below, and waked up next morning without pneumonia, much to my surprise. My shoes had been set above the floor lamp to dry the night before and were not much too tight the next morning, so I decided to hie myself off to the likeliest looking place on the map in search of better weather.

Just because I had heard so much about the yodelers of St. Gallen, and because I thought that if people can sing like that they must have something to sing about, after a breakfast of delicious hot Swiss rolls, curly little decorations of good butter, coffee with cream, and marmalade that would almost make me love Switzerland, all of which was included in the 8 francs ($2) I paid for my room, including the drying service, and the two feather beds—I started out on tram 14 for the station, and thence to St. Gallen.

I got wet again, but this time I beat the racket. I took an extra pair of stockings, and my house shoes to put on while my shoes dried as best they could on the train. It was still raining, and I should have sense enough to stay in a dry hotel room, but curiosity was hurting me, so off I went to prove that the Swiss weren't so good after all.

To be sure of right connections I asked three different people what time the train left for St. Gallen, and on what track. It was to leave at 9:19 on Track 1. Now of that I could be sure. I sought out Track 1, walked down between two trains, got on, and was in place by 9:01. I had only 18 minutes to wait. Margaret had insisted that actually all trains leave exactly on time in Switzerland. I had coordinated my Swiss watch with all the Swiss clocks in the station. And there I was. At 9:20 I was still sitting there. So was the train. Others pulled out. But mine still set. Ah, the Swiss could be wrong!

By 9:22 I was gloating. A man sat down across the aisle. I wigwagged, pointed to my watch, and said with a question mark "St. Gallen?" He pointed to the empty track beside ours, and said, "St. Gallen gone!" And dis train goes to Lucerne at 9:25. Hurry."

He helped me get bag, baggage and wet shoes off on the platform just in time to catch his Lucerne train before it moved out at exactly 9:25. I walked gloomily up to the sign that said Track 1. It was still there and empty. The train I had boarded had been on Track IA! How dumb could I be? I didn't say any more to myself just then that the Swiss could be wrong.

I asked three people again what time the next train would leave for St. Gallen. The answer was 10:17, on Track 1! I got out my guide book, sat down on a bench, house shoes and all, to wait until I was sure the engine had its nose budged right up against the sign that said "Track 1," merely that and nothing more! I would mind my ABC's from then on, for I believed that the Swiss mean exactly what they say.

I can't say that the trip up was uninteresting. In fact it would take three stories to tell about it, but my mood wasn't for writing just then. At St. Gallen there were some changes made—but not in the weather. I changed my shoes, changed some money, and almost changed my mind when I sat down to a lunch in the station's 3rd class restaurant.

There were Swiss thick soup, Swiss roast pork, Swiss fried potatoes, Swiss chard, Swiss Ice Cream, and all together it didn't cost more than 3 francs.

It was still pouring down rain outside, so I didn't hunt up any yodelers. The atmosphere and fog were so thick I doubted if sound could travel; I was wondering, along with the Swiss, perhaps, just when that London fog would go home.

I asked two people what time the next train went back to Zurich. One said 1 o'clock, the other said 2 o'clock. The track number was the same in both instances, so I decided that both might be right. They were. But I was ready to take the first train, which I shouldn't.

The idea over here is that you don't take the first train, but if you really want to get there, you take the fastest; and on that you'll get there "firstest."

I should have been warned when I passed the baggage coach and saw all the milk cans inside. But I hadn't read far enough in the guide books. I went on and got in the first coach next to the baggage car because that was the only other coach (or wagon as they say, and it really was almost that).

I heard some goats bawling and some calves doing the same. I looked up on the hill, but the fog was too thick to see them. Yet they seemed closer than the hill. When the door was opened and the wind changed I found that they were closer than the hill. They, like the milk, were in the baggage coach ahead.

The train pulled out on time, just about the time I discovered that I was on the "local," the very local, MILK AND GOAT SPECIAL!

We had a marvelous ride together, however, the locals and me and the goats. We changed trains twice because the Special didn't go any farther that way. Then we changed to a sweaty bus, and rode that for a while. And back on another

MILK AND GOAT SPECIAL, with seats as hard as the others. And it rained all the way. The streams I had expected to see as beautiful blue-green were the color of the coffee I'd had for lunch.

We arrived in Zurich, still in the rain, at 5:30, two hours after the second—and faster—train had come in. But really we'd had a lot more fun.

I'd spent a rainy day learning one lesson: Any time you think the Swiss are wrong, you'd better search yourself.

THE DAILY HERALD
COLUMBIA, TENNESSEE
WEDNESDAY, JULY 29, 1953

Country Woman Finds New Home Charming

Mrs. Knox Likes Bad Nauheim Terrace

BY LERA KNOX

Bad Nauheim, Germany—

Friends, Columbians, Country People!

Having just returned from Italy I feel inclined to orate, like Mark Anthony "Friends, Romans, Countrymen!" However, Romans wouldn't be interested in what I have to say; and if I single out CountryMEN, some of the Rural Dames might be inclined toward jealousy. So for these reasons I cannot speak to you as Mark Anthony might have done. Besides, I have been so mixed up on languages for the past two weeks I had to look in the dictionary to see how to spell "friends."

For about ten days I was in Italy, traveling all the way down to the "ankle" of the boot. Venice, Bologna, Florence, Rome, Naples, and even on out to the Isle of Capri (pronounced there as "Sapry." Of course we stopped at Vesuvius where I picked up an authentic pine cone and some lava rocks and at Pompeii, where I further loaded down my luggage with a handful of cinderlike, and very light, white "ashes."

Coming on back up the west coast we stopped on the Italian Riviera, and spent a night at one of the swankiest hotels in one of the swankiest resorts on one of the swankiest beaches. Boy, it was really ritzy. It had hot and cold running water, instead of merely cold and cold.

It gave us a chance, also, to see how the other half (or tenth) lives. And after seeing some families living in not much more than dens and caves in Southern Italy, this was interesting, not to mention a welcome change.

With the ten days in Italy, and about two in Switzerland, and two more on the road to and from back "home" in Germany, I was rather ready, I thought, to really "unlax." But when my daughter Margaret, met me in Frankfurt and gave me the news, I found that I was somewhat like the boll weevil in the old song. I wasn't quite sitting on a fence, was I in the process of "hunting a home."

My army son-in-law had been transferred from Battalion headquarters in Budingen to Regimental Headquarters in Bad Nauheim, and Meg had at last found us a house in the new town. Even when she met me she had the clock and the radio on the front seat in the car, her most-likely-breakable dishes and bric-a-brac on the back seat; her sewing machine, hand loom, dress form, and other et cetera, between the seats, and most of my movable wealth together with her pots and pans, a frozen chicken, a box of eggs, a loaf of bread and some canned milk in the trunk. These army people must keep themselves "mobile," you know.

Everything in the house at Budingen was all packed up, and she had been sitting on the doorstep, reading the *Digest*, and waiting for a truck for a matter of three days more or less. The army takes its time, you know. However it always gets there eventually. So next morning the truck arrived, and in a couple of hours we found ourselves cleaning windows in the new very old house in a lovely new old town.

It is marvelous! I was so excited I didn't "unlax" at all. In fact I had to take a sleeping pill that night to make me stop washing windows.

I could write books and books about this old house and this old town, and about how happy we all are here. But time and space and previously-made reservations don't permit right now. So I'll just put the whole sensation into one short sentence: I am sitting now on beautifully old and weathered terrace of the new home of some of the folks I love best in all the world, overlooking a magnificent view of one of the towns I love best in all the world (I was here last summer and fell in love with Bad Nauheim). The sun is exactly right. The temperature is exactly more so, about 65 degrees I would guess, anyway a sweater doesn't feel bad, yet I could take it off and not notice the difference. The radio is playing semi-classics.

The noise from our nearest neighbors is just loud enough to be interesting but soft enough to be noticeable.

I am looking out on a cherry tree that seems like jade set with rubies; two pear trees, heavily laden, and two apple trees, the same, are in tempting distance, and a grapevine is stretching itself out over part of the terrace. Besides all that as though those things were not enough, there are birds singing in the trees, and children playing in the sandboxes and in the grass just down below the trees.

I really tried to put all that in one sentence. But who could? Try it yourself.

Of course the windows are not all clean yet. The curtains are not up, and most of the furniture and practically all of our bags and baggage are piled up in the middle of the floor. But we can save those things for a rainy day. Margaret and I have been like two kids playing house in trying to put things into place as best, we could. But painters will be here in a few weeks (we hope) so we can't put things away too permanently. Besides, things that are packed away don't have to be dusted or pressed as long as they are packed.

Meg has had to go to Frankfort today to attend to some red tape. Stan is off on maneuvers, or somewhere. And so I can feel "sole owner" of all I can see. And I look at only what I want to.

One excuse for my staying at "home" this morning is to welcome the plumber who is supposed to come and put in a new sink. But when that musically tingling door-bell rings and I open the door, if it should be St. Peter, or the Angel Gabriel, or whoever is supposed to come to Bad Nauheim from that Supposed-to-be-above-Land, I'm afraid I'd have to shake my head gently and respectfully and say, "Sorry; Sir, but I just can't leave this place until we get all the windows cleaned, the curtains up, the pictures on the walls, and all the furniture in the places where we think it looks best. I am having too much fun "playing house" to be interested in another Heaven right now.

A plane just flew over "my" terrace, and I didn't even bother to look up. If it had borne the insignia of that red hammer and sickle that I saw so much in Italy; and if it had shaken a bomb at me, I would have been obliged to wig-wag with my "thinking cap," "Sorry, sirs, I just can't be bothered this morning. I've got windows to clean."

Furthermore, and I believe this is true, if the S.S. *United States* herself should come sailing up this hill this morning, even with Old Glory waving in this perfect breeze, and offer me the privilege of using my return ticket to America today, I'm afraid I'd say, "Oh fellows, let's don't be in too big a hurry. Just take somebody else who doesn't have a sunny terrace this morning. I'm obliged to get some red geraniums growing in Margaret's window boxes before I leave, and I've got to finish cleaning windows and get some curtains up and hang some pictures on the walls. Thank you sincerely, and much obliged besides, but after all, that ticket is not really good until September 24. And I believe I can wait that long. Besides the pears and apples won't be quite ripe for a few days. And the cherries are ready for preserving, and pie making. And my daughter is still a Young thing and cannot be left by her mother—not until a rainy day anyway.

P.S. It may rain before morning according to the radio so maybe I sent that ship "S.S. *U.S.*" back too soon. There are sunshine and folks I love in America, too.

THE DAILY HERALD,
COLUMBIA, TENNESSEE
FRIDAY, JULY 31, 1953

Country Woman Likes the Way the Swiss Tip

BY LERA KNOX

I had just started out to tell you in the previous article what a "paradise" I found in Italy; then the paradise I found in Germany after getting back home again got in my way so completely I couldn't look back clearly on that Italian and Swiss tour. But I'll try again.

Ordinarily my homesicknessing hormones have a tendency to work back toward the place I left last, but it was very hard for me to feel homesick for Italy after I got back safely over the border into Switzerland.

The two countries, to my way of thinking, are different enough to be sisters, which indeed they are, to a certain extent.

Switzerland is a sort of step-sister or half-sister to three other countries, Germany, France, and Italy, but don't you ever think that she doesn't get along very well with her step-kin, as well as her kin and her un-kin.

If you remember what you were supposed to learn in school, which I don't very much, you will recall that the northern part of the mountainous little country, the part which joins Southern Germany, is very much like Germany, even to speaking the same language.

The western part, that which joins France, is like France, even to speaking the same language, and doing the same kind of cooking. And as I said, the Southern part speaks Italian and eats Spaghetti. But there the similarity stops.

Yes, poor little Switzerland, a very small but very independent country built mostly straight up and down, doesn't even have a language of her own, not one she can speak with one national tongue. But never forget this: Switzerland tells the world!

What she can't say in words she tells with red and pink geraniums, immaculate cleanliness, conscientious integrity, and unexcelled courtesy nicely blended with respectful dignity; and a tremendous amount of good old-fashioned common sense.

Now certainly I am no career diplomat, and no politician, and no philosopher; just a plain (very plain) country woman, I proudly admit. But it is my plain-country-woman opinion that if we other people, individually and nationally, would use more courtesy and common sense with a lot of cleanliness, integrity, and geraniums thrown in for trimmings, we should be a lot more able to live as happily and peacefully as the Swiss.

Does anybody want to tell me why not?

Of course, Italy has geraniums, too. And they also are pink and red, but even if the Customs Men forgot to ask us questions and stamp our passports, we'd know by the geraniums when we crossed the international border between the two countries.

The Italian geraniums grow up or down, right or left, bloom or droop; they get rid of yellow leaves or spent blooms as best they can. But every geranium in Switzerland seems perked up and on parade. They all look as though they were "at attention," or as someone said, they seemed to be expecting the Chief Inspector of Geraniums at any minute. But confidentially, I don't believe there is any Chief Inspector of Geraniums, and neither the Swiss nor their flowers are expecting inspection. It is just that their standards of integrity are so high that they try to make even the places where gods alone may see "beautiful, entire, and clean."

Certainly I am no judge nor critic of men or nations, but being a woman I just have to have my say; and being a country woman (plain) I can only say what I see as I see it, with a tiny bit of exaggeration of minimization (I don't know whether that is a good word or not, but it says what I mean) of facts to get enough color for emphasis.

(Frankly, I do confess to using overstatement and understatement as I'd use cake-coloring in decorating a birthday cake. If it weren't for that tiny bit of pink and green in the Sweet peas and roses and leaves on a decorated cake, the plain white cake would seem just like a plain Sunday cake that you wouldn't remember any longer than next Sunday.

And because I'll probably be able to make this trip and tell you about it only once in a lifetime, I'd like to give it enough color to make you remember it longer than until next Sunday. But you know that I know that you'll know that the sweet peas and roses and leaves on these "word cakes" I offer you are slightly artificially colored in spots. But you can tell the difference, I am sure between the tinted flowers and the sincere, factual white "icing.")

Now for instance this statement is slightly colored with exaggeration, but for emphasis only, and with malice toward none and apologies to all.

It just seemed to me that almost every hand in Italy is stretched out to tourists, palm up, and mostly dirty.

That is the flower—now here's the factual "icing." The difference in the attitude of these two semi-sisterly sister countries toward soap and water is plainly noticeable. And certainly no less noticeable is their two very different attitudes toward the tourists' money. They both get it, of course, but oh, by such different manners.

I am reasonably sure that the proud and dignified little sister, Switzerland, gets more tourist dollars, francs, marks, kroner, and shillings than does the much larger and somewhat vampish begging sister Italy. And the money Switzerland gets is passed over so much more gracefully, generously, and satisfactorily, that I might almost say it seems a pleasure and a privilege to spend money in Switzerland.

How do they do it? Well, it's hard to explain. The easiest way to say is to say it's because the Swiss just act so much like the Swiss. But that wouldn't explain much, I'm afraid.

So maybe I'd better illustrate with the matter of tips. You'll never see a Swiss service person, porter, maid, or taxi driver look as though he'd expect you to tip him, simply because he doesn't. And you just don't. That is, unless you are a thick-skinned, stupid, ignorant, show-off American with "much, much money." There are those, you know, even in the best of resorts, or perhaps I should say mostly in the resorts. But if you are sensitive; or maybe I should say common-sensitive and if you notice where you are, and keep an ounce of wits about you, you'll no more tip your maid, porter or taxi man in Switzerland for kindly services rendered than you would tip John Finney or Herbert Sowell, or Mr. Ross, or Cliff Parsons, or your doctor, for the kindly services they have rendered.

I would suggest that a large part of Swiss success with guests is largely due to this fact that it seems a "Land of No Tips." I've seen that tip problem threshed out so much on board ships, in England, in France, in U.S. and other places, it was really a refreshing relief to get to Switzerland.

Of course, you pay for goods and services in Switzerland, just as you'd pay for goods and services anywhere. But the point I am trying to make is that you pay for services with the same dignity that you pay for goods. It is all as simple as that. Now isn't that a beautiful idea? And it seems thoroughly Swiss, and very commonsensible!

Furthermore, you pay fair prices for services, just as you pay fair prices for your groceries, clothes, or medical supplies, and with no more embarrassment to either seller or buyer. When the porter delivers your suitcase, you do not turn your head slightly and slip him a couple of francs. You say, "Thank you, what do I owe you?" And he tells you to a centime just how much it is, for he and the other porters have a set price for each size bag and the distance carried. And you pay him that price just as you would pay interest to your banker for the service he had tendered in lending you money.

You don't slyly slip 15 cents under your plate for the waitress; and you don't hide a dollar under your pillow for the chambermaid, not in Switzerland, if you are as commonsensible as the Swiss, and if you don't want the waitress and maid to pity your lack of good up-bringing.

No, you do it differently if you want to keep your self-respect and their good will. When you go to the desk to pay your bill, the hotel-keeper figures very accurately the cost of your "bed and breakfast" (which are always counted up together), your extra meals, your extra baths, bottles of wine, telephone calls, and what not. And then when it is all added, he adds an extra 10%, 12% or 15% (depending on how many days you've been there, as the percentage goes down the longer you stay), and you pay that percentage under the heading of "Services," and that's all there is to the Swiss System of Tipping, or that's the way it seemed to me.

Sometimes they make it even a little simpler than that, and price your bed and breakfast, your meals, and shoe-shines with the phrase "all inclusive," or "including gratuities." And with that you know at once how hard or light your visit will hit your budget. Now that's what I call common sense in business, especially in tourist business. And certainly Switzerland knows that business.

My greatest wish for all the rest of the world, regarding the Swiss, is, "May Their Tribe Increase."

THE DAILY HERALD
COLUMBIA, TENNESSEE
MONDAY, AUGUST 17, 1953

Mutual Good Will Links U.S., Germany

Country Woman Cites News Article

BY LERA KNOX

Dear John, and ilk (meaning "of the same kind," if such there be):

I am very glad you asked that question, "How about GI's, or even officers—how do they live in Germany, and the German people, etc." It gives me an excuse to write an article which should be very easy to write, for you see, I am going to let someone else answer the questions. Other people seem qualified in a different way from what I am.

It just so happened that at about the time I came over here another editor evidently asked the same question that you did. He is the editor of der *Frankfurt Rundschau.* And if you don't know what all that means, I can tell you that it is a newspaper in Frankfurt.

He sent his girl-reporter over to Budingen, a charming and typical little German town about an hour's drive from his city, to see just what might be going on between the GI's, the officers, and the Germans.

The young lady approached Col. Bond, who was in charge of the 2nd Infantry Battalion at Budingen and Col. Bond sent her on to Margaret Morgan, my daughter, and when we returned from London we found some copies of the article on the German page, a translation into English, and also a letter from the reporter.

I'll copy them verbatim as her expression in many instances is much better than mine. Besides, she has a style of her own, as you shall see.

(Letter from German girl reporter of der *Rundschau*)

> Frankfort, 15.6.53
>
> Dear Margaret,
>
> Since I have not heard from you sin ce you have been in Grafenwar, I assumed that you went to England to fetch your mother. Enclosed you will find my story on my visit to Budingen—and I translated it so you may read it without too much bother. Hope you don't mind my writing about you! Please give Col. Bond a copy as I think he might be interested in knowing what appeared in the paper about him.
>
> I hope that I will see you soon. Did your Mother yet arrive?
>
> Affectionately,
>
> JMB
>
> P.S. Hope you do not mind the copypaper—but as usual I am in quite a hurry—and this happens to be handy.

The reporter enclosed the following article:

Understanding Strengthens Cooperation

About 2,000 Americans in Budingen.
American Families Shop in German Towns

The little town of Budingen is the residence of 6,500 inhabitants and about 2,000 Americans, members of the Armed Forces and civilians as well. Since both units—artillery and infantry—are on maneuvers most of the time, they do not influence the life of the town more than in any other place. The good will of Germans and Americans to establish "good neighborhood" is very much to the advantage of the population. Also Lt. Col Bond, CO of the Infantry Battalion, is of the opinion that with a little understanding on both sides, a good relationship can be established.

Lt. Col. Bond, with many interests and a good knowledge of German music, has known Germany in three different phases: twice before the war as a tourist and in the first years of the occupation and at the present time. He studied German during his university time. "I like to talk with German people, visit German restaurants, and take trips through your country," so he said, "in order to know Germany and its people."

Col. Bond and his officers try to cooperate with the German authorities and the population in order to avoid unpleasant incidents that used to happen some time ago. These facts were acknowledged by the mayor, Mr. Emil Diemer. "We all know," said the Bergermeister, "that an occupation is never a pleasant affair for both partners. However, one has to make the best of it. Our town is economically very prosperous by the presence of the Americans, as they not only patronize our restaurants, but their families buy in German food stores, butcher shops, textile and leather goods stores. Since "Little America" was built, about 60 American families are living there who employ German household personnel. Furthermore, about 300-400 Germans are working in the barracks.

"These figures are very important since one-third of our population are refugees. However, we do hope that the 48 houses still under requisition will be released real soon."

When I asked him about the touchy question of the "Frauleins" and serious incidents I received very pleasant information from the mayor: "The soldiers behave themselves in good discipline. Every incident is being punished most severely by the officers of the troops. As in each military post, we also have soldiers remain in contact with the city for ever," stated the mayor, "and since spring 1952, 23 American-German marriages were registered with my office."

The American women all live in "Little America." In one of the apartments located in one of those white blocks—typical for the family quarters in each American post in Germany, I met some dependents. Many of them are taking German lessons and like to have some German friends in case they did not yet make contacts.

Two of the "infantry women" have taken over responsibility for the care of the Budingen orphanage. They arrange parties on holidays for needy persons and take gifts to the orphans.

A great pleasure for me was the chat with Mrs. Margaret Morgan, the wife of Captain Morgan attached to the staff of Col. Bond. She is free lancing for various American magazines and newspapers. I had the opportunity to read some of her articles about Germany.

Mrs. Morgan was living in a German hotel in Budingen before moving into her quarters, so she could learn German life from first sources. In her stories Mrs. Morgan tries to further German-American relationship.

After my visit to Budingen I was convinced that with a little bit of good will on either side German-American "co-living" can be tolerable if all parties concerned will always try to see the human side in everything.

JMB

THE DAILY HERALD
COLUMBIA, TENNESSEE
THURSDAY, SEPTEMBER 17, 1953

Industrious Germans Erasing Scars of War

Hammers, Saws Busy Night And Day

BY LERA KNOX

I am glad to have had such a large part of two summers in the same part of Germany so I could better evaluate and appreciate the tremendous amount of progress the German people are making in coming out of their war trouble and rubble.

The progress they have made is almost unbelievable; the change from last summer to this is astounding. But when you hear daily and hourly the sounds of hammers hammering, saws sawing; when you see people hurrying; working early; working late; and when you know and understand the German people and their ways of doing things—you can say, "It is just as I might have expected."

My son-in-law, Capt. Morgan, was here during the war. My daughter Margaret came over shortly after. One of the first letters Margaret wrote home gave a small word-picture of the way things were then. Because of the fact that Margaret does a lot of her thinking and concluding from the clothes people wear, she naturally expressed her opinions in that way. She said something like this:

"Stan had told me that it is somewhat colder in Germany than in Tennessee; that the summer is more like spring and fall at home, so I should bring my warmest woolens. As you remember most of my woolies consisted of the things I wore while I was at U.T., plaid skirts, gay sweaters, and bright coats. But I did something today that I won't be guilty of again:

"I went down town wearing a bright plaid skirt, a yellow sweater, and a red coat—but never again—not while I am in Germany.

"The women here are all dressed in black, navy brown, or some of the colors, or non-colors, in between. With their somber black coats, black stockings, black shawls over their heads, they made me feel more conspicuous and more embarrassed than I have ever felt anywhere. I shall either have my old college clothes dyed dark, or I'll send them back home to make gay wool rugs and get myself something that looks in keeping with what other people over here are wearing." That was in 1946.

When Margaret and Stan returned to Germany in 1951, she wrote: "Things are brightening up over here. Women are wearing tan raincoats. I do not see nearly so much black, navy, and sad brown on the streets."

Last year I could see for myself. Women were wearing raincoats of brighter blues, greens, and even a few reds. On bright days when the raincoats were left off I could see far fewer blacks, and many more bright colors in dresses.

This year if you can walk down the street in Bad Nauheim and see just one woman not dressed in a brightly flowered dress with or without a very gay coat, I'll buy you a coca-cola—if we can find one.

But it is not in women's clothes alone, although I think those serve as very good barometers of the people's moods and pocketbooks; it is in everything, everywhere, that you see the people are coming out of their doldrums and leaving the terrible war-torn war-worn look.

The war-made ruins are melting away, also, but of course gradually. There are places which may or may not be touched for years; but a remarkably large number of old haggledy looking walls are either being torn down completely or are being straightened, braced, and added to.

We were in Frankfurt yesterday and the din of building is almost deafening. So many hammers and saws are going you don't notice traffic noises at all.

Many people who obviously have not been able to do anything yet with their ruined houses have pushed back the broken bricks and stone and have built little roadside market-sheds in their front yards.

From these they sell fruits or vegetables, evidently grown in their little back yards or in those of their neighbors. Or they will be selling newspapers, souvenirs; trinkets, clothing, anything they can think of or find to offer the passer-by for a few pfennigs.

Some who have not opened shops in their yards have taken the loose and broken brick bats and have walled up the gaping windows of the front walls of their houses and have posted brightly painted bills and signs on the drab walls. The contrasts are startling in some instances but interesting in all.

Many of the former business houses are rebuilt only in part, the lower floor, front part. The stark standing walls have been either torn down or made steady and the rubble from the front of the lot either hauled off or pushed back, so that now under bright and attractive new awnings you can see brand-new show windows filled with interesting merchandise.

Sometimes, of course, if you go into one of the stores you will find that there is not much behind the store windows, perhaps a row or two of shelves, a cash register, some very polite salespeople neatly dressed and eager to serve. But you can hear the sounds of hammers and saws working away at the back walls. You can very well understand that each time you come back into that store the floor space will be larger and there will be more shelves and counter space.

Coming back this year to the same stores I visited last year, I can see astounding progress, great improvements in the quality and the quantity of the merchandise offered; but the greatest improvement is certainly to be noticed in the faces of the people, and in the laughter of the children on the street. I would say that there is always hope, much hope for a people whose children can still laugh, shout, and sing, and the German children are doing that.

THE DAILY HERALD
COLUMBIA, TENNESSEE
WEDNESDAY, SEPTEMBER 23, 1953

Country Woman in German "War" Area

Mrs. Knox Set to Sail Home Last Sunday

BY LERA KNOX

Dear Homefolks:

Now it can be told. I suppose it has been or will be in all the newspapers anyway.

The reason you have not heard from me in such a long time is (in addition to the fact that I thought you needed a rest from this sort of stuff I've been writing) that I have been in the midst of a big and almost real-like war.

No, it wasn't a bullfight in Spain. It was an army-fight in Germany. Don't be uneasy. Most of us came through without scars and I doubt if many of us will get Battle Stars to add to our "Fruit Salad" decorations, or whatever it is that soldiers wear above their left coat pockets.

We've been surrounded by the famous "Monte Carlo Exercises," the biggest war game or maneuver since the end of World War II.

Of course we've been in maneuvers of one kind or another all summer and my busy army son-in-law has been out in the field a great deal of the time. Of course I don't know anything about the army and can't tell what I do know (for security reasons) but I've been very glad to be here with my daughter while he has been away.

All these maneuvers have seemingly been boiling up to come to one big "head," and that head busted about 4 days ago.

For the past month we've been scarcely able to get any mail, or to send any, because our post office was "in the field." And it was only occasionally that we could make contacts. So if you haven't heard from me, you can remember also that I haven't heard from you. So we're even.

The Monte Carlo "war" is supposed to end today. So I imagine that APO 39 will be back in headquarters by Tuesday anyway, and I'm expecting a whole bundle of good reading. It won't come much too soon, either, for come next Sunday I expect to start out, on the long and long-awaited trek back home. I'll have about two days in London, and sail on the S.S. *United States* September 23, arrive in New York September 28, and I imagine from there I won't be long getting home. Perhaps about October 1. And believe me it has been a long, delightful, and most interest-full summer,

Four months ago today, May 13, I arrived in London, lost and not knowing where to go nor what to do. But I managed to make that, with the help of good English hospitality and showmanship, one of the top-notch months of my whole life, I soaked up a whole coronation, as well as one of the largest and most interesting cities in the world.

On June 13 (notice how this 13 is playing along with my luck) I came to Germany; had a nice rest, which I really needed, then went to Switzerland and to Italy for a ten-day tour, came back to Germany, and started out on July 13 for a trip back through Holland and England to Ireland, dear little lovely land, and then to Scotland; back to London, Holland; and Germany again.

Since that time I have been gadding about over Germany, part of the time almost "in the field" with the army, and finally I've been through the military climax of the post-war period, "Exercise Monte Carlo." It has all been more wonderful than words, but I'm ready now to come back home and start washing dishes all over again.

For the past four days we have been expecting to be "captured" at any time. We live on the edge of lovely Johannesburg Mountain just above Bad Nauheim. Troops seem to have been encamped all around us. Of course everything was so well camouflaged and so immensely secret we didn't know anything about it, not officially, that is.

We could hear planes, and perhaps a few firecrackers. And one night I unmistakably heard footsteps running across the little porch beside my window—I got up and closed the window! But altogether I've managed to stay off the "casualty" list.

All I know that I can put in the paper is what I've read in the paper, the local *Stars and Stripes*, which we get every morning and read avidly, not only to learn what has happened to Little Abner's baby, but also to know how likely we are to be "Prisoners of War" before morning.

In the next article I'll tell you some of the stories that are permissible to print right now.

Sincerely,

Your "On The Spot War Correspondent" L.K.

THE DAILY HERALD
COLUMBIA, TENNESSEE
THURSDAY, SEPTEMBER 24, 1953

Country Woman Sees Johnnies Jeeping Home

Mrs. Knox Says Military Tactics Exciting

BY LERA KNOX
("WAR" CORRESPONDENT)

Exercise Monte Carlo (On the Spot, or near several important spots): It seems that the Fates, or the Gremlins, or the General Manager of all extraordinary things that happen to ordinary people, has decreed that among the many interesting things that should happen to me this summer, there should be a war (just a playlike one, of course) right in my own back yard, and front yard, too.

After the war maneuvers had been going on all summer over here, all the maneuvers came to one big climax, the biggest ever since the last real war ended.

Because much of the information I don't know, and what I do know I can't tell, I must pass on to you only the things that have already been released to the papers, but here so close to the center of the big to-do it has been very interesting and almost exciting.

We have been getting bulletins such as these: "Westland" armored vehicles came into play today after a daring "Eastland" early morning paratroop raid on the headquarters of the U.S. V Corps proved unsuccessful.

French and Belgian armor swept along the northern sector in the "Exercise Monte Carlo" area and maneuvered into positions just south of a Frenkenberg-Alsfeld axis. Meanwhile, it seemed apparent that the U.S. 2nd Armored Division would be thrown into action shortly, as it was attached to the U.S. V Corps and took up positions about 10 miles south of Alsfeld.

"Westland" armor slashing well into "Eastland" positions on the southern sector of "Exercise Monte Carlo" tonight, but their northern sector units temporarily were bogged down before the "floods" created by the "blowing" of the Edersee Dam.

At 12:01 a.m. today, "Eastland" defenders "blew" the dam, closing routes to the northeast. More than 50 square kilometers were "flooded" by the "overflow" of the Eder and the Fulda rivers.

(This simulated destruction of the dam is of some historical interest because, during World War II, the RAF destroyed it with a torpedo attack. Power sources virtually were eliminated by the attack, handicapping German war industry, particularly tank production at Kassel.)

"Westland" aerial reconnaissance estimated that Kassel would be "under two feet of water" before the waters subsided and predicted that the "flood" will delay advances up to 40 hours in the affected terrain.

"We held back the 'Westlanders' for 3 1/2 hours," said a private of Company B, 4th Engineering Battalion, 4th Infantry Division.

"We blew up a road at this intersection with 560 pounds of crater charges, and sure stalled that 2nd Armored Cavalry crowd.

"The umpires ruled that it would take a squad of about 12 men, a bulldozer, and three trucks to fill up that "hole" and make it passable in that length of time."

Near Bad Nauheim, the 12th AF Jet Wing "battered" the "enemy" in ground raids. The fly-boy jet-jockeys racked up 80 sorties for the day in support of the Army's request for air support.

After a briefing in which it was announced that there would be no parachutists dropping in this maneuver, there came a real surprise. Suddenly "Eastland" parachutists dotted the sky. About 40 troopers, including their officers and even their mascot, began landing in the surrounding area. There was quite a chase, in which many of the troopers were captured, searched, and "processed." They were found to have maps, and were trying to capture the general of the "enemy" forces.

The umpires ruled the paratroopers "eliminated" before they reached the headquarters area.

It is only natural that the army wives, feeling alone and defenseless while their men are away, should be somewhat nervous. Rumors circulate that prowlers are around when the men are in the field. Extra precautions are taken to bar all doors and windows, to leave porch, kitchen, and bathroom lights on all night. And some of the women take turns about spending the nights with others who are likewise afraid.

Some nervousness is experienced in daytime, too. But the girls are usually briefed on what do to in emergencies. One of our neighbors was going quietly about her household duties one day during the maneuvers, when she heard a loud noise as of something hitting her house. Immediately she telephoned the Military Police, and alerted her family for whatever might be about to happen to them.

While waiting for the protectors to arrive, she was peeping out the shuttered window when she saw a flour-sack mock-bomb fall in the shrubbery of her yard. She realized then that it was probably a "bomb" of the same kind that had fallen on the roof and made such a frightening noise. Yes, we've been "bombed," too!

So it has been big men playing games during the maneuvers, it seemed to us womenfolks. But we watched them play all around and above the woods and fields with their guns and tanks and planes and "chutes," and we were pleased when the umpires reported the games "well done."

Throughout the entire exercise, we were indeed very thankful that the entire maneuver was "playlike" and not the Real Thing, the horrible terror that war is.

I don't know what arrangements have been made for an "armistice" between the "Eastland" and "Westland" troops, but I do know we've been having a lot of celebrations since our "Johnnies" came jeeping home.

THE DAILY HERALD
COLUMBIA, TENNESSEE
SEPTEMBER 25, 1953

Country Woman Goes High Hat by Accident

Mrs. Knox Stays in Waldorf on Way Home

September 21, 1953
Room 316
Waldorf Hotel
Aldwych, W. C. 2

Well look what those blessed, pesky, gremlins of gadabouts have done to me! I arrived from Holland this morning on my way to catch the liner S.S. *United States* at Southhampton Wednesday and found London hotels fuller than a bushel basket with 6 pecks of sweet potatoes in it! Imagine my surprise.

I was so sure I'd have the whole town to myself now that the coronation is, or should be, over, I did not try to reserve a room in advance. So it was the Waldorf or a park bench, and the Waldorf won. Believe me, I won't try to slip up on New York that way; am writing tonite air mail for room at the Bristol on 49th St. I expect to arrive in N. Y. Sept. 28; may stay a couple of days there.

Will try to get in home about Oct. 1. If there is anything I can do for you in N. Y. you can contact me c/o S. S. *United States*, c/o United States Line; I'll be in Room 35, Deck Tourist Class. Will return to Columbia by way of Washington and Knoxville on Greyhound.

The number "13" is still keeping my luck good. Thought last night I would have to sit up all night on the Channel Steamer, but Room 316 turned up vacant so I got that, and notice that if you reverse the number I have (last room in London tonight it seems) you'd get 613.

Saw "Ol Vic" players in *All's Well That Ends Well* tonight and am getting "standing room" for *Hamlet* tomorrow night.

Best to all

LERA KNOX

P. S. By the way, take this for what it is worth—and I don't know what it means or what its news value is—but I've been trying all day to get rid of some French Francs and banks in London won't touch them—they say they have orders "because of the conditions" in France.

From what I can gather off my own particular unofficial grapevine (branches are the people I meet in Europe) France will be the next "blister" to bust in Europe. It's really a sore spot.

THE DAILY HERALD
COLUMBIA, TENNESSEE
MONDAY, SEPTEMBER 28, 1953

Mrs. Knox Bringing Two German Families

Country Woman Locates Real 'Souvenirs'

BY LERA KNOX

I've never been much of a souvenir collector, not that I don't see a lot of things I'd like to take home, but when I look them over and consider their size and estimate their weight I always wonder how I'll get them home.

Of course I have a sprig of heather from Scotland; a spoonful of sand from the North Atlantic; a pebble from the Thames, near London; a bit of seaweed from the Mediterranean; a ruby blown-glass vase from Venice; a plaster leprechaun from Connemara; a painted plaque from Assisi; an apron from Capri; a wooden hand-carved donkey from Bavaria; a chocolate candy bar wrapper from Switzerland; a shamrock leaf from Dublin; a wooden shoe from Holland; and pictures and postcards from everywhere I've been.

But I believe I'm breaking all records in the "souvenirs" I'm trying to bring back from Germany—two whole families of what might be called "displaced persons."

Ever since I got first-hand knowledge of the way German people work—first from the Prisoners of War who were on our farm during the last war, and later during last summer and this summer, in their own homes and on their farms here in Germany, I have been wanting some German families to help us out at Knoxdale.

I thought it would at least do no harm to make inquiries here. The American Embassy told me that the quota for German-born emigrants is not filled, and that there are many families who can't go because of crowded conditions.

The man at the Embassy told me that if I could find people who were qualified and would pass tests they could be issued visas. That seemed a big part of the battle. All I had to do was to find the "needles" in the tremendous "haystack" of European over-population.

First I asked American Express how to go about it. Somehow over here we get in a habit of asking American Express for everything. A man there suggested that I contact one of the church organizations. He gave me the name of a personal contact in the Lutheran World Federation near Frankfurt. But that "contact" was away from the office. I tried another office at Stuttgart; failed again as that contact was also on vacation or a field trip.

Next I went to the Society of Friends, or Quakers. I had heard that they have been successful in relocating several families in America. There I failed again. I tried the Red Cross in Frankfurt, but they could give no immediate assistance as their work is mostly with American Servicemen and their problems. Of course, it didn't help matters any that everyone with whom I tried to talk was German, and I could speak only Tennessee English. To put it conservatively I'll confess that my blunders were myriad.

The next attack was on the Catholic World Council in Frankfurt. There, as luck would have it, I met a Mr. Shaw, genuine American. He had no suitable family on his list, but he referred me to World Council of Churches in the same building. He introduced me to Miss Asta Gangjetzean, whose business management is as efficient as her name is unpronounceable. She had on her desk a huge stack of applications from families who were wanting to emigrate. There were pictures and detailed information about each family. Her secretary called our attention to a family which she thought would most likely fit our needs. And it so happened that they lived just a few blocks from the office.

Miss Asta (I'll not try to spell or pronounce that last name again) right then walked over to the house with me, but nobody was at home, everybody off at work!

I'm sure that Miss Asta was somewhat disgusted at my Scottish persistence, but I told her to go on back to the office and I would sit on the doorstep until somebody came back to that apartment, then I would bring that "somebody" to her office for explanations.

Fortunately, however, a woman in the same apartment house knew where the man of the family was at work, she went to bring him back. Everybody in Germany is extremely helpful in all matters I find, when they find any matter in which they can be helpful. This woman herself had an application in for emigration and she was glad to help her neighbors.

I'll never forget the smile and the light that shone on Mr. Steinbeck's face when Miss Asta mentioned the word "America"! He and his family had been driven out of their home in East Prussia in 1945. They have been "transients" ever since. In 1948 they thought they had everything ready to go to Canada, but the "red tape" got tangled up or quota filled or something before their application went through. He said they had about given up hope, but they seemed to be still trying and praying.

The extreme pleasure on his face paid me well for all the efforts I had made. Arrangements were made for him to bring his family to see me on the following Sunday when they could all be off from work.

When I got back to Bad Nauheim that evening I found a call from the Red Cross secretary in Friedberg, that she was bringing a family up to see me that night. They came and arrangements were made for them also to come over and talk further about the matter and to meet the other family on Sunday. Meanwhile we all got busy on "papers." There were applications, references, and affidavits galore; and all of us must go through a certain, or uncertain, amount of investigation before visas and other things can be straightened out. But as things stand now (and we all have fingers crossed) the two families will be able to be at Knoxdale in about three or four months more or less.

I have learned from the Council of Churches in Germany that there are many families over here who are very anxious to go to America to live and work, and from the American Embassy that the German quota is not yet filled. So if any of you homefolks should be interested in trying an experiment such as I am making, you might write to this organization about sponsoring requirements.

As I understand it you must guarantee that the family will have a home and work, and will not become a public charge on the United States. There may be other requirements which I will learn as I go along. But that's mostly what I know now.

You can write to the American office which is: National Council of Churches of Christ,. Central Department of Church World Services, Att. Mr. Ronald Elliot, 120 East 23rd St., New York 10, N. Y.

Or if you want to write directly to Frankfurt, the address is Miss Asta Gandjetzean, World Council of Churches, Sandweg 7, Frankfurt, Main, Germany.

Of course there may be much uncertainty as to how the human "souvenir" project will work out, but at least it seems a lot more interesting than postcards and vases and heather.

THE DAILY HERALD
COLUMBIA, TENNESSEE
THURSDAY, OCTOBER 1, 1953

Mrs. Knox Back from Four Months in Europe

Alex Knox, Mrs. Knox, and Mrs. Elsie Burt

The Country Woman is back home again!

Mrs. Lera Knox, whose second trip to Europe this summer covered more than 10,000 miles, stepped down onto Maury County soil for the first time in four months this morning—fresh as a daisy despite a long bus ride from New York and a harrowing storm experience at sea earlier that delayed the mighty S.S. *United States* no less than four hours.

Hailed joyously by her husband, Alex Knox, and her sister, Mrs. Elsie Burt, she was met also by representatives of the *Daily Herald*, for whom she has written some articles about her experience in this, her second European tour, and for whom she promised to write at least one more—about the storm at sea.

Incidentally, she hurriedly reported that the travel magazine *Ireland* was asking permission to use some of her *Herald* articles on the Emerald Isle for its readers.

She was then whisked away to her beloved Knoxdale, to resume the life of the Country Woman At Home after weeks upon weeks of experiences abroad that included the Coronation in England and a long stay with her daughter in Germany, besides trips to Ireland, Switzerland, Italy, and other European countries.

And almost her first words to *Herald* staffers were "Here, please take this cap to Tillman Moore." She then turned over for delivery the battered baseball cap that had seen the coronation of a queen, the beauty of Ireland, the dirt of Italy, and the cleanliness and thrift of Germany, all in a short 4-month span.

Her boat trip back had ended Monday four hours late, and staying overnight in New York, Mrs. Knox "saw five shows and about three publishers" before embarking homeward by bus at midnight Tuesday.

Her phenomenal luck still held, for she was late and missed the first bus that night because of seeing *The Quiet Man* and found it threw a wheel before reaching Washington while hers was on schedule.

She also saw *The Robe*, the new type Cinemascope film, in its New York premiere, the stage show *Picnic* and the movie

From Here to Eternity while shopping and sightseeing in New York.

"I'm dying of the heat," she explained as she hit the hot pavement this morning at 11, explaining that nowhere this summer had she found the mercury above 75.

"Maury County sure looks fine—it's the best place after all," she said, explaining that all the way down she had been thinking about how America would look to the two Germany families she has arranged to bring here a few months from now.

Already talking about "maybe a trip to Mexico while my bags are packed," the globe-trotting Country Woman was back home fuller of pep than when she left, and still looking ahead to new ventures—all to be recounted, when made, for the benefit of *Herald* readers.

THE DAILY HERALD
COLUMBIA, TENNESSEE
SATURDAY, OCTOBER 3, 1953

Mrs. Knox Scared Stiff by Storm at Sea

But She and Other News Folk Are Curious Ones

BY LERA KNOX

I thought I had seen about everything in the way of weather this summer while traveling in Europe. I was thoroughly soaked six times in the Coronation rain; thoroughly windblown on the peninsulas of Ireland by Atlantic gales; drenched again by "unusual" downpours in Switzerland; dried out again by basking in the sunshine and breezes of the Italian Riviera; tossed topsy (and almost turvy) in Naples Bay. I climbed into a snowstorm on August 1 (that truly "cold day in August") as I went to the top of The Zugspitz, the highest mountain in Germany. In fact Europeans bragged and bemoaned the fact that 1953 has given them "the worst weather in years" and I took or was taken in by the best and worst of it.

The thermometer in Frankfurt one day reached an unprecedented 91 degrees Fahrenheit, and practically covered Page One of every newspaper with headlines, as well as jamming radio weather reports.

But it was not until I started home that Old Dame Weather really kicked up her heels (and a lot of salt water) at me.

We were all sitting around in the lounge of the S.S. *United States*. Some were playing Bingo; others Bridge; some were watching the "races" of cardboard horses on a "fast" linoleum track.

Suddenly the "horses" all fell flat on their sides with an awful flap. Then every loose chair and unattached piece of furniture began to rush in a great hurry toward the north side of the room. Passengers began to grab at posts, at tables; anything that seemed stationary, even at each other.

Before the chairs all got across they suddenly started skidding back toward the south wall. Passengers were still grabbing and holding.

Faces first looked amazed, then frightened; then when something popped or banged outside on the deck like a cannon or a ship breaking in two, faces began to "freeze" in horror.

My first thought was of an iceberg—remembering the *Titanic*, as everyone else must have been doing. I asked the purser, who happened to be standing near my post. He said we had just been slapped by a wave.

I couldn't tell whether his face was frozen or not. It was pleasant and inscrutable until a bellboy brought him a note, and my imagination told me his expression changed after that. Of course all imaginations were working fast and overtime in those few minutes. I did hear him give orders to the effect that every man was to do his duty, or something like that.

I remembered that my life jacket was five decks below, but I didn't dare turn loose the post I was hugging to try to go down those rocking stairs to get it.

My observation of the other passengers around me was that we were all scared stiff. The red and white faces of two fat women near me looked like pink and white marble. That thought sort of cracked the "ice" that must have been my face, so I made some sort of silly remark to them. One woman smiled slightly. The other looked beyond or through me. She seemed unable to hear or appreciate my pseudo-joke.

I must have looked as scared on the outside as anybody else. But actually down on the inside of me I was more curious than scared. In fact, I think that curiosity was my saving grace at that particular time.

I knew that the ship had gone through four days of hurricane coming over. I wondered if this was another hurricane; if it were worse or better than the other one. Most of all I was wondering all the time what would happen next; whether the chairs would make it all the way across the room next time; who'd pick up the poor flattened race horses; whether said horses would make it to the end of their linoleum track faster on their sides or on their pedestals; whether we'd be slapped again on the right side or whether the next wave would hit on the other side; whether the seam of the ship would hold.

Boy that was the loudest boxing match I'd ever heard or heard of. I wondered if the waves were hitting as hard on the upper decks; whether they were going over the top or not.

The purser cautioned everyone to get something steady and hold fast. Was he kidding? Those were wasted words! Everybody was holding fast to everything, except their supper. The purser called for more porters for cleaning detail. He was told that all porters were already busy. I could see that.

There were some instants between the slaps and rockings when we might for a second turn loose a post and grab a table, and thus work around to the door, to the rail, and start down stairs. The stairs soon were covered with suppers, especially the stairs going down.

The stairs to the upper decks seemed clearer of people and porters and suppers, so those were the ones I chose. I wanted to know what was going on at the top.

Besides the more sick some got, the more some got sicker. If you can figure that out!

I managed to stay rather stubborn as to seasickness, remembering that I had a good reputation to keep up and an excellent dinner to keep down. I was determined that if the Atlantic fishes got my dinner they would have to take me along with it.

Folks were scooting down the stairs like rats down a roll-a-coaster, stopping at every landing, and sometimes between, to leave all or part of what they had to give.

I couldn't anticipate any satisfaction in following that crowd, so I continued to climb, noticing that my only company on the upper landings were members of the crew, especially the ones with caps marked "Fireman." I noticed that the little cat-hole doors in the bottoms of the big "Fire Station" doors had been opened, probably, I thought, to let the big snake-like fire hose come sliding through.

Everybody was leisurely rushing, trying to look as though nothing was happening. It must have been funny to see us trying to fool our stupid selves when that ship seemed standing first on one ear and then on the other. Officers were giving quiet orders as though on the sly. I was probably in the way of operations, but what chance does a crew have against a woman's curiosity? I wanted to know if it could be as bad at the top.

I might have known what I'd find in the enclosed navigating Bridge—and was I glad that place was enclosed! I found Sally McDougal, my roommate, who for untold years has been star feature writer with the *New York World-Telegram-Sun.* Also there was a chipper tom-boy photographer, named Phyllis, also of the *World-Telegram-Sun.* And a girl from the *N.Y. Times.* And Harriett, who was once a newspaper woman, but is now doing publicity for a fabric firm. I didn't ask but I'll bet every one of them had printers ink in the veins.

All were holding on for dear life to the rail around the room, and six faces were flattened against the windows watching the spray. Phyllis was fidgeting more than anyone else.

"So inconsiderate of that darn storm to happen at night when a fellow couldn't get a decent picture, darn it!" what would a snap of spray in the dark look like on Page One? Silly stuff!

This story is getting too long. But if I wrote on until tomorrow night I couldn't make the article as long as that night seemed. It was just one slap after another; and two rolls after each. I went to bed and slept and prayed until morning.

And believe it or doubt, I didn't ask anybody any questions until after breakfast when things had quieted down and the purser had his fair-weather face back on again.

I learned that what we had been in was not a hurricane, but a Storm! One of the worst in anybody's recollection. The worst thing about it was that it had come up suddenly, as a surprise to everybody. There had been no warning to anybody from anywhere.

I heard by grapevine that it had been even worse a hundred miles to the north, and that two crew members had been washed overboard from a British freighter. I said another prayer of thanksgiving that our navigating bridge had been enclosed with stout walls and tight windows, and that I hadn't tried to go out on deck with Phyllis to try to get a picture of spray in the middle of the night. Silly stuff—or are we just silly folks?

EPILOGUE

After braving that storm, Lera Knox returned to her country life in Columbia, Tennessee. In the sixties, Mother and Daddy sold their restaurant and farm and moved to Sarasota, Florida. In 1968 Daddy was injured in an automobile accident. He died two years later, two weeks short of their 50th wedding anniversary. Mother died in 1975. Son Jack passed away in 2000 at 79. His widow, Betty, lives in a retirement community in Terre Haute, Indiana. Their youngest child died in a California scuba diving accident in 1988. The other grandchildren live in Illinois, New Jersey, Indiana, and Tennessee.

Stan and I evidently inherited Mother's love for traveling. After Stan served in Vietnam, we visited China, Thailand, India, Australia, New Zealand, and Europe again. Having had several "careers," at 87 we are happily ensconced in a Gainesville, Florida, retirement community.

Margaret Knox Morgan

www.ingramcontent.com/pod-product-compliance
Lightning Source LLC
Chambersburg PA
CBHW020651270326
41928CB00005B/72